Christmas in Rarotonga

Christmas in Rarotonga

THE JOHN WRIGHT STORY

With Paul Thomas

MOA Publications
Auckland
New Zealand

ISBN 1-86947-062-1

Published in 1990 by
Moa Publications
P.O. Box 26092, Epsom, Auckland 3,
New Zealand.

Typeset by
Typeset Graphics Ltd, Auckland

Printed by
Singapore National Printers, Ltd.

To my thigh pad

ACKNOWLEDGEMENTS

I thank all those who have helped with my book

Sue, my wife, for her support
Paul Thomas, who so ably put my thoughts on paper
Peter Marriott, for the statistics

All the lads
Alan 'Bud' Hill
Bob Cunis
Frank Peach
Gerald Mortimer
Mark Plummer
Peter Borrie
Roger Bhatnagar
Warwick 'The Fox' Larkins

All the photographers named or unknown

C O N T E N T S

INTRODUCTION

I've never actually spent a Christmas in Rarotonga but there was a time when it seemed like a good idea.

It was during our tour of India in late 1988. We'd lost the first test at Bangalore. A lot of us got ill during that match and at one stage we had a television reporter at cover point and a radio commentator (admittedly a former New Zealand captain) at mid off. The pair had to field for a while because we simply didn't have eleven players out of bed.

Half an hour before tea on the first day of the second test at Bombay we were 158 for eight. In technical cricketing jargon we were up the creek. I'd been watching in the stand which wasn't very comfortable because the seats were hard on my dodgy back. I went into the dressing room where the team coach Bob Cunis was watching the action on television and having a quiet cigarette.

The tour was the first time the pair of us had performed our respective roles of captain and cricket manager outside New Zealand and as Danny Morrison made his way out to the middle to join John Bracewell, you wouldn't have bet the family silver on either of us growing old in our jobs. We both knew the pitch was going to turn and that we could kiss the series goodbye if we didn't get some sort of score in that innings.

As we sat there watching television, Bob took a reflective drag on his cigarette and said: "If things carry on like this, you and I better think of spending Christmas in Rarotonga. It mightn't be such a good idea to go back to New Zealand."

As it turned out, Danny and Braces put together a ninth-wicket record partnership for New Zealand against India to get us back into the game and we weathered another half-dozen crises to emerge victorious. It was the most memorable match I have ever played in. There were outstanding individual performances within a total team effort. It was a tremendous demonstration of that resilience and character and ability to perform under pressure which have become the hallmark of the New Zealand team in the last decade.

When I was trying to think of a title for this book – (if we'd lost that game, it may well have been called 'Wright Off') – Bob's phrase came to mind. To be frank, it was about all that did. It contained some of that dry, ironic – sometimes black – humour that seems part and parcel of cricket. When cricketers are telling stories about the game, the ones that get the most laughs are usually the ones about cock-ups and disasters, about batsmen wearing bouncers between the eyes and bowlers being flogged all over the park.

I don't know whether cricketers have better developed – or more perverse – senses of humour than other sportsmen in other codes; I would like to think that the nature of the game attracts people who don't take themselves too seriously although there are a few exceptions to that, particularly at international level. One of the good things about cricket though is that no matter how serious the situation, there's usually someone like Bob Cunis there to make you laugh, even if it's the last thing you feel like doing.

After we'd lost two tests in three days on the Australian tour in 1980/81 John Bracewell confided to a shell-shocked dressing room that he would tell his grandchildren that New Zealand still played three-day test matches when he first got into international cricket. In a one-day game in India in 1988, the Indian opening bat Kris Srikkanth was going for it even by his extravagant standards and thrashing the ball to all corners. By halfway through his third over, Willie Watson's figures were looking like a computer error. I asked him how he felt. "Bloody hell," he said, "it's like bowling in the highlights."

Or take the case of my Derbyshire team mate David Steele. Steeley had silver hair and steel-rimmed spectacles and looked older than 33 when the English selectors picked him to add some intestinal fortitude to an England team which wasn't coping with Lillee and Thomson too well. The papers called him 'a bank clerk going to war'. To a man who'd grafted away unrecognised for many years in county cricket, going out to bat for England for the first time – and at Lord's to boot – was going to be the highlight of a career, a moment to savour. Steeley had never used the home dressing room at Lord's before and when it was his turn to bat, he went down one flight of stairs too many and ended up in the kitchen while a restless crowd and a curious Australian team waited for him to make his appearance. When he finally got out into the middle, Aussie wicketkeeper Rod Marsh greeted him with the words: "Where've you been, Grandad?"

Although a dour and gritty performer on the field, Steeley was a character and the central figure in much of the Derbyshire team's dressing room banter. He was extremely careful with his finances – we used to say he had tarantulas in his pockets – and loved batting more than anything except pound notes. Among other things it meant that when the dust cleared after a mix-up in the running between the wickets, the player heading for the pavilion with his bat under his arm and a face like a squeezed lemon was very seldom D.S. Steele.

Another of Derbyshire's England players was the all-rounder Geoff Miller. Geoff was a good bat but he'd been around for a while without getting a first-class century. This became a source of constant comment for the media and something close to an obsession for Geoff. Whenever he got to 75, people would be going round in the dressing room saying "For God's sake, when he comes in at the break, don't say anything about a century."

Sweet victory – Paddy Greatbatch and Smithy give the umpires a hand with the stumps.
ALL SPORT

On one famous occasion he'd reached 89 and looked certain to lay the ghost when Steele mucked up a call and the pair of them ended up heading for the same end. Steele won the race because he launched himself into a fast, flat dive about three yards out from the crease. His explanation/apology was classic Steele: "I'm ever so sorry youth, it quite destroyed my concentration – I felt bad for three balls. Then I thought, it's a good wicket and I have to get my head down."

Steeley wasn't unduly troubled by his conscience. For another who drew the short straw in similar circumstances, he had the consoling message "that's show business". A couple of innings later he pushed one into the covers and took off for a regulation single only to find, when he got down the other end, the non-striker still in his crease, leaning on his bat, and showing no interest whatsoever in Steeley's predicament. Steele wasn't the sort to give up his wicket without a fight and tried to push the other batsman out of his ground before accepting the inevitable and trudging off. The rest of the team greeted him in the dressing room singing "There's no business like show business".

This book is essentially about the two types of cricket I've spent most of my adult life playing: test cricket and English county cricket. County cricket was a major part of my career and had a significant – and not altogether positive – influence on my development as a batsman. Coming from a farming background, I've always recognised the place of rain in the grand scheme of things. It would be fair to say that 12 years on the county circuit enhanced rather than diminished my appreciation for this gift of nature. My county, Derbyshire, wasn't exactly a glamour side. I realised that in my first season there when our fast bowler Mike Hendrick broke down and had to be carried off the field. A couple of officials came out with a door because Derbyshire didn't have a stretcher.

Occasionally there were times when I could have gladly quit county cricket. Yet there were a hell of a lot of times when I thought how lucky I was to be paid to play a game I loved in an extraordinary and unique competition and to represent the warm, loyal, salt-of-the-earth folk of Derbyshire. I wouldn't have missed it for the world. I hope that the section on my experiences in county cricket provides an insight into a professional cricketer's life: what he sees and learns; the pressures and rewards; the intense frustration and deep satisfaction; the tedium and the good times; and above all, the talented, eccentric, and very funny people he sees at work every day.

Of course the point of view is that of a Kiwi professional cricketer. For me, being a Kiwi came first and being a pro followed because the attraction of county cricket was that it would make me a better player and help me not only to play for my country, but also to play well for my country. That has been the motivation which has driven me.

It's been great to have played for New Zealand and to have been part of a tremendous era in our cricket. Every cricketer aspires to perform, to test himself, in the international arena; it's a hard and unforgiving environment where success and all its rewards can only be obtained at the expense of others whose desire to succeed is just as strong. The pressure is relentless and the hardest opponents to overcome are within.

In section two I look at the things which have left an impression on me – including cricket balls propelled by a variety of fast bowlers, each seemingly bigger, uglier and quicker than the last – during my time in international cricket. In part three I discuss the people I've spent that time with – the guys in the New Zealand team: as Bruce Springsteen said about the E Street Band, they're all about the best bunch of people to have at your side.

Oscar Wilde couldn't play the guitar to save himself but he did have a way with words. Arriving in the USA, he told customs men: "All I have to declare is my genius." What I have to declare is the experience of being

John Wright, cricketer. That's what this book is; it's not an autobiography in the chronological 'everything you wanted to know about J.G. Wright' sense. What people want to know about me would make a pretty slim volume, occupying no more space on the bookshelves than 'Geoff Boycott's Book of Drinking Songs' or 'A quiet life' by Ian Botham. That means you won't find out how old I was when I got my first jockstrap or what I had for breakfast before playing a legendary innings of 15 at Heanor in July 1987.

Those looking for sensational revelations of the 'I saw Ewen Chatfield buy a Sex Pistols album' sort will also be disappointed. It is not widely known that cricketers are generally intensely shy people whose preferred form of relaxation is curling up in their rooms with a cup of cocoa and a well-thumbed copy of the MCC coaching manual.

Assuming that anybody who has read this far has actually bought the book, I can confess that what it does contain are the reflections of a bloke who's played a fair bit of cricket with and against the best of his time, in various parts of the world and, as he approaches the end of his career and faces the appalling prospect of having to do some real work, is trying to squeeze a few more bob out of it.

Once a pro, always a pro.

CHAPTER ONE

Another day, another dollar

I never had a single-minded ambition to play county cricket; my cricketing ambitions were more focused on playing for New Zealand and it was only the belief that playing in England would help me to achieve that aim which took me there. I had some lucky breaks and when the chance presented itself, I grabbed it. But becoming a professional cricketer in the fullest sense of the word was like puberty: it happened gradually, then I woke up one morning and discovered that everything had changed.

I played for Derbyshire from 1977 to 1988. The first three years were tremendous and gave me a platform for the rest of my career. Looking back I've often felt that playing over there for no more than two or three years, the way Greg Chappell and Martin Crowe did, would be a better way to do it. You learn so much and you don't get sick of it. England is really the only place you can practise the trade of professional cricketer.

County cricket and international commitments effectively mean you play 12 months a year. The longest break I've had from the game is six weeks and 1989 was my first winter at home since 1975. I had to make the transition from amateur to professional and that meant playing when I didn't really feel like it, which was totally new to me. Before then I'd eaten, slept, breathed cricket and to get sick of it was quite out of character.

There are times when I knew I really needed a break but that would have meant taking a New Zealand season off and I felt I could never justify playing county cricket but not being available for New Zealand. If I'd never played county cricket, I probably would not have suffered, as I did from time to time later in my career, from the feeling of lacking sharpness and appetite for the game. The whole experience definitely affected my attitude to playing cricket. Nowadays if there's a choice of things to do, I wouldn't be the one saying "let's have a game of cricket".

When I first started playing, I couldn't get over how much cricket was played. I remember getting out halfway through a session and making the excuse that I could have got runs but didn't feel like it. The Derbyshire captain Eddie Barlow gave me a real dressing down. He said I'd made the choice to be a pro and I had a responsibility to perform every day, give 100 percent and have pride in my performance. The real pros, batsmen and bowlers, compete regardless of the state of the wicket or any other factor. Some of the quicks only run in when the ball is flying about; when the wicket is flat, the Colin Crofts of this world don't want to know. The good sides perform day in, day out and generally the most professional sides come through.

Even in my very first year it was difficult mentally and I had to get accustomed to batting or fielding when it was freezing cold and there were three men and a dog watching. Bob Taylor, the Derbyshire and England wicketkeeper, had a catchphrase 'QC' – quality counts. He'd get into you if he saw you with your hands in pockets or yawning. He had tremendous pride in his performance and it showed in his game. For years he went on tours as Alan Knott's deputy but was still totally involved; if he wasn't playing, his job was to help those who were.

David Steele, another Derbyshire teammate, would never moan about a wicket and played every day as if his life depended on it. He used to say he'd play with a square ball. Early on I remember him telling me in no uncertain terms that I'd got out playing a bad shot and needed a bat handle shoved up my bum.

Unfortunately county cricket does tend to make you a bit of a run counter. You're always looking at your average and how the season's going because that's how you're judged. Barlow used to say that if everyone could win two games a season, the team would do well but players don't really think that way.

Being the overseas player I always had extra pressure especially as overseas players are regarded as match winners. I could not afford the luxury of having a game when I just went through the motions. I had to perform otherwise I would have been averaging 32 which wasn't good enough. I wanted to be in the top 20 players in the country each season. I often thought the English players were a bit lucky in that respect: they could always take the easy option and say they were just having a bad trot.

But a bad trot couldn't become a gallop, not unless you had a rich family or other qualifications to fall back on and not many county players, particularly Derbyshire ones, had either. In 1977 Freddy Swarbrick, the Derbyshire left arm spinner, was being talked of as a future England player. That season he took 65 wickets at 24 runs apiece. Two years later something went, mentally, and after seven or eight years as a pro, his career was on the skids and the dole queue was beckoning. If you get dropped, you could be out of a job. You could be due a benefit in a year or two but if you're not performing, then there's no reason for the county to keep you on its books. When cricket pays your mortgage and feeds your kids, getting dropped is a lot more than a blow to your pride.

Then there are the youngsters who come straight from school with some ability and heads full of dreams but without the mental attitude, the ability to perform under pressure, that you have to have. A lot of them would spend two or three years in second XI, trying to get a spot in the first teams. But their game would actually decline because they weren't being extended by first team cricket.

The thing I always liked about county cricket is that it's a unique competition and a tremendous industry to be part of. I made a lot of good friends. There are pretty strong codes of behaviour and certain limits. It's played competitively but most batters walk, which is not generally the rule elsewhere although the older guys say it's on the way out there too. You get in a lovely rhythm playing day in day out – you pick up from where you left off and it just flows. Conditions are so consistent compared with New Zealand or at least they were before teams started doctoring their home pitches to suit their bowling attacks.

I also enjoyed living in England, watching Derby County and Nottingham Forest, going to Wimbledon, our local pub, English beer, Sunday papers, and many other elements of the English way of life. I always felt at home in England and the feeling extended to cricket: I felt more comfortable playing in England for some reason and played my best cricket there. It was good too, to have six months in both countries and the chance to travel.

In those days the New Zealand cricket fraternity didn't exactly greet its professionals with open arms. The cool reaction of the non-professionals in the New Zealand team surprised me: I didn't think that my attitude had changed, that I didn't try as hard, that playing for New Zealand meant any less to me because I was playing for money; the money didn't even come into it in the first few years. Perhaps because of Glenn Turner's professional attitude to remuneration for playing for New Zealand, the non-pros thought of the pros as different, as people who wanted special treatment, and I got lumped in with Turner, Geoff Howarth, and Richard Hadlee. I didn't see it that way; I was younger than the others, much less of a name, and all I wanted to do was play for my country. Now of course all the New Zealand players are professional.

Some people didn't seem able to see past the 'play for pay' thing to what being a professional meant in cricket terms. Administrators who'd played first-class cricket or maybe the odd test match would give me the benefit of their knowledge and experience without appearing to appreciate that cricket was my job, that I spent ten months of the year playing it and because of that exposure, I knew a reasonable amount about it. You see so many angles, incidents, matches, it's like studying full-time and the game and its lore almost become second nature. Nor did such people understand the commitment required to play all the time.

I played county cricket for three years not for the money but because I wanted to be better. It was important to me to improve my game and play for New Zealand, to try to be the best opener in the world. I didn't succeed but I gave it my very best shot. After four or five years I realised I wasn't going to be the best in the world and I started thinking about getting out and playing just for New Zealand. That's when the realisation hit me that

Go the ball! – New Zealand v England at the Oval, 1978.
PATRICK EAGAR

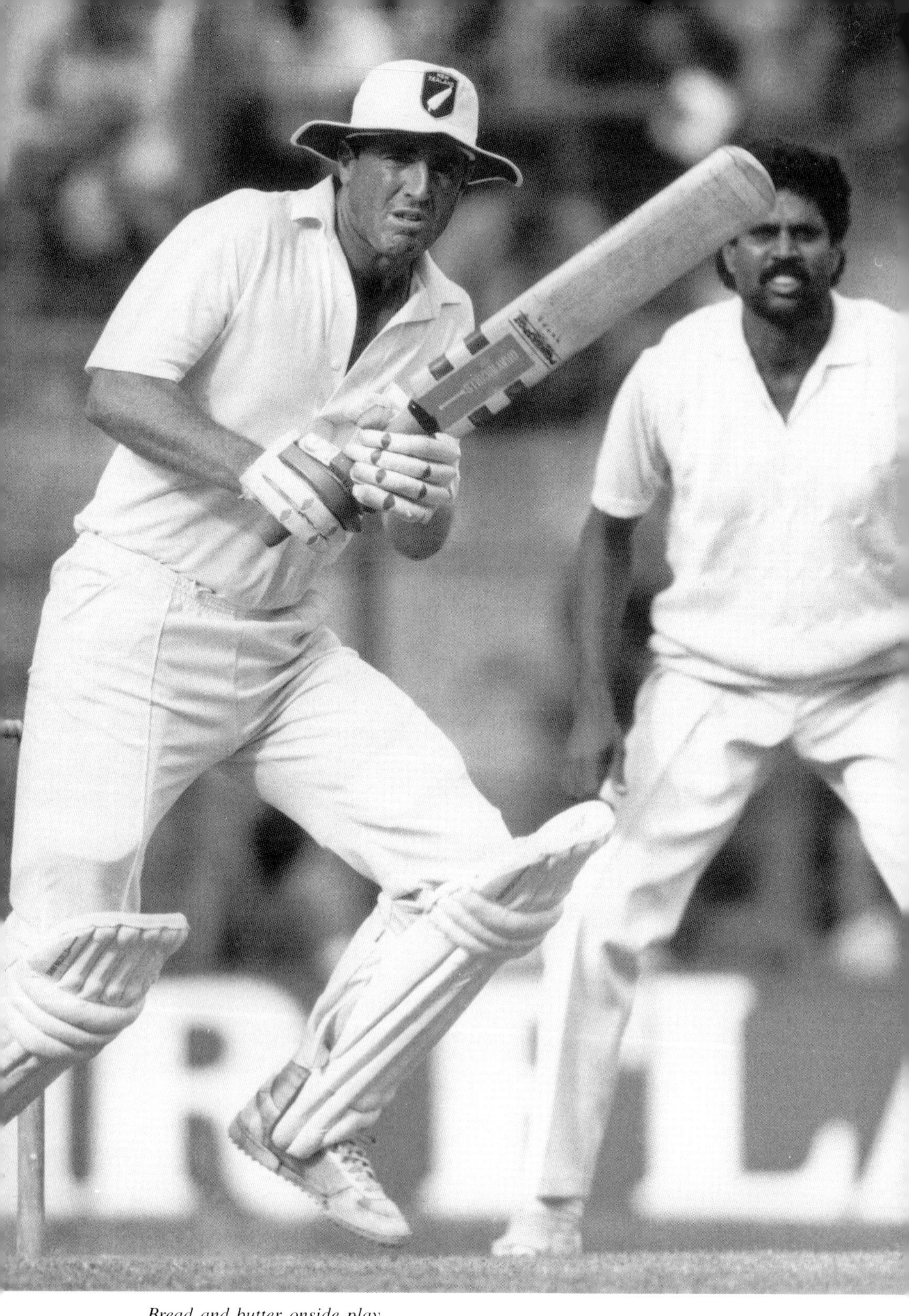

Bread and butter onside play.
ALL SPORT

More runs in the bank – 185 not out for Derbyshire against Northants in 1982.
JOHN GRAINGER

cricket was not a pastime or a hobby, it was what I did.

Then I thought 'well if I'm going to carry on, I may as well make some money out of it'. At that point you become a professional in attitude as well as in fact. That's when it becomes a job. I also had a determination to hang in there and see it through to prove I could do it. The South African Peter Kirsten, who was Derbyshire's other overseas player, quit after five years then wanted to come back.

In the end what was I going to do? You realise it's not such a bad job after all. There were many times when I felt like chucking it all in, when I felt it was detracting from my performance for New Zealand, which was more important. Then I'd think of the tax-free benefit I was due after ten years.

It wasn't a game anymore and I had to get used to the fact. But if I had to choose between being a cricketer or an accountant, I'd be a cricketer. It's an open air job and it's very honest: you can have the cleanest gear, the best bat, the right background, and an uncle on the committee but it doesn't count for anything when you get out in the middle.

On the other hand, if I'd been a reasonable rock 'n roll guitarist, I'd have chucked it in years ago.

CHAPTER TWO

England made me

At school and afterwards I was a pretty successful cricketer without being a stand-out like Martin Crowe. I scored two or three centuries for my school, Christ's College, and got a lot of runs in Brabin tournaments. I was always pretty determined: I once batted five hours for 90 in a Brabin game to win the tournament. The odd comment was passed about me one day playing for New Zealand although some may have suspected my ambitions. One year I made myself unavailable for a Brabin Under 20 side, instead going to the first Ngaruawahia rock festival, but I couldn't get into the Canterbury squad, which limited my chances. In my last year at varsity, 1975, I was so keen on making the squad, I used to drive from Dunedin to Christchurch to play club cricket. The Canterbury openers at the time were Peter Coman and Barry Hadlee so making the actual side was one thing but I've never really understood why I couldn't make the squad. The previous year I'd been on the B trip and been top batsman.

An Englishman, James Graham-Brown, came to Christchurch for the 1975/76 season and played for my club, Old Collegians. He'd been on the Kent staff for two or three seasons and, like a lot of English players who come over here, he was a big star and automatically went into the Canterbury squad which annoyed me. Brownie knew I was interested in playing in England. He said he could organise me some club cricket, maybe a couple of second XI games, and perhaps even fix it for me to attend pre-season training with Kent.

That season, frustrated with apparently being unable to get anywhere with Canterbury, I'd moved to Gisborne and made the Northern Districts team. The contact had come through ND selector John Guy via Roddy Fulton with whom I'd played at Christ's College. I can't remember how people reacted and I didn't care. I'd worked so hard and not got the breaks with Canterbury that I felt I had to do something. I played five games for ND that season, averaging about 25.

At the end of the season I went to England, the first time I'd been out of the country. I wanted to go to England anyway, with or without cricket, and just thought I'd combine the two. I was pretty keen to further my cricket but if it didn't work out, I was going to play club cricket and look around. When I got there, I stayed with Brownie's parents and he'd arranged for me to go to Kent pre-season training at the St Lawrence ground. I also joined the Holmesdale club and played in the Kent League. When I played my first game, it was so cold my fingers were numb when I batted. It was brilliant to go to Kent's training with seven or eight internationals on the staff. We trained at the gym in the morning, had a three-course lunch with cheese and biscuits, then had nets or open wicket practice in the afternoon. I got a bat if I was lucky. We used to drive down to the ground with Bob Woolmer, who was then playing for England. The thing that struck me was how good the wickets were.

I'd never had anything specific in mind when I went to England although I can remember saying to Brownie what a great life it must be, playing professional cricket – the best thing you could ever do. That year the West Indies were in England with Richards making plenty of runs and Holding taking wickets and I watched a lot of it, mostly on television.

The summer of 1976 was superb, the sort that comes along once a decade then gets talked about fondly until the next good one. The wickets we played on in the Kent League were good, a lot of them in fact were county grounds. I didn't play regularly for the Kent seconds at the start of the season – they had a staff of two dozen and I got asked to play only if there were injuries. My first game was against London University and I batted in the lower order because I was just filling in.

A bunch of us went over to France for what was meant to be a ten-day holiday and ended up being a bit longer. I got my introduction to French wine and food. After ten days we rang Mrs Graham-Brown and said we'd been a bit delayed. She rang Kent and told the selectors I wouldn't be available for a little while yet. When I got back Colin Page, the Kent secretary, said to me "either you want to play or you don't. If you do we'll pay £5 every day you play plus expenses."

So I started to play regularly for Kent seconds. We had Chris Tavare, Chris Cowdrey, Graham Dilley, and Paul Downton, all of whom went on to play for England. Javed Miandad and Kepler Wessels were playing for Sussex, Mike Gatting and John Emburey for Middlesex, and Graham Gooch for Essex. It was a great summer and the wickets were excellent till August when they turned square. I got runs – 500 averaging 52. Then I played a game for a Derrick Robins' XI against the Kent county side. I batted with the South African Kenny McEwan, and we both got centuries. I was playing a lot more cricket – four or five days a week – and of a higher standard than I thought I'd get. I was getting runs and it was helping my game. I was playing with guys in my age group who were there for the same reason – to improve their game – but I wasn't a threat to them because I was an overseas player and Kent already had three overseas players.

I was very well treated: got my second XI cap, went to Lords with the Kent side when they beat Worcestershire in the Benson and Hedges final, and out to the victory dinner afterwards when Norman Graham slipped cutlery into Derek Underwood's jacket and warned the waiter to keep an eye on him. When Derek went to leave he was stopped and they found a knife and an ashtray in his pocket.

The thing about Kent was that they were extremely positive. I had mates of my age and there were also the guys who'd made it like Alan Knott, Underwood, and Brian Luckhurst. I got an insight into how a club was run. Mike Denness was captain and he wasn't that popular although he was very good to me. I used to travel a lot with my gear and whenever I'd spend a couple of days in London, I'd leave it in a locker at Victoria station. I was late for a game once and I rushed to Victoria, jumped on the train, and was starting to relax as the train chugged out of the station when I realised my gear was still in the locker.

Playing for Holmesdale was fantastic. We played on lovely grounds and although it was competitive, you enjoyed yourself socially afterwards. It was a great club and I still have contacts there and a lot of Kiwis have played there since. The thing that struck me later was the difference between Kent and Derbyshire. Northerners were much more straight up, much more like Kiwis. People in Kent didn't quite look down their noses but they were reserved. Derbyshire was essentially working class, harder and tougher. Kent was a wealthy county and it was like going from the smartest house in town to the worst.

At that stage Derbyshire was the only county which didn't have its quota of overseas players. On the advice of people like Brian Luckhurst, Page, and Norman Graham I wrote to them and asked them for a trial. The secretary David Harrison wrote back saying thanks but no thanks – we're only interested in test players. I thought that was it. Then towards the end of the season, Kent played Derbyshire in a John Player league match at Folkestone. During that game Page and Luckhurst mentioned to the Derbyshire people that they should have a look at me. Derbyshire got back in touch and asked me if I'd like to play in a couple of trial games. Page said he'd told the Derbyshire secretary that I was a good player and all I had to do to get a contract was go up there and hold a bat. I didn't believe that.

I went up by train. I'd never been north of London and immediately noticed the difference between north and south. I carried my gear to the hotel and that night I was ill and I can remember thinking 'I've come all this way and I won't be able to play.' Next morning I felt okay and got a taxi to the ground in Heanor, a mining village. I was early and the only other person there was an old bloke with a flat cap, a tweed jacket, a whippet and smoking a pipe. He was a cricket nut but he went on about how overseas players were ruining the game. I didn't say too much in case my accent gave me away.

It was a second XI game, Derbyshire against Nottinghamshire. They had Kenny Watson who played for South Africa; we had Alan Ward, who'd played for England that year. It was a good wicket on a small ground. I told them I was an opener and they let me open. I didn't think I had anything to lose: for the other second XI guys it was just another game, but there was a lot riding on it for me. I got 159 not out. I knew it was an important innings but it was just one of those days. In another innings I got 73 out of 124 and in my three trial match innings I scored 239 runs at an average of 119. Eddie Barlow, the great South African who'd come over to captain Derbyshire, was watching and I was offered a one-year contract. It was quite simple: if I hadn't have got runs, there wouldn't have been a contract. The deal was £1800 and a one-way air fare. Barlow was on £10,000 a season. They got me on the cheap but it was the biggest break I've ever had. Besides, there weren't any other counties chasing me. So I went back to New Zealand with a contract to play county cricket in my pocket, having played just five first-class games.

Each season in county cricket you play about 70 days of first-class cricket plus at least 20 one-day games in three competitions. One year there is the equivalent of three seasons in New Zealand. From that point of view it's like a fast track. During the year you encounter all sorts of different conditions: you might start out playing on a slow seamer at Derby and end the week playing on something lightning quick at Hove.

As a pro I was paid to play cricket and nothing else for five and a half months. I was always in the first team and could concentrate the whole time on improving my cricket. In the seconds you have to coach. As a 23-year-old in 1977, it was a fantastic place to improve your game.

My first game was against Minor Counties, who are amateur players. I dropped a catch and lost £10 to the bus driver, Ivor, playing cards. Next game we played Worcestershire at Chesterfield in a Benson and Hedges 55-over game. There were eight test players taking part: they had Glenn Turner, Basil D'Olivera, Vanburn Holder and Norman Gifford; we had Barlow, Mike Hendrick, Geoff Miller and Bob Taylor. It was a bit daunting. There was always a lot of pressure on you as an overseas player, especially being an unknown. The way I looked at it I was only on a one-year contract so I had nothing to lose. It was a great challenge, a fantastic opportunity, but I didn't know if my future lay in county cricket. I got 102 in 178 minutes at Chesterfield where people had been a bit critical of me being signed. I'd replaced Ron Headley and at the first committee meeting after I'd got the contract someone said "who the hell is he and why the hell did we get rid of Ron Headley?"

I got a great reception from the team. When you go in as an overseas player, they're wondering what they've got so there's that sorting out period, but they were very helpful. When you are a young guy coming into a team, it pays to sit in a corner and shut up which is what I did that first year.

The first problem I had was with my running between the wickets. I had three or four run outs early in the season. Against Kent I was run out by Alan Ealham, the best cover fieldsman in county cricket – one writer said that taking a quick single to him was like dicing with a rattlesnake. Eddie Barlow had told me before the innings not to bother coming in if I was run out again. Fortunately he was the incoming batsman as I came off but the lads hung a noose from the ceiling so it would be ready when he returned. It was just a case of adjusting to limited-over cricket and to the fact that it never rains but pours.

My third first-class game was against Hampshire, who had Andy Roberts, who was a lot quicker than anything I'd faced before. He had a very good stare, never said much, and generally knew where it was going. I faced him a lot that day but it was a very flat wicket. After a few games I was in the top five in the national batting averages which gave me a lot of confidence and went some way to keeping the critics happy. I was capped on May 28 after five first-class games for the county. I had no idea what a cap was all about and found out later that some players wait three or four years for their cap. I got it at lunch on the first day of a game against Kent after getting a quick 40 odd. My wages went up from £1800 to £2300. It's also ten years from the day you are capped until you're eligible for a benefit.

For a young man, playing county cricket for two or three years is a tremendous opportunity to improve your game because you get such a lot of experience in a short space of time. You're playing consistently good opposition and you're enthusiastic: it hasn't become the way you learn your living. I've always thought young English players who get on a staff don't realise how lucky they are. So many New Zealanders would love the opportunity to be paid to play for five or six months. The standard of play is good. You face the best bowlers in the world – most of the counties then had two overseas players one of whom was a bowler – and you watch the best batsmen. I saw Barry Richards score three hundreds, one of them before lunch. You learn a lot just watching a player of that calibre.

Barry Richards was probably the best player I'd ever seen. After he'd got a century before lunch, we put the field back and he lost interest. His batting was effortless. I faced John Snow when he was trying to bowl quick in a limited-overs match and got an idea why he'd been so effective in Australia in 1970/71. He hit the wicket hard and got a lot of bounce. He was sharp and bowled straight at you, always coming in at the body. You weren't trying to get on the front foot to him.

Viv Richards got 104 against us in a limited-overs game – it was unbelievable. His first 50 took 46 minutes, his second 28. We got 238 off 40 overs which was a Derbyshire record for the John Player League but Somerset won. I can remember fielding on the deep square leg boundary when he whipped one round the corner. It hit the fence only five yards from me but I didn't have a chance of stopping it. You saw some tremendous cricket, particularly batting. By the middle of the season the wickets were flat, the batsmen were in a rhythm, playing with a lot of confidence, just picking up where they left off the game before. I saw some really remarkable innings.

Geoff Boycott didn't play a remarkable innings in the sense of spectacular shots but he was amazing in his own way: you could be at the ground at 11.15 and he'd be on five and come back six hours later and he'd be on

155 and he'd still be doing the same things. He was so methodical. He did accelerate a little bit but not dramatically. He was an accumulator, a real professional, a run getter. When these players get in on flat wickets, it's really up to them – how many risks they're prepared to take. Boycs was a low-risk player. He was brilliant at manipulating the strike and could always get the single when he wanted to face the bowling and when he didn't.

Boycott took his batting so seriously. I once played in a benefit game for Bob Taylor against a village side in Yorkshire who would have struggled to win an under-14 competition. The wicket was terrible but it was an afternoon out to help Bob get a few quid. It was a 40-over game and I got out after four or five overs for 20 odd. After 32 overs Boycott was still there and I don't think he'd got 50. He played it as if it was a test match against the West Indies. People accepted that that was just Boycott. I used to marvel at his self-discipline, how he turned himself into a machine. He didn't show emotion, didn't allow himself the luxury of risky shots or going down the wicket even after he'd passed 100 and despite being quite capable of playing shots.

I quickly realised that it didn't matter how hard I practised or how well I played, I never would, never could bat like some of the players on the circuit. Viv Richards did the most extraordinary things, getting away with things I wouldn 't dream of doing. I used to think I was playing a different game from guys like Ken McEwan, Alvin Kallicharran, Zaheer Abbas, and Gordon Greenidge on their magic days. Glenn Turner came into this category particularly in his last few seasons when he expressed himself, scoring his runs in incredibly quick time and probably enjoying it a lot more.

Then there were the characters and the old pros. Norman Gifford was as tough as anyone on the park but he had great humour. Once we were batting out time when Ole Mortensen, our Danish fast bowler, came in saying he was going to play a few shots and then proceeded to block five overs from Giffy. Giffy wanted a fielder in at bad/pad. The bloke he asked wasn't very keen and Giffy said "the way he's batting you could put a Ming vase in there". He was one of the spinners I learnt a lot from.

The Essex bowler John Lever played so well for so long that he had a second benefit season. He was the best left arm quickie I ever faced and used to sort me out. Geoff Cook of Northants was a tremendous pro, a good bloke to play against, and would always have a laugh afterwards.

In my first season I topped the Derbyshire averages and aggregates, 1080 at 32.7, just a reasonable first year by some counties' standards. I knew I had to perform but everything was new and I just played cricket and didn't worry about the pressure of being an overseas player. I enjoyed it more than any year at Derbyshire.

The players were generally very helpful. Early on I'd ask Geoff Boycott about opening and John Hampshire about how he coped with playing all the time. After play you have a pint in the changing room then a drink in the bar with the opposition and the main topic of conversation wouldn't be the stock market. There would be a lot of discussion about technique which was excellent for a young player if you were talking to someone of vast experience like Dennis Amiss.

It was also interesting playing at the different grounds. You had a list of what was important: what's the wicket like? What are the changing rooms like? (You'd turn up at some of the small grounds and find that only half the team could fit in the dressing room at one time.) What are the lunches like? Some of the grounds were very depressing – Coalville was in the middle of a colliery; Aberystwyth was awful, playing against Javed and getting smashed all over Wales by a Pakistani. The festival weeks were good with tents all over the ground and invitations to the sponsors' tents for a drink.

'Bunter' Barlow was definitely the best captain I've played under and from my point of view it was a tragedy that I had only one season under him. He was ruthless – he sacked Alan Ward and Phil Sharpe, both England players, because of their attitude to training, not their lack of ability. They weren't too keen on running up hills and we did plenty of that. The pre-season training was very tough. He was in his late 30s then and I remember him leading us on five-mile runs. Runs were a great means of getting everyone on the same level, going through a bit of physical pain together.

A couple of times in training I was ill from exhaustion, and he commented that Kiwis were pretty soft. Late in the season a game was cancelled because of rain. We trained and this time Bunter puked. I said the South Africans seemed to get soft as the season went on. We were in the middle of shuttle runs and I had to do the last one and then a two-mile run and he was there with me. He could handle himself and he enjoyed life – he was about as positive off the field as on it.

One of Barlow's legacies to Derbyshire was the emphasis on physical fitness. After a session of shuttle runs up hills, David Steele and I were lying on the ground exhausted. He said: "Wrighty you know I'll be really pissed off if I have a heart attack before the season starts. I tried to bat in the nets yesterday but my legs were too tight and I couldn't get the front one out to play forward." I told him that if he did croak, I'd like his bat. We had people who could do 200 sit-ups, 80 press-ups, endless star jumps, but couldn't bat or bowl.

Bunter was very positive – we could be 80 for eight chasing 220 and we'd be winning the game – and very strong on discipline. He was attuned to the various stages a game goes through and wouldn't let it drift away. If you missed a single at cover he'd remember it and have a word with you at tea. He didn't get many runs but never considered himself in bad nick and he was an excellent bowler, never afraid to take a guy on. He once bowled four bouncers in a row to Wayne Daniel, who was very quick. I don't think Daniel forgot. He certainly repaid the compliment to the Derbyshire openers.

When I first started Eddie told me I was one of the best young players he'd seen. No one had ever said that to me and it made me think he really believed in me. It probably wasn't true but it was good for my confidence. We'd have changing-room discussions and everyone would give their point

Eddie 'Bunter Barlow' is the best captain I've played under – Derbyshire's and South Africa's answer to 'Grizz' Wyllie.

My first test series – 1978 against three of my Derbyshire teamates: Mike Hendrick, Geoff Miller, and Bob Taylor.

of view. He'd listen then do exactly what he wanted to do. You could have a disagreement with him but he never held a grudge. I had a few fairly heated discussions with him; I remember him arriving at the wicket in a limited-overs match after we'd had a slow start and demanding to know what was going on. I told him to get off down the other end and we had a bit of a shouting match. He was pugnacious, like Alex Wyllie.

He loved to compete. I found that South Africans had a lot in common with Kiwis in that sense: because the South Africans couldn't play test cricket, county cricket was like a world stage for them and they were incredibly competitive. It would have been great to play longer under Bunter. He was very popular at Derbyshire, looked on as the man leading them out of the wilderness. He was the ideal bloke to lead a struggling side but maybe not the guy to play under for five years. He was probably more ruthless in terms of looking after his own interests than I ever realised.

When I first started, I wouldn't say much for a whole day after I'd been dismissed. Failure affected me too much, I got really down. Gradually I realised I couldn't afford to do that, that I had to be more philosophical about it because it would end up affecting my next performance. I managed to get out in lots of different ways. In my first season I nicked a ball and it lodged between my legs. The 'keeper Roger Tolchard trampled all over the stumps to get to me and grabbed the ball.

On the other hand, you couldn't get carried away with success. I got 169 against Pakistan and failed in my next three digs. Barlow used to say: "If you take the piss out of cricket, it'll take the piss out of you." Most of all, you couldn't afford to lose your hunger for success and achievement. Because you were playing all the time, a particular innings or game could easily lose significance and you could take the attitude that there's always next time. That attitude can make you easy on yourself, more tolerant of failure. I felt I had to perform. I was in a side with shortcomings, often out of the one-day competitions early in the season, so it was important to have an inner drive and your own standards so that at the end of the season you could feel you'd done a good job and were worth what you were being paid.

County cricket isn't as antagonistic as other types of cricket. There's not so much sledging although there are personality clashes, people who hate each other's guts. The umpires are excellent and disciplinary rules are pretty strict: you get reported for showing dissent, questioning umpires, running on the wickets. Things that go on here wouldn't be tolerated. I'm far more aggressive to New Zealand umpires than English because discipline standards there are much stricter. Most of the umpires there are ex-players so they know what's going on and they're pretty relaxed. When you're batting, it's easy to have a conversation with the umpire, ask him "am I coming in straight on the ball, am I lining up on off stump?" The bowlers do the same.

I never had any problems with the Aussies and that aggro thing. It goes on and you accept it but when it goes over the top, it's just boring and becomes monotonous. It's part of gamesmanship and putting people off. In county cricket it's much more subtle. You have to play these guys three or four times a season, have a drink with them, so you have to learn to co-exist just like competitors in any industry.

Oddly enough that darling of the cricketing establishment Mike Brearley used to annoy me. I found his public school manner a bit hard to take – he referred to me as a colonial once which was hardly the way to start a beautiful friendship. Most of it was simply good captaincy, trying to unsettle me. He was very good at picking up where you didn't want fielders put and upsetting your game that way.

I learned as I went along, mostly from the old pros, the 35-year-olds and over: they've learnt the little tricks such as when you get in on a flat wicket, you make the most of it because next week you could be facing Sylvester Clarke on a green one at the Oval. That was one of the things Steele taught me.

You learn to sum up the options, work out what the opposition is doing, choose the low-risk course of action. If you're facing a guy you know will bowl a loose ball regularly, you wait for the gift. You become a technician. You discipline yourself not to play shots for the sheer hell of it, because you enjoy playing them. My job was to score runs and win games if we got in a position to do so. You measure success in getting 50 rather than playing shots. A first-class cricketer in New Zealand can have a poor season and go back to his job thinking "I'll have another crack at it next year"; in England if you don't perform, you go back down the pit. You learn to play within your limitations. The limited-over game has changed things though: fielding has improved, batting is much more aggressive and there's not so much of the old professional approach.

The thing about professionalism is that it's not necessarily the way you play: it's an attitude, attention to detail. The England wicketkeeper and my Derbyshire colleague, Bob Taylor, was a great example of a totally professional cricketer. His high standard of performance and total commitment were the same day in and day out. There were other players and sides who always won from certain situations: Knott, Amiss, Keith Fletcher. Essex were a tremendously professional side. They'd grown up together and had the ability to enjoy their cricket. Fletcher was a very good player and captain – it was a real mistake for England to drop him as captain. Middlesex under Mike Brearley were the same. It wasn't surprising that professional outfits started from the top, from the committee and the chief executive and his staff through to the captain and coach.

To state the obvious, being a pro means you play cricket for a living, and you become more conscious of the importance of making a living as you get older. It's a case of getting satisfaction out of it rather than enjoyment. When it's your livelihood and your working life, you have to have that attitude. I have a reputation for being very untidy because I never used to worry about packing gear. I've learnt that it pays to be methodical about small details. I remember knocking up with Glenn Turner and being amazed how methodical he was. He hit the ball the same way day in day out.

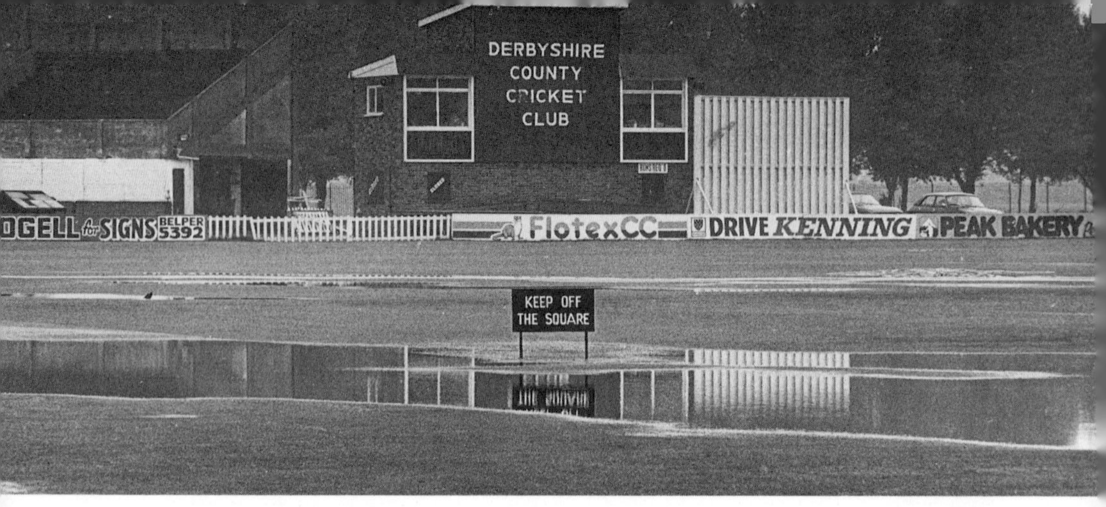

Get the cards out!

There's inevitably a negative side whenever you're doing something because you have to, rather than because you really want to. 'Rain stopped play' is a well-loved phrase on the circuit; hoping for rain because you don't want to play can become a habit if you're not careful. One of the interesting things was that sometimes when things were least in your favour, you succeeded, and then other times it didn't matter how good you felt, it didn't go for you.

Despite fluctuations of mood, attitude, and form my game never really fell apart. I never lost a sight of the simple, relentless requirement of the job: you're a pro, you've got to score runs. In the end it comes down to mental attitude and a solid method: playing straight, keeping your head still, full face of the bat: showing them the maker's name, as David Steele used to say. I don't play spinners all that well but I've had enough exposure to have a method that enables me to stay at the wicket and score runs. I don't use my feet but I commit myself a long way forward in defence and score off the back foot, cutting out the high-risk shots. You watch a guy like Keith Fletcher and see how late he plays the ball. You learn what you can and can't do, what shots you can and can't play.

You bat with a guy like Barry Wood who gets out cutting off spinners and you learn that cutting the ball coming into you isn't such a good idea after all and you stick with a straight bat. The bowlers tend to bowl at the stumps so you become a good legside player. Players get to know you too which makes it interesting. The big thing for me was to get through the new ball. The class performer gets the new nut and there's not so many good spinners around now.

In county cricket you don't get a chance to work on technical things because you're always playing rather than practising and experimentation in mid-season is a dicey business. I did more of it than most and sometimes took it to extremes. Steeley and I used to talk about hands a lot, about our grips and whether our hands were working together. I got so worried about the position of my hands at one stage that I glued my gloves to the bat handle. I got a century but it was bloody awkward carrying the bat while running between wickets.

CHAPTER THREE

Derbyshire

Derbyshire County Cricket Club is one of the perennial also-rans of English cricket, usually to be found bumbling along at or near the foot of the championship table. The club has won just two trophies in its history – the championship in 1936 and the Natwest limited overs competition in 1981.

It wasn't fashionable and had no right to be. It has a reputation for producing fast bowlers – Les Jackson, Cliff Gladwin, Mike Hendrick, Harold Rhodes, the Popes – its most famous player is probably Bob Taylor the ex-England wicketkeeper and holder of the record for most first-class dismissals. Derby is a football town and when I arrived Derby County had just won the league under Brian Clough and had a great side with players like Archie Gemmell and Frannie Lee. Cricket wasn't a big deal in the county.

At one time we had the most unpopular ground on the county circuit – Derby Racecourse: exposed, very cold, a desolate place, and without decent changing rooms. When the Aussies played there in 1981, they were not impressed, Dennis Lillee in particular. The question "How the hell do you play here?" was constantly on their blue-tinged lips.

It could be bitterly cold there, often sleeting during the early season games. We played a two-day practice game against Northants in late April. They rang up on the second morning and said they wouldn't be fronting up – and it was their turn to bat. Fielders were known to wear long johns and thermal underwear, two T-shirts, a shirt – sometimes with a parka underneath it – and two or three jerseys. A quick who'd been running in like greased lightning down south would get there and seize up. Amazingly, people used to come and watch when it was freezing. There was a bloke called Geoff who'd turn up and pretend it was summer. He'd sit there in his short sleeves saying wasn't it wonderful that summer had arrived.

We used to change where the jockeys did and there was one window to watch from. I was flatting in Chesterfield and I'd drive 25 miles, train for three or four hours, then have a lunch of a couple of cheese cobs and a pint of shandy at the Grandstand pub because the club didn't provide lunches. In a strange sort of way I grew to love the ground. They've made many improvements over the last ten years – notably a new pavilion – and it's not a bad ground but a lot of people hated playing there.

For the first three or four years I just got on with my cricket; then I started thinking about what could be done about the things I could see were wrong and that the players found so frustrating. With Eddie Barlow in charge that first season, there was a sense the club was going places. We had a good side with Barlow, Hendrick, Taylor and Miller and finished seventh – the best placing for ages. Another eight points and we would've been fourth. It was a happy side.

I don't know too much about what happened the next year – I was on tour with New Zealand – and at the end of the season Barlow left. We lost the final of the Benson and Hedges competition, supplied three players to the England team, and finished 14th. Then the changes started: in the first six years I was there, the club had two chief executives, five chairmen, and four captains. After another change of captaincy, a newspaper compared the comings and goings at Derbyshire with those in television's 'Dallas'.

A club is like a business – standards are set at the top and if the board of directors (or in this case the committee) is good and makes the right decisions and the right appointments, starting with the chief executive, you have a good club. And like a business, a club has a bottom line which is the playing results. If you're winning, you attract sponsors and members. Derbyshire had fewer members than any other county.

Admittedly some clubs have more assets than others because of tradition and location. Those with test match grounds have commercial advantages and they attract players who want to play at those grounds. Then there's the London factor: if you play for Middlesex, you've got a better chance of playing for England because the cricket writers on the big, national, London-based papers – and some of the selectors – don't want to travel outside London too much. It's a bit like Auckland in New Zealand rugby.

The county clubs are run along the same lines as some charities here. The Derby president was the Duke of Devonshire, then you had the chairman and the committee of 10 or 11 people. Committee members were elected by the members and were amateurs, not involved professionally with cricket. The committee really made the decisions that affected the club and the players.

The club's 'management' consisted of the secretary, these days known as the chief executive, a treasurer in charge of the finances, a sales manager in charge of commercial things including sponsorship, a catering manager, office staff, then the coach, groundsman and playing staff.

There were two types of committee member: one attended a third of the meetings and was seen only at the important games when he'd roll up in his XJ6 looking immaculate and condescend to talk – as if he knew it all – to the guys who'd done well in that game; a regular at test matches where he'd make the most of the hospitality provided by the host county's committee members. The other was retired, chairman of the grounds committee, made the PA announcements during the game which would include weather forecasts, and spent most of his daylight hours at the club working his guts out to make it better.

Some committee members were motivated by parochialism – there was a rivalry between Derby and Chesterfield because Derby was chosen as the headquarters although Chesterfield had the cricket tradition and the nicer ground. That was the sort of nonsense that went on. I don't think anyone on the 1977 committee had played first-class cricket; by 1987 there were three out of 14. That's certainly not the only criterion but it does tell a story.

With all the changes, the club lost direction. The players generally got the raw end of the deal: they were the hired help. I always felt that there wasn't enough interaction between the committee and the players in the decision-making process. It was only when Kim Barnett became captain that I was asked my opinion. It was far easier to quantify the players' deficiencies – you just have to look at the averages at the end of the season – than to assess how the administrators had performed. But the lack of accountability is demonstrated by the fact that there was a bloke in an important position in the club whose nickname was 'Slightly', 'Totally' or 'Absolutely' depending on what time of day it was.

Peter Kirsten, the most brilliant batsman I've played with, left because he just got fed up with the way the club was run. We used to talk about how things could be improved but eventually it got to him. It was a mistake for him and a mistake for Derbyshire. If his registration hadn't been cancelled, both of us could have played when Michael Holding wasn't playing.

However, the people at the club were very loyal to me. They could have hired just about anybody instead of me and once I was there, they couldn't have been more friendly and helpful. But there were one or two people who were a waste of time and who did not have enough cricket experience and knowledge. There also wasn't enough interaction with the local club leagues. A lot of the clubs reckoned they were better run than the county. At the end of my time there was only one bloke on the playing staff who was Derbyshire-born and -bred. On the county circuit we were known as the League of Nations.

If you can't attract good players, there's no point in having three or four mediocre ones. If you sign a 17-year-old, give him a chance for two or three years, then realise he hasn't got it, you've actually lost double that time because you've got to go through the process again. Identifying talent is absolutely crucial. Not enough attention was given to young players' mental make up and how hungry and and ambitious they were. Derbyshire wasn't attractive to ambitious young players because it didn't win trophies. The whole thing is self-perpetuating: if you're not a good club, you can't attract good players. Really good management is the way to reverse the cycle and at no stage did I feel we had that.

Players didn't identify with the club enough. To perform day in, day out, you've got to have pride in the club because that brings out the best in most players, particularly if they're not self-disciplined enough to set

A delicate matter – Barry Wood moving the two short legs.

The day after the night before – Derbyshire, 1977.

Vic the butcher – my landlord.

"Ay up, me duck! The bitter's good tonight."

Team photo Sunday lunchtime.

Early April and it's cold! The Derbyshire County Cricket ground.

There's plenty of room on the carpet – David Steele.
GEORGE HERRINGSHAW

their own standards. You see this with Essex, Liverpool and the All Blacks – it means something to play for teams like that; there's a tradition of success to be maintained and that has created large and loyal followings who demand nothing less than success. People want to play for these teams because they are the best and that perception of being the best extends to the individuals within the unit.

I would have liked to have had a much bigger input especially after I'd been there for a few years. I honestly felt it wouldn't have been too hard to have made the club perform better. You had the squad for six months and could work with them. The time I could have been more involved was before Peter Kirsten left. When Holding arrived and I was playing part-time, it was out of the question.

The players, crowds and fans were fantastic to me. I played my best cricket there, especially with Kirsten. Derbyshire had never had an overseas player who'd stayed longer than five years and although I wasn't a match winner in many respects, I think they appreciated honest effort. I've got tremendous respect for them and very fond memories because they were so long-suffering. They didn't have much success, and the club had poor facilities, but they turned up. They were really nice people. In a way the whole club was too nice. They'd have done better if they'd been more ruthless. If I'd have been in charge, I'd have got a quick bowler from overseas. Derbyshire signed two batsmen – me and Kirsten – as its overseas players on the theory that we'd get the runs and they'd attract English bowlers to the club. It didn't happen. They should've got rid of one of us and got a match-winning bowler.

But if Derbyshire was short of some things, it wasn't short of characters. We had a spin bowler whose opening line to large ladies was: "What do you do love? Kick start jumbos?" He once referred to a southern titled lady as a 'pig with lipstick'. He'd interrupt a young single bloke chatting up a woman to say the guy's wife was on the phone or just stand there with a strand of chewing gum hanging out of his nostril.

Mike Hendrick was very down to earth. When we roomed together during away games I wouldn't dare wake him up if I came in late but if it was him, he'd come crashing in and turn on the light and the radio. I was very much the junior. He was very helpful but stood no nonsense – if you played a bad shot, he'd tell you. He was one hell of a bowler, the best seamer I've played with. He left the club because he didn't see eye to eye with Barry Wood. Woody insisted we turn up at 11 a.m. for John Player matches which didn't start till 2 p.m. Hendo claimed that meant he couldn't go to church, a story Woody believed for a while because he was new to the club. A less likely churchgoer than Hendo would be hard to imagine. Hendo and Fred Swarbrick once gave the PA announcer at Derby a note saying that Ivor Biggun and Hugh Jarsoll were wanted at the secretary's office. It was duly broadcast.

There was an off spinner called Bob Swindell who lacked confidence. We were playing on a square turner and he knew there'd be pressure on him to deliver, so before we went out to field on the second day he had three double brandies to stiffen his resolve. He was never called upon to bowl.

When Barlow left, David Steele, a wonderful character, came from Northants to captain the side. He'd been in the game a long time and his views on pre-season training were the exact opposite of Barlow's. He enjoyed a benson and lots of cricket and there was a clash between the Barlow doctrine and the Steele doctrine. He lasted three months.

He was sacked from the captaincy after a game in which we ended up chasing 217 in 117 minutes and 20 overs – about 73 runs an hour. We lost a wicket in the third over and he went in and closed it up. He batted for 50 overs of which 17 were maidens and was 66 not out at the close. One of the reasons he did it was because Wayne Daniel had given our batsmen a hard time but it caused quite a stir. He wasn't totally suited to the captaincy.

He used to read the bowling figures out: "Hendrick, 15 overs, three maidens, three for 38 – well bowled"; there'd be the same sort of thing for a couple of others then: "Wincer, 17 overs, one maiden, none for 125 – knacker's yard".

Steele was the sort who'd say, when you came into the dressing room really pissed off after getting out, "Shit shot Wrighty". He also had a lot of trouble with names. He was once interviewed on TV and asked about prospects for the season. He said we had a lot of promising players: "There's Kim Barnett, there's. . ." and his voice trailed off in mid-interview. He confused me with Alan 'Bud' Hill, the other opener, and called me 'Bud' for a while.

We were 290 for two one day, needing four off the over for a last batting bonus point. Kirsten and Steele both had centuries. Steele blocked five then tickled one to fine leg for a single. Woody was furious and so were the rest of us. When Steeley came in he said: "Sorry skip, I could feel a big one coming on". Usually when we were chasing, he'd whack a couple over the top to show he was really trying but his philosophy was 'there's plenty of room on the carpet, no need to go aerial'. He was a great player of fast bowling, taking it on the front foot, and was the sort of guy you wanted around when the going got tough. He never gave his wicket away.

He wasn't a bad left-arm spinner but sometimes his arm would hit his ear on the way through and the ball would bobble down the pitch giving the batsman a free hit. He'd run after it and dribble it away before the batsman whacked it, or 'spot' it and send the field back. He had a no-ball problem which he once tried to solve by wearing a size 12 boot on his front foot. He looked like Donald Duck waddling around the field and needless to say, he still over-stepped.

During a test he roomed with Mike Brearley. They weren't exactly soul brothers; Brearley, who had a bad back and had to sleep on a board, objected to Steeley smoking in their room. On the first day Brearley got a duck and Steele 90 not out. He'd recall how that night he thought to himself: "Here I am, lying on a fairydown, enjoying a smoke, and thinking about getting

Power struggle – new captain Kim Barnett and ex-captain Barry Wood.

90 and there's Brearley, lying on a board, breathing my fumes, and thinking about getting nought. That's life."

We once put a kipper under Steele's bonnet, on the manifold, and he drove halfway from Hampshire to West Wales with his head out the window because of the pong. He thought there was something wrong with the engine but he was the sort who wouldn't stop to find out.

Steele should've played a lot more for England. He was their top batsman, averaging 40 in eight tests, in two series against Lillee and Thomson in their prime, then the West Indies. He was picked late in his career and only because Tony Greig the captain wanted him. He was English sportsman of the year after his first season for England. Then he was dropped for a tour to India because they reckoned he couldn't play spin but as Steeley said: "Couldn't play spin? I'd play with a square ball if I had to." He would've succeeded because he had the temperament but he was unfashionable. He was too big a man to let it bother him. We became very good friends. One of the great things about playing county cricket was meeting blokes like Steeley.

Geoff Miller was the next skipper and his problem was that he wasn't himself. He was playing for England at the time and couldn't work out if he was trying to be Mike Brearley or Eddie Barlow. Being captain of a county team is bloody hard, the hardest job in cricket. It's constant – you've got the first team to lead, the second team to keep an eye on, and all the things going on at the club which shouldn't affect you but do.

Mills never really got to grips with it. He was succeeded by Barry Wood who came from Lancashire in controversial circumstances, leaving straight after getting a £62,000 benefit. When he signed we all knew he'd be the captain.

Woody was the little general. Under him we had the best Derbyshire side I played in and we won the Natwest and were fourth in the John Player

League. When we were batting together he'd walk down the wicket and say: "I'm a great player when I'm going, beautiful to watch."

Chris Tavare once got 156 against us which Woody described as the worst 156 he'd ever seen. He was a controversial captain. Kirsten didn't get on with him and they used to have arguments on the field. He could bring the best out in the team because he was cocky but then he'd fine people for turning up without a tie or jacket. When you're playing day in day out you don't need those sorts of regulations. He didn't want the coach interfering but the committee overruled him and he resigned. After he'd resigned as skipper, they wouldn't pick him – they said he was upsetting the team – so he left the club and retired. It was a waste of a fine cricketer because he still had a lot to offer.

Alan McLelland, a second string wicketkeeper, was called 'Snatch'. He had a gruesome afternoon at Taunton once and said afterwards that he'd dropped everything but his pants. Another time Steeley was bowling and Snatch had already missed a stumping and a catch off him. Vanburn Holder ran down the wicket, had a huge heave and let go of the bat which ended up sailing over mid on. Snatch dropped the ball and spent so long fumbling with it that Holder had time to walk back into his crease leaving an exasperated Steele on his knees in the middle of the pitch.

At most other clubs even the second team had sponsored cars; at Derby the top players did. Bob Wincer had a three-wheeled car whose shock absorber had gone on one side. We called it the plastic pig. In a pub once Bob called the waitress and complained there was a worm in his pie. "No love," she said, "that's fat." "I'm not bloody surprised," said Bob, "it's eaten half the meat."

Mike Deakin kept wickets a few times when Bob Taylor was on test duty. He was a cocky little fellow who drove a flash car and reckoned he was going to be a millionaire at 25. He used to walk out for warm ups with his wicketkeeping gloves on, smoking a fag. In a one-day game against Somerset Viv Richards smacked us all round the park and was still there when they needed only six to win with overs in hand. "Now then Viv," said Steeley, thinking of his bowling figures, "six singles will do it." "Sod that," said Deaks and bet Richards a fiver he couldn't hit the first ball of the over out of the ground which absolutely outraged Steele. Sure enough Viv hammered the first ball over the stand, tucked his bat under his arm, and walked off without even looking to see where the ball had gone.

Bob Taylor must have seen everything and played in a lot of bad sides during his 20-odd years in the game but he remained a real gentleman, the total professional, and a superb 'keeper – the best I've ever seen – who kept his own standards throughout. He was a tremendous team mate, the best pro of them all. I'd come back here to find 'keepers wouldn't bother to take throws on the half volley at practice. Bob took everything. You never remembered much about his performance because he made the difficult things look easy. He was very dapper and had more blue shoes than anyone I've come across.

Supporters' joy – Woody with the Natwest trophy.

Derbyshire Natwest Trophy Winners 1981.
Standing: *Peter Kirsten, Kim Barnett, Colin Tunnicliffe, Steve Oldham, Paul Newman, Me, Bud Hill.*
Seated: *Geoff Miller, Bob Taylor, Barry Wood, David Steele, Mike Hendrick.*

Ole Mortensen, our Danish fast bowler, was named 'Stan' after the English footballer. He was very intense and this, coupled with his Viking looks, caused the Essex team to call him Eric Bloodaxe. He was a very good bowler, quicker than Willie Watson, and tremendously competitive: our best bowler and best competitor after Holding. If something went wrong he'd scream "Satan" in his guttural accent which was pretty unnerving and he'd sledge batsmen if they played and missed – "You're useless," he'd say.

I admired him greatly because he'd come from Denmark with no cricket background and forced his way in. The standard of cricket in Denmark can be judged from the fact that Stan had a top score there of 230 and he was a county number 10 or 11 batsman.

He suffered from a bad back and in my last game for Derbyshire when I was captaining the side, he also had a groin injury. I bowled him right through the morning session because there was no way he was going to bowl again if he came off. He had a hot bath at lunch but when we got out on the field again, he said he couldn't bowl. I asked him to try: he made two attempts to get up to the wicket and each time he stopped halfway. The third time he made it and bowled one that was so slow, the batsman missed it completely. That was all he needed. He'd taken three wickets in the morning and he went on to take another four in the afternoon bowling on one leg and determination.

When he first arrived, he didn't understand the field positions – he could be put at backward square and end up at back stop – and he didn't consider it was his job to field a ball unless it came straight to him.

Stan took things pretty seriously and for that reason used to get a lot of stick from the other lads. We were playing Kent at Canterbury and John Morris and Bernie Maher messed up his gear. I was walking down the stairs when a brawny arm gripped me around the throat, nearly decapitating me. "Did you mess up my gear Shake?" he growled in my ear. Being completely innocent, I didn't take too kindly to this so a little later I put some liniment in his jockeys. Five minutes after he'd put them on, he was hopping around then he dived into the shower to try and douse the fire down below. That night I drove him back to Derby. He was convinced Bernie had done it and kept saying he was going to kill him. I was saying "Yeah Stan, it was a terrible thing to do." Luckily I didn't play in the next game when the lads told him I'd done it.

They were a great bunch of lads but you played cricket, had a few beers and that was it. In some ways it could be a lonely existence and Kirsten and I became good friends. We had a flat above a butcher's shop and used to get woken up in the morning by the clanking of the hooks as they put the meat on.

After we were married, Sue and I had a flat in a village called Duffield and we had our favourite pub, The Woodlark. The regulars there weren't really into cricket; they were working class Derby people who loved their football and it was a great place to get away from work.

CHAPTER FOUR

A week in the life

T*uesday, 10 July 1979:* We finish a match against Yorkshire at Chesterfield, losing by nine wickets. Boycott got 167 and 57 not out, I got eight and three. After the game we're thinking about the drive down to Hampshire and facing Malcolm Marshall. It's far better to make that sort of trip when you've scored a few runs or had a victory. Three of our players – Hendrick, Miller, and Taylor – are away on test duty so we're not as strong as we should be.

I'd come to the ground with my gear packed so it's a quick shower and change then into the car. It's a five-hour drive and we'll hit some rush hour traffic. I travel with Peter Kirsten as usual. Over the season you usually travel with the same people: some like to go straight through, some want to stop for a pint and a bit to eat. Some prefer pub grub and others like motorway cafes which are renowned for greasy food. I drive because Kirsie has a habit of falling asleep at the wheel. I'm not a good passenger anyway. I've got a sponsored car so mileage doesn't matter and I'll make a little bit on the petrol money.

It's important to get a good start to the county season: you get runs in the book and confidence to kick on. Games when you get eight and three aren't what you want. So far I'm averaging about the mid-30s which isn't brilliant. I'm well aware that I didn't perform and that we lost and now I've got to get it right.

Basingstoke is known as a turner, a real 'bunsen', not a great batting strip. It's not a regular county ground – it would have one or two games a year – but Marshall's playing so they might have left some grass on it. Hampshire's one of my good teams: I usually do well against them.

We talk about the game a bit then Kirsie sleeps for a while. We stop at a pub for a bar meal and a pint and get into Basingstoke at 11.30. Check into the Post House, not a bad pub, better than some. The standards of the pubs depend on the resources of the county – the richer counties can afford to put their players in better accommodation. Kirsie and I room together. Get to sleep about 12.30 a.m.

Wednesday, 11 July: The first thing you do when you wake up is check the weather: it's a beautifully fine day so we'll start on time. I enjoy a wet day more than most but you've got to face facts – we'll be playing. Quite often you get to games and it'll be raining and you hang around, maybe make a start with an hour to go on the first day. Everyone wants to call it off so you can get away but the umpires can't do it because of the rules.

Now they have these motor mops – you think you won't play for a month of Sundays and suddenly you're out there three hours later. When the rain's poured down, dressing room talk often turns to sabotage. Some days I just don't feel like playing and would love it to rain especially when we've got a day in the field. In England it rains so much, you half expect it. It's easier mentally somewhere like Australia or India because you take it for granted you'll be playing.

Derbyshire blazer and tie for the first day of a game. The familiar problem of slow service at breakfast. We've still got to find the ground and be there by 9.30. At the ground I have a run-in with the coach, Phil Russell, a good bloke and a great Derbyshire man, but this morning we don't see eye to eye. He insists on us wearing sprigs for fielding practices. Since the ground is really dry and it's a fine day, I don't think it's that important and we have a slight altercation. Having that sort of professional difference of opinion before play starts never helps.

The guys who got to the ground early have scored the best spots in the dressing room. It's perched on top of the pavilion and it's minute: by the time everyone and their coffins are in, we're falling over each other. The wicket looks like it will turn early but at least Marshall's going to struggle to get it past my earhole. We have a knock up and do our looseners. We seem to alternate between doing the looseners individually and as a team. I think it's good to do things as a team. Miller's away so Kirsten is captain. He wins the toss and we're batting.

I like to get ready half an hour before and then I get a bit uptight, particularly if I haven't been getting many runs. It's not going to turn square straight away so there's an opportunity in the first innings. I would've liked a net but there aren't any at the ground.

The lads give me a wide berth as I sit there. They know how to treat different players before they go in to bat and they know I like to be left alone. The only trouble is everyone's falling over the coffins. The bowlers are in shorts doing the *Telegraph* crossword and hoping the batters are going to stay out there all day.

I'm opening with Bud Hill who tries really hard. He normally goes out there and sticks around, a good gutsy player. Before we go out Bud and I have a short but serious discussion on my running between the wickets. (In the match before the Yorkshire game I ran Bud out; in response to my call he changed directions three times before being run out by half a pitch going for a single.) I tell him not to worry, if it happens again I'll buy him a motor bike for his birthday.

He takes the first one. I prefer to let the other guy take the first one;

My favourite batting photo – Natwest final at Lord's, 1981.
PATRICK EAGAR

My best mate – my wife, Sue.

Mum and Dad.

Tall stories with the Woodlark's landlord, Norman.

Not much grass on this strip – with Peter Kirsten outside our flat in early May.

"How do you think it'll play, Wes?" "John, your guess is as good as mine!" Wes Armstrong, my favourite groundsman.

Lining up for the aftermatch presentation – New Zealand's first test victory over England, Basin Reserve, 1978.

PETER BUSH

it gives you a bit more of a look at it. If the other guys feels the same you alternate but Bud doesn't mind. Marshall opens the bowling and doesn't get a lot of bounce. He's still pretty quick though: even on a wicket like this, he puts in the effort. We'll have to watch him. We put on 22 in four overs before Marshall bowls Bud for three.

Mike Taylor, a dribbly medium pacer comes on for an over so the quicks can change ends. I feel in quite good nick, having played a couple of meaty cuts. Taylor bowls one down leg side, I go to smack it away backward of square, miss, lift my back foot and get stumped, a smart piece of work by George Stephenson. It's bloody disappointing and I'm thoroughly pissed off and do a bit of swearing when I get in the dressing room. I got a start on what isn't a bad track, felt in reasonable nick, and got out to a basic error, probably going for it too much.

"Hard luck" from the guys. Apart from Steele, they don't really make much comment. If you're hard on yourself, you don't need someone else to tell you what you did wrong. It's only if you keep on making the same mistake and don't care about it that you need a rev. I'm getting a little more philosophical but it's only my third year in county cricket and I still don't take failure that well. I compete with Kirsten a bit, us being the overseas players. I feel he's got the edge, he's a more talented player, but I keep at it.

It's a good time to read the papers out on the balcony, write a couple of letters home telling them what a wonderful time I'm having over here not getting any runs, take a £5 double on the 2.30 at Thirsk – the horse will still be running at tea time. Then I watch the game and hope like hell that seeing I got out early, the other guys will get plenty so I can have a day in the sun. At lunch we're 100 for two with Steele and Kirsten looking good. Not a bad lunch out in the marquee. I always have a big lunch when I'm not batting. There's nothing worse than getting out early, being set for a big feed, and finding that lunch is lousy. This one's soup, salad, dessert, cheese and biscuits.

After lunch Kirsten and Steele go on to 118. They've put on 96 in two hours. Then there's a mix up and Kirsten is run out for 50. It's disaster. Kirsten is not pleased and, in his absence, Steele gets called some unflattering names. Being run out when it's not your fault is the most frustrating way to get out and Steele won't be expecting Kirsten to shout him dinner tonight. Then we collapse – six wickets go down for 33 in an hour. So much for a relaxing day on the balcony.

The ball's already turning and Cowley the offspinner has five wickets. Steeley's definitely not flavour of the month now. Our left arm opening bowler Colin Tunnicliffe, who's broad of beam and an extremely good striker of the cricket ball, is joined by Snatch McLellan who's filling in for Bob Taylor. They add 47 in 14 minutes, Tunner's getting 43. It's not a big ground and he hits four sixes in eight balls and gets to 50 in 24 minutes with five sixes and two fours. He's hitting straight, high and handsome and it's compulsive viewing for the boys on the balcony. John Southern, their left arm spinner, goes for 38 off four overs.

We're all out for 209, Cowley records his best figures – five for 44 – and we're in the field before tea knowing 209 is not enough on a wicket that's going to turn square.

At stumps Hampshire are 141 for two. We're not that well equipped for a turning wicket. Fred Swarbrick is really struggling with his bowling so it's Kirsten's part-time off spin and Steele's left armers. Fred's been bowling well in the nets but can't do it in the middle. The situation isn't helped by Tunners, exhausted from his batting, straining his groin after one over. Rice and Greenidge open. Gordon is limping which isn't a good sign: when he limps it usually means he's going to crash it everywhere. He doesn't go mad but he's 57 at stumps which is ominous. I drop David Turner in the gully, a sharp one but I should've caught it. I've definitely had better days.

We have a pint in the changing room, have a shower, then go to the sponsor's tent. They have them at festival games and at grounds that don't get a lot of cricket. It's a good way to relax and wind down. I have a few pints of bitter – it's taken me a couple of years to get used to bitter but now I'm a big fan. 'Where are we going to eat?' is always the question: some guys will eat fish and chips for four days to save money from their meal allowance. Steeley has mates all around the country who take him out for a meal which saves him a bit of dough. A few of us have a meal in a cheap Italian and try and forget about the day although the conversation keeps coming back to cricket. I get a reasonably early night because I'm knackered from the night before.

Thursday, 12 July: Same routine: at the ground at 9.30, warm up – this time in spikes, reluctantly. The coach gives us a team talk. We have some early success and get Greenidge – if he'd got set, we'd have been chasing leather all day. Turner, the guy I dropped, gets out at 30 which is a relief. There's no worse feeling than dropping a catch, especially if the guy goes on and gets a big score. At 174 for six there's a glimmer of light but the tail wags and they end up with 328 – 119 ahead. Steele and Kirsten have bowled 72 overs between them and taken nine wickets. Swarbrick got seven overs. We didn't bowl that well.

We're batting again before tea and the wicket's taking quite a lot of turn. Our attitude is to block out the game. Bud Hill gets out to Marshall again for another three. It's unusual because he's a good player of the quicks. No one tries harder – he goes to bed early, trains hard, works at his game. He's the sort of guy you don't want to see out in this situation because he can bat for ages. As usual when he gets out he looks to the heavens in sheer bloody horror and walks off very slowly. Once when he was doing his slow exit, a spectator yelled out: "Someone get a fishing rod and reel him in."

I'm concentrating hard, trying to get a big score. Their spinners, Cowley and Southern, aren't great bowlers, just good county pros, and although the wicket's taking turn, it's quite slow. Then I mistime a drive and get caught and bowled. I was caught in two minds whether to block it or hit it hard. I've made 17 in an hour. It's disappointing but not as bad as the first innings because I concentrated hard and gave it my best shot. It's easy to say I was done by the pitch but what's the point? I ballsed it up, should have blocked it. Kirsie gets 51 and at stumps we're 44 ahead with four wickets in hand. Their spinners are doing it again.

In the evening we go to a fun fair in Basingstoke. Snatch drops his wallet and we spend hours looking in a hedge for it. When I know I'm not going to bat the next day, I loosen up and a few of us have a beer or six and a few more back at the pub where a lot of rubbish gets talked about cricket. We're not exactly fancying our chances in this one. Steeley complains that he's too knackered to bat because he's doing so much bowling.

Friday, 13 July: Unlucky for us. We got to 196 for nine when Snatch and Bob Wincer come together. Wincer's called 'Back and across and run it down' because he's full of theories about batting. Snatch is dropped before he's scored. They go through to lunch at 249 and eventually put on 79. It's not enough. Hampshire, needing 158 to win, get them shortly after tea for four wickets. There's an air of inevitability about it all, including Steeley's 11 no balls and Snatch's missed catch and stumping. The stumping chance was Trevor Jesty who gets 68 in 76 minutes. Jesty's a very dangerous batsman on his day, a good timer and a clean hitter. If we'd held our catches we could have put them under pressure – Greenidge was dropped twice getting 33. They shouldn't have got the runs as easily as they did. It's the second game in a row we've lost and I haven't got runs. We leave Basingstoke around five for the drive to Liverpool.

County cricketers spend a lot of time driving. It could be worse – Yorkshire, Somerset, and Glamorgan being out on the extremities have it worse than us. A four-hour drive isn't much to look forward to when you come off the field but no one was complaining about leaving Basingstoke. Thank God for the motorways – it must have been awful before they existed.

We get to St Helens just outside Liverpool at 11 p.m., stopping at a motorway cafe for a change of diet. The sponsored cars are Cortinas which are fine. One year we had Anglia vans which the lads called milk trucks. I don't mind driving too much as long as you don't have to go into big cities. And the distances aren't that great compared to New Zealand – Basingstoke to Liverpool at 200-odd miles is one of the longest ones. Travelling and playing the next day isn't fun but it's a fact of life.

I've never been to Liverpool before so I'm looking forward to that but the hotel turns out to be not much more than a bed and breakfast. It's noisy and has saggy beds, both of which I hate.

Saturday, 14 July: A great English breakfast – eggs, bacon, toast and marmalade. There's a lot of racing on so we get the picks sorted out. The waitress is a real Lancashire lass; I could hardly understand her and she had communication problems with Steeley as well. He asked for two on a raft – two poached eggs on toast – and from the way she reacted, she must have thought he was suggesting something filthy.

Barry Wood – "I'm a great player when I get going."

Stumps drawn at Derbyshire. Alan Hill and Kim Barnett return to the pavilion.
JOHN GRAINGER

Steeley gets lost on the way to the ground and keeps on having to ask the way. He finally finds someone who knows the way and after he's got directions, he asks what the wicket's like. "It's a belter" is the reply so he takes off in a hurry, anxious not to miss out. Finding some of these grounds can be a problem though, especially in big cities and if they aren't signposted. I still get lost in Manchester and usually get different directions from everyone I ask.

The bloke who gave Steele directions is right about the wicket. One look shows it's full of runs. The changing rooms are good too, in a big old building, sort of a club with a bowling green out the back, a couple of bars and a restaurant. It's a beautiful day. We have a knock up, get the car springs out of the system. They win the toss and bat – not surprisingly. We've had a change in the team from the last game: Tunners has taken his strained groin home and for some reason they've replaced him with a batsman. That leaves us with an opening attack of Wincer and Walters. Wince is in his first year; he's developing and he's got some way to go. Walters is really a first change bowler. It's the sort of attack the Lancashire openers will be looking forward to facing: not a West Indian speed merchant in sight and three spinners who won't be much use on that wicket. It's a threadbare attack, especially given that Swarby got seven overs on the square turner at Basingstoke because of his problems. Losing the toss isn't such a bad thing because a last innings chase is our only chance of winning.

We've got top umpires: Dicky Bird, who's the best and Alan Whitehead, who's pretty good too. It's good to strike umpires you get on with. After three overs including five no balls and two wides – Wince is struggling to get his line – Lancashire are 28 when Dicky discovers that the two sets of wickets aren't correctly aligned. As Wince is running up to bowl Dicky calls out in his Yorkshire accent "the wickets are not straight, they're not straight." Leg stump at one end lines up with off stump at the other. We've got to start again much to the annoyance of Barry Wood and David Lloyd, the Lancashire openers. While they straighten them, Kirsie gives us a team talk on the theme of what rubbish we've bowled and how we've got to make the most of the second chance. At lunch Lancashire are 121 without loss.

Soon after lunch John Lister, who's called 'Myxomatosis' because of his bulbous eyes, chases a ball with such enthusiasm that he trips over the boundary rope and goes headfirst into the hard part of the deckchair, collecting four stitches in his lip. He's a bit accident prone; the phsyio reckons he's got a medical record as long as his arm.

We spend the day chasing leather. Woody gets 126, playing well especially as he's been going through a bad trot. He's one of those players who can annoy you because he always seem to be brimming with confidence. They tick along at four an over. Frank Hayes, who's a bloody good player and can really smack it, gets 72 and at 240 for two Clive Lloyd, just the bloke you want to see in that situation, lopes in. He has a look then gets stuck in. Fielding at extra cover is like being the goalie in a penalty shoot-out. Wince keeps bowling short and Clive keeps playing flat pull shots which are still rising when they hit a stand of conker trees about 70 yards away. Finally Wince says "Eh up Clive, it's only July. You're not meant to pick conkers till September."

They declare at 406 for four, Lloyd 104 not out, 29 no balls. Steeley has bowled 34 overs to follow his 61 at Basingstoke. It's not long since he was sacked from the captaincy and late in the afternoon he said to me: "I came to this club to toss the coin and ended up bowling 30 overs a day." When we got off the park, Kirsie gives us a bollocking for poor fielding. In fact we fielded bloody well; it's just a frustrated captain letting off steam. It wouldn't have mattered if we'd had a couple more players on the field.

At stumps we're 48 for none; I've got 27. The pressure's on and I didn't feel like failing again. Their attack's not that strong: Willie Hogg's slippery but all over the place and Paul Allott is inexperienced. No nasty fasty. I'd rather not have had to bat but when you're not out at stumps, you're pleased you had to. It's extra good to be not out on a Saturday night because you can have another look at their attack in the John Player League game on Sunday and pick it up again on Monday. It's almost like a net. A few of us go out for a restaurant meal and get back to the hotel at 8.30 p.m.

Sunday, 15 July: Sleep in because it's a 2 p.m. start then read the Sunday papers – a bit of upmarket stuff and some sleaze as the lads say taking off the tabloid's posters: Pope rapes Queen: We have pictures. The game's at Old Trafford in Manchester which is a 25-mile drive. It's our seventh day of cricket in a row but I'm still feeling good. It's not uncommon to play 20 days on the trot at some stage of the season. I'm really pleased to be not out and determined to do well because there's a whisper that the coach was thinking of dropping me for disciplinary reasons over the sandshoe episode.

It's another fine day. We have lunch at midday then go to Old Trafford. It's one of the best grounds in the world with fantastic changing rooms and great viewing positions. They have a good crowd who know their cricket, parochial but fair and witty.

Some players and sides don't like the 40-over Sunday league because it's a bit of a hit and miss affair; some sides specialise in it. It can be very frustrating because it's so compressed. We've lost four out of six games so we're basically out of it. Lancashire are a good one-day side but haven't been having a good season at home.

We lose the toss and get put in to bat. I get 44 out of 65 and am fourth out, playing quite well and feeling in good touch before I get out chasing a wide one. We end up with 154 which is the bare minimum score, probably not enough.

Steeley has been getting a hard time for no-balling so he tries his doomed experiment of wearing a size 12 boot on his front foot. The crowd must have wondered what on earth was going on when the whole Derbyshire team fell about laughing when he bowled a no ball in his first over.

Lancashire get a good start, everyone chimes in, and they win by five wickets with 2.3 overs to spare, much to the delight of the crowd. It was just a professional job; there was no need for anyone to go mad. We finish at 6.45, have a beer, then back to the hotel for an early night because I'm not out and want to have my act together tomorrow.

I had a chat with Fred Swarbrick; he's pretty unhappy and knows, as we all do, that if he can't get it together soon, it could be the end of him. He never really related to Eddie Barlow and feels his game didn't develop as it should have done. It's strange because he's such a competitive guy which comes out when he's batting but he just seems to have lost confidence in his bowling. In the nets he bowls as well as ever.

We've always thought he'll snap out of it because he's that sort of guy but it's a vicious circle: the longer he goes on bowling, the less of a bowl he gets. The closest he got to a bowl in the first innings was collecting David Steele's cap and handing it to the umpire.

Monday, 16 July: It's a cloudy day with the odd shower about and there's a slight delay. An English guy living in New Zealand comes up to me before play starts and wishes me luck. It's nice when they say g'day and good luck and leave it at that. Some of them want to spend the next couple of days and nights with you.

It's a good wicket so it's a case of just hanging in there and taking my time. I face a lot of Jack Simmons, a good off spinner known as 'Flat Jack' because he's pretty tight and doesn't give it much air. He's got me out before but there's not much turn today and I play him well off my legs. He still bowls 15 maidens in 41 overs. I'm pleased with the way I played him. I'm still learning about playing spin.

I get better as I go along and end up with 117 in 232 minutes with 19 boundaries. Life is good when you do well. When you're a pro and doing well, it's the best job in the world. Performance is everything – that's what you're there for. It's hard when it's not right, you worry about it, but when you do well, it gives you confidence and a lot of satisfaction from knowing you're still up there, you've still got it. It was a flat one and not a great attack but I still had to do it.

Bud Hill found himself at eight in the order after opening on a turner against Marshall the game before. It's the flattest track we've struck all season and he didn't get a bat. We declare at 300 for four just after tea and the opening bowlers get clobbered again: Lancashire are 63 for none after nine overs. Wince goes for 82 off 15 overs. They get 139 off 31 overs and the game is set up for a last-innings chase as it was always going to be.

Tuesday, 17 July: Lancashire add another 92 in 65 minutes then declare. Fred has a bowl and it's obvious he's completely lost it. He bowls an over to Bernard Reidy, who's a big strong lad and gives it a thump, which is half double-bouncers and half full tosses which go right over Reidy's head. Bernard just about ruptures himself trying to thrash the first few out of sight but can't connect properly, then decides not to risk making a fool of himself and blocks the rest. It's the most bizarre maiden I've ever seen. The Lancashire lads are falling off their chairs on the balcony and we're trying not to laugh. Later David Lloyd gets his century by back slogging a high full toss past Snatch's left ear with leg slip taking evasive action. It was tragic but funny.

A few weeks before Fred had gone to a bloke who'd given him a pebble to carry around, suggesting that if he rubbed it between balls, it would help him to relax. At one stage Kirsie, completely hosed off with this lack of bowling resources, said through clenched teeth: "Go on Fred, rub the ball and bowl the bloody pebble."

'Welder' Walters runs in from the third-man boundary to field a ball, turns himself inside out, and twists his ankle so he is out of it. It wasn't a great loss because he'd gone for 24 off six overs.

We're set 338 in just over four hours and get a good start. I get 63 before top edging a sweep. I played really well and am disappointed because it's the sort of wicket that once you get in, it's there for you. I could have got another century if I'd been a bit more patient. At one stage we're 205 for four and the win looks on but then a couple of wickets go and at 245 the chase is called off. Bud goes out to bat at eight under instructions to block it and smacks one from Jack Simmons off his toes. It hits forward short leg – a sub – in the guts and sticks.

Our next game's against Kent at Chesterfield but we've got a couple of days off before that and I'm looking forward to them. I never used to sleep during the day before. Since I started playing county cricket, I seem to do more and more of it.

With Viv Richards and Peter Kirsten after Derbyshire's victory in the Natwest final at Lord's, 1981.

Peter Kirsten – little man, big bat.
BOB THOMAS

The Aerial Route.

CHAPTER FIVE

Cap in hand

A benefit is normally granted about ten years after the player was awarded his county cap. That would mean he's been a regular member of the first team and obviously performed quite well. It works on a strict seniority basis: if player A got his cap two months before player B, A would generally get his benefit first. There have been examples of blokes playing for their county for seven or eight years then being sacked before their benefit; others who play long enough – Geoff Boycott for instance – get two.

Getting capped is crucial. I did that early on but some players wait for three years or more for their cap if they're not holding down a regular first-team place. If you're not capped till your mid or even late 20s, you've then got to battle the ageing process to secure a benefit. It requires a pretty clinical assessment; I was capped early on, played full-time for six years, then part-time for four. My salary dropped a little bit when I was part-time but I kept on playing because of the prospect of a benefit. It was like a carrot to a donkey. I was lucky that Derbyshire didn't have a lot of capped players who'd hung around for ten years. There were only five benefits in my time there whereas some counties have them every year.

A benefit runs for a full calendar year and is granted at the discretion of the committee and county club. During that year the beneficiary is allowed to organise functions and events, make a benefit tie and produce a brochure. Derbyshire is one of the few counties that doesn't grant the beneficiary the gate takings from a nominated match which makes it one of the worst places to have a benefit.

People don't actually buy any of these things; they make a donation to you which means every penny you get is tax free. That goes back to a House of Lords judgment in 1927 which decided that the proceeds from a benefit match were not subject to income tax and that subscriptions by the public to a benefit fund should be treated as a gift rather than remuneration.

There are several key factors which determine how much you eventually make from a benefit:

- The size of the county's catchment area and population base. The southern counties tend to be richer than the northern although Lancashire and Yorkshire have very strong traditions and large memberships. Derbyshire has the lowest membership of any county and that, and the lack of a benefit match, is reflected in the size of the benefits: the Derbyshire record is Bob Taylor's £54,000 while some of the star players at southern counties have raised over £150,000.
- How well the county team does that season. If the side does well, interest is increased, the followers are more enthusiastic and crowds are bigger.
- How well the beneficiary himself performs.
- How well organised the benefit season is and how much time is put in laying the ground work.

Because I wanted to play against the West Indies, I came home during the English winter when most players start preparing for the season. Generally the earlier you start the better. You're told you've been awarded a benefit a year in advance but I discovered a bit later than normal because a certain Derbyshire official, who may have been slightly, totally or even absolutely at the time, sent the letter informing me that I'd been awarded a benefit in 1987 to New Zealand by seamail. If I'd been given the nod early on I could have done some preparation during the 1986 season.

I played in the West Indies series and cut short my benefit in September instead of it running the full year to play in the World Cup in India but I still managed to miss some international cricket: the tour of Sri Lanka which was organised in January 1987, six weeks before it started. I was already committed to getting back to England and running the benefit which would have been impossible if I'd been on the tour. I must admit to having been pretty unimpressed with the way the tour was arranged at short notice – it probably cost me the captaincy but I would've been letting people in England down if I'd gone: the benefit season launch dinner took place before the tour even started. It wasn't an easy decision to make but I'd been a pro for long enough to put financial considerations first. As it turned out the Sri Lankan tour didn't last past the first test: someone hadn't done their homework.

The first thing you do is form a benefit committee which raises funds and organises things on your behalf. Some guys employ full-time fund raisers although it's actually illegal. You're also meant to confine your activities to your county although that doesn't always happen either. Some of the international stars top up already huge benefits by encroaching into other counties and that causes problems. I know I wouldn't have been very happy if some big star had come into Derbyshire and organised a dinner. After all you can sell only so many dinner tickets.

I was lucky that I had some good mates who were tremendously

"I've just bought his tie."

supportive and did a lot of work. The committee started with 15 and dwindled to about 10 who did all the work. We made a rule at the start that whatever we did, we weren't going to rip people off and we'd make sure everyone had a good time at the dinners, dances, race nights or whatever and I think we achieved that. Some people on the committee were influential businessmen which was important because they knew people who'd happily spend £100 on a dinner and buy £10 raffle tickets. Others were just ordinary people and the thought often crossed my mind that they were working to make money for J.G. Wright who was already better off than they were.

The brochure is a big revenue earner. Jeff Humphreys, a sub-editor on the *Derby Evening Telegraph*, did the layout. My committee chairman, Vic Brownett, had a label-making company which did the artwork. My role was writing to a lot of cricketers asking for articles. Most of these tend to be numbingly predictable so I asked contributors to make them a bit different from the usual brochure crap: "Anything you like but none of that 'terrific player, wonderful human being, devoted family man and kind to animals stuff."

I never realised how much work was involved in getting advertising for the brochure. Sue and I must have written 600-700 letters to potential advertisers plus the committee tapped all the contacts they had. We raised about £16,500 in advertising revenue which meant we netted £12,500 after printing and other costs.

We printed 5000 and had to get some back to New Zealand because we had advertisers here. Somehow the decision was made to air freight 1000 copies out which cost £1 a copy. To this day I have a stack of very expensive brochures in my wardrobe.

Then we tried to design a benefit tie which was like Barry Crump trying to be Pierre Cardin. A factory made up our original design and you wouldn't have been seen dead in it. Eventually we copied one we found in a certain internationally famous department store and it was a best seller.

The benefit started with a winter dinner, before I'd got back from New Zealand, which was a great success. After that it consisted of dinners with speakers and raffles, celebrity golf tournaments, games against clubs, six-a-side games in which business house teams, each of which would have a star playing for them, competed over a day, a midsummer ball at a stately home, race nights, a competition for local clubs, a spot the ball with a Mini as first prize, black tie dinners, and a brass band performance which netted £120.

I did everything: sold tickets, made speeches, organised matches, jacked up speakers, selected menus, rounded up players, visited pubs. I spent an unbelievable amount of time on the phone. It was almost 24 hours a day and I'd never do another one. You can always tell a beneficiary: overweight, because he's been drinking five or six pints a night, and capable of falling asleep on his feet. It's very hard to perform on the field because everything pales into insignificance compared to the benefit.

You rely a lot on your fellow players, especially your team mates. If there are a few stars on display, people are more likely to go to your dinners or whatever. Most of the players are helpful but there are exceptions and you sort out your mates very quickly. Most of your team mates are in the same boat, hoping they'll get a benefit. Those that are capped and are looking ahead to their benefit tend to be more helpful than those that aren't.

I arrived in Derby at 6 p.m. on a Saturday in late March, having travelled from New Zealand. Next day there was an indoor cricket tournament. It was a disaster, making a profit of £15. The reality of it came home to me. It hadn't been well organised and some people had put themselves out to be there. I thought to myself, "the whole year could be like this." I learnt that you may as well do it well if you're going to do it at all. Next day I had a speaking engagement in Bradford, Yorkshire. I was jetlagged and knackered. No one had given me directions and in the end when I got to

Bradford I had to pay a taxi driver £10 to guide me to the venue.

I had some good mates in Chesterfield who were great organisers and had wealthy contacts. They belonged to the Chesterfield Gentlemen's Luncheon club, a very social organisation which got together regularly at a pub called the Fox and Goose for various reasons: they didn't need much excuse for a celebration. We had three very interesting days when they put together sides of 13 or 14 players who'd pay £100 each to play the Derbyshire county side in a 25-over match. It would start with a morning tea and maybe a spot of brandy if it was cold. We'd play at Queen's Park, which is the county ground in Chesterfield which the fellows enjoyed. I'd captain the Gentlemen's Club and we'd have stretching which was a bit of an ordeal for them as they were mostly 40 to 50 and not that fit. Derbyshire would bat first and score something in the region of 324 for seven. Two members of my team would pull hamstrings sprinting round the boundary and several others would narrowly avoid serious facial injury trying to catch the many skiers that went up. There'd be blokes who'd drop three sitters then hang onto a screamer.

There'd be 20 minutes for the change of innings, then they'd have the dubious pleasure of going out to face Michael Holding. We'd usually manage 120 and be all out on the second to last ball of the 25th over. Then we'd all change into ties and blazers and reassemble at the Fox and Goose for refreshments and a buffet and sometimes live entertainment of the sort appreciated by broad-minded chaps.

It was a great day out for them, meeting cricketers and talking cricket. It gave cricket nuts a chance to play against England players and face the West Indies' opening bowler and at the end of it they'd have a photo of the two teams to show that they'd really played against a county side. People came from all over England and one from Ireland to play in these matches.

When Derbyshire played in the Natwest Trophy quarter-finals we put up a tent and hosted local businessmen who could sit and watch the cricket, eat smoked salmon and drink champagne for £25 a head. As the game wore on and they relaxed, one of my committee members, Gravity Newman, so-called because he was an expert on the specific gravity of bitter beer, sent some models around to sell raffle tickets. They were rather attractive young ladies and the raffle tickets sold well. One of the models happened to mention when she was in the tent that her ambition was to be a page three girl so a bloke bet her £10 that she wouldn't streak topless across the ground. She did and two days later she was on page three of the *Sun*.

The golf days were fun. They were run on celebrity pro-am lines. We had one at a course called Matlock with 34 teams and a celebrity in each. Fred Trueman was supposed to take part but he couldn't make it and the team that was expecting to have him ended up with a young lad who was struggling to make the Derbyshire side. Situations like that required a bit of diplomacy.

At another golf day, a Derbyshire player called Ian Anderson was drawn to play with the golf club captain who greeted Ian by saying he'd been looking forward to playing with him for two months. Ian didn't have the heart to tell he was a god-awful golfer but after he'd shot a nine and ten on the first two holes, his previously enthusiastic partner stopped talking to him. Three Derby County footballers were meant to take part in that game but when I arrived the organiser had a deathly look on his face: their car had broken down and they were going to be late. They never made it and in the end I had to pay South African cricketer Craig Lowe £10 to play some extra rounds. He ended up playing four rounds of a nine-hole course in one day.

You've no idea how many phone calls it takes to get 15 guys to play in a golf day and then no matter who's there, the first question is always "Is Ian Botham coming?" The soccer players used to enjoy the golf and I had internationals like Tony Currie and Peter Lorrimer, and Willie Thorne the snooker player.

The dinners were a big thing. Derbyshire wasn't a wealthy area and the speakers generally cost between £200 and £400, some more. We started off at £15 a ticket; in London it would have been £30. When it's getting close and you've sold only half the tickets, you have to start discounting: six for £60. Often the same people would turn up to support me.

Spot the professional – a benefit golf day.

I had a dinner in a little pub in Heanor while we were playing Hampshire there. An irate publican came down to the ground demanding to know how much meat would be needed. In a couple of phone calls to the people who were organising it, I discovered that they'd forgotten to inform me or the publican that they'd sold only 15 tickets. We had what could be called an intimate evening with two guest speakers and ten empty tables. The evening ended with a joke-telling competition and the loss of £160.

At the dinners, the idea was to have a celebrity at each table – you couldn't put Joe Bloggs on a table that a company's paid £500 for. I had people like Brian and Nigel Clough, Fran Cotton, Clive Rice, Allan Lamb – quite a number of the England players helped out. The more celebrities you have the better: the English seem to like to be associated with stars.

The most notable thing about the dinners was the incredible standard of after-dinner speakers: there was Stan Taylor, president of the Golf Comedians Society, who'd do a commentary of a Scotland v Brazil soccer match with an Italian referee; David English, who used to manage the Bee Gees, once drove for five hours to make a speech for three autographed bats and £100 then drove home again; Wandering Walter, a Blackpool comedian and cricketers like Peter Parfitt and David Lloyd.

I had a tremendous dinner at New Zealand House organised by the London New Zealand Cricket Club with Henry Blofeld and Brian Johnson as speakers and attended by the New Zealand High Commissioner, Bryce Harland, Eddie Barlow, Lamb, Mike Gatting, and Keith Fletcher. The Kiwi connection was a big help. The New Zealand House dinner raised the equivalent of five dinners in Derby and I had a six-a-side tournament at the Maori Club in London, again through the LNZ Club. Kiwis playing in England were a tremendous help, especially guys like Willie Watson and Tony Blain, who were over there playing league cricket. I took Blainy home from a celebrity dinner in Hull but when we got to Leeds at about 1 a.m., he'd forgotten where he lived and we drove around for two hours till we found it. That didn't impress me greatly because I was playing the next day.

Then there were the matches against club sides. We were to play Clifton Cricket Club, a lively little outfit in the Peak district, in a twilight game after our county game finished. There'd been a lot of organisation and a couple of meetings with the Clifton guys who were really looking forward to it. There'd been an awful lot of rain and the county match was called off at 3 p.m. At lunch I'd had a message to say that Clifton had cancelled and told the Derbyshire lads the game was off. I was disappointed because of the loss of revenue but the lads were happy because they could slip off home.

When I got home, I rang Vic, the chairman of the organising committee, to say what a pity the game was off. "That's strange," he said, "I've been talking to them and got the impression it was on." I rang the Clifton Chairman chairman who said it had definitely not been cancelled. It was 5.10. Clifton was 35 minutes' drive away. There was no way I was going to get a team together and up there for a 6 p.m. start. The Clifton chairman implored me: "You've got to come," he said, "otherwise who'll eat all the food?"

We got a team together of all but two of the Derbyshire side. Johnny Morris' Dad played – we said he was a famous cricketer whose name for the moment escaped us – and a young lad who worked at Derbyshire who we said was a promising young player and a county under-18 rep. It turned out that the false cancellation call had been made by a disgruntled member of the Clifton club.

David Steele always enjoyed playing in benefit games. He liked to bat at three and, because he came all the way from Northants, he liked to have a good stint at the crease so he was often not out at the end of the innings.

Stan Mortensen didn't like playing benefit games. He was pretty serious about his cricket and took a bit of persuading to take it easy on club batsmen. His idea of a good benefit game was to open the bowling, take five wickets for three runs in two overs, then go home. There were a lot of club batsmen who were desperately keen to take a few runs off the county attack. Stan would whistle a couple past their nose then spreadeagle their stumps which from my point of view wasn't a nice way of saying thanks for supporting my benefit. He did it to the captain of a club, a guy who'd been one of the organisers of this particular game and was really looking forward to it. Stan was in one of his Eric Bloodaxe moods and fired one at the bloke's Adam's apple then knocked his off pole out of the ground. It was pretty hard to apologise to the poor devil and explain that Danish quickies don't understand the finer points of benefit matches.

I struck a wet summer. One day we batted through a deluge to give some club bowlers a chance to bowl at county players and when their turn came to bat, we had to abandon the game. I had four consecutive Sunday games washed out. One club had put in so much work that when it was rained off, I arranged to take a team back there for a game the following year.

It was a great experience to organise something from the bottom up and actually run events. It improves your organisational skills. You have a lot of fun, meet a lot of new people, and have a lot of laughs. Norman Anderson, whose son played at Derbyshire, was the treasurer and a marvellous one. He had brilliant attention to detail. He'd done it for Bud Hill's committee and a number of Bud's team did mine as well. A few members of my committee are now on the Derbyshire committee which is good for the club because they're great operators.

It consumed a lot of time and running it in a compressed time frame meant things couldn't be spread out. After a few months it became a hard slog although by then I was hardened to the things I had to do. It didn't do my game any good. I averaged 37 and I didn't find it that easy to play although I had a few knocks in benefit matches to keep my eye in. By the end of the season I couldn't wait to get to India and to not have to ring people up and ask them for things any more.

I'm not sure that it's the best system. In Australia they have a sort of super scheme, a fund for international players after they've spent so many years in the side. County cricketers aren't highly paid in the main. At the end of their playing days – usually the mid-30s – they have to look for a new career whereas in most walks of life, if a person is good at what they do, they're about to enter their peak earning period.

I think benefits are a good idea in New Zealand to reward players who've put a lot into the game, particularly those who perhaps weren't regular test players but have made a big contribution. I think it's important that benefits are confined to the beneficiary's province unless there are special circumstances. Ian Smith is an example of a player who might deserve to be granted a nationwide benefit by the New Zealand Cricket Council because he switched provinces well into his career. He might not get a benefit from either province but he's contributed a lot to New Zealand cricket.

In a way you're better off in this country: a player here gets a benefit after about 80 games whereas in England you have to play about 250 plus all the one days. It's probably more lucrative here too if it's in one of the main centres and well-run although it wasn't so good for Bruce Edgar who had his straight after the stock market crash.

The Sunday benefit match. Bob's opening the bowling.

Ideally the remuneration would be sufficient to leave players comfortably off when they retired. Geoff Howarth had a benefit in England but missed out here when benefits were just getting started. He was one of the most deserving cases. A case could be made for players of previous eras and for those in other sports in terms of the time spent and the sacrifices made. New Zealand's top sportsmen and women don't as a rule have a lot to show for their efforts. Because I played professionally for 12 years, my attitude is more professional in the financial sense as well as the playing sense. I've been extremely lucky to have played a sport that is professional and to have had a benefit in England where the system has been around for a long time and is accepted as a normal part of a player's career so there's no stigma attached to it.

In a way the benefit rounded off my county cricket experience. It was almost a finishing school. I used to look at Bud and wonder why he was so tired and hangdog. I thought surely it couldn't be as bad as that. My benefit was well organised and I had a great chairman and a good committee but after a few months of it, I was in the same state. I wouldn't consider myself a really social person, although I'm the sort who doesn't want to go out but once I'm there, will generally end up having a good time. However, I didn't enjoy continually going out, giving up my privacy, always asking people for favours: to have 16 celebrities at a dinner – one at each table – you had to ask 72.

In England benefits are an accepted part of the system but I still found the whole year incredibly discomforting, continually going to functions and being very pleasant to people because I was dependent on their generosity and good will. I was also conscious of not being a local and not having roots in the community. I was always asking for things, which is an uncomfortable sensation – it was as if I'd become a charity organisation for 12 months. I got hardened to it as the season went on. As the old cricketers say: "You've got to make every post a winning post."

CHAPTER SIX

A bad workman blames his tools

A bat is like your best mate, like a dog to a shepherd. When things go wrong for a batsman, the first thing he invariably does is start looking suspiciously at his bat, looking for the crack that's not there. He's thinking that the bat has stopped 'going'.

Batsmen have a fetish about bats. Go into any changing room around the world, particularly in England, and you'll see guys picking up bats, settling down in their stance, practising shots, like a shadow boxer. Usually it's someone else's bat they're using. At Derbyshire Bud Hill did so much of it that Eddie Barlow banned him from the dressing room. A bat to a batsman is like a paddock to a farmer: someone else's grass is always greener, someone else in the team always has a bat you fancy.

My best-ever bat weighed 3lb 1oz and took me ages to get used to. I kept it in the bottom of the gear bag because it was too heavy for me. I thought, "I just can't handle this machine." Then one day, in desperation because I wasn't getting any runs, I used it and whacked a quick 30. It felt really good. So I used it again and got a big hundred and after that the bat and I were inseparable. A lot of players prefer a certain balance and weight and won't use something that feels really awkward when they first pick it up but the bottom line is that if you're getting runs with it, it starts to feel good and vice versa.

The first bat I ever had was a size three Bert Sutcliffe autograph which my parents brought me back from a holiday. Bert was my absolute idol even though I never saw him bat. I went to a country school where there wasn't much gear – the wicketkeeping gloves were my mother's rose-pruning gloves.

My next bat was a size six Colin Cowdrey Slazenger which I had till my second year at college. Then, like every other kid, I had a Cannon harrow. At Christ's College in Christchurch there was plenty of gear, mostly Gray Nicolls, so I used that. I was quite happy to use gear bats – even as a kid I used my bat only at home.

You always see youngsters using bats that are too big for them which isn't a good thing. These days though, they're such an expensive item, kids probably have to grow into them.

At school I won a Gary Sobers harrow which was a good stick and I went through a phase when I thought the Gray Nicolls bats with the sloping shoulders were incredibly classy looking although I never actually had one. Then I had a Duncan Fearnley which was too heavy and I never really came to terms with it. I didn't use a full-size bat till my last year at school because I was still pretty short.

I took a Gray Nicolls to most of my Brabin and Rothmans tournaments and through varsity I used what was in the gear bag. Then when I moved to Gisborne to play for Northern Districts, I ended up working for John Guy in his sports shop. He was importing Crown Sports bats, which Glenn Turner was using at the time, and he gave me one.

When I got to England, a couple of the Kent guys took me down to the Gray Nicolls factory, in Robertsbridge, Sussex. In those days it was just a collection of five or six little sheds in a little village. It was very quaint, almost like a cottage industry. At that stage GN bats were absolutely superb and were acknowledged as the leading brand in England. They gave me a couple of bats and I've used them ever since. And ever since then, I've enjoyed going to bat factories, smelling the willow.

All the batmakers have a stash of bats set aside for the pros and they're generally the best. After a while they get to know what the individual players like. I'm very particular about my bats and I've been known to use another brand of bat with the GN sticker on if that suited me better.

In England it's a case of which batmaker is first to the woods. After that, the pressing of the wood is the key. Some players prefer soft bats on the theory that the ball tends to come off a nice, soft bat more sweetly. I like a hard-pressed bat because I find that, as an opener, the new ball really flies off it.

Pros and top players are generally contracted to batmakers and in some cases get an endorsement fee. It's only in the last few years that it's started happening in New Zealand although we're not a big enough market to make endorsements that lucrative. In England £10,000-plus a year is not uncommon for the top players and a leading Australian player recently got a contract for $150,000 over three years to endorse a new brand. Players are getting more pragmatic these days and it's not uncommon for leading players to endorse a brand for a season or two then switch to a competitor. Viv Richards, for instance, has changed brands several times in recent years. It makes it an expensive business for the batmakers but there's no better way to advertise a brand than to have a top player like Richards or Martin Crowe out there smacking it around with your bat. If the bat spends a lot of time in the middle and on television, then it's money well spent.

A maker who has got players like Graeme Hick and Crowe in his stable will generally make sure they get the best of the willow. It's in the batmaker's interest to keep these guys happy because they give his products the best

The backyard bat.

School bats!

exposure. Martin Crowe will go to the factory, talk to Duncan Fearnley, watch the bats being made and go away with six or seven from each visit. He gets some magnificent sticks – I know because I've used some of them.

Bowlers tend to get fewer bats from their makers; they're usually more interested in the quality of boots, pads and thigh pads anyway. When you see a test player using a stick without a maker's logo on it, it generally means negotiations have reached a crucial stage.

I think incredible marketing opportunities are wasted because of the restrictions on the size of the stickers on bats: a team sponsor could have its logo on each player's bat. The same restrictions didn't apply in India where Richard Hadlee flourished a bat adorned with a company logo.

At any given time one brand will be the market leader: it was GN in the 70s and Fearnley for a while in the 80s but it sort of rotates. It's a very competitive business, almost like winemaking. One particular brand will have a good year and the players will start to say that "so and so's bats are going well this year". The pros know whose bats are hot at a particular time. If you're hitting it well they'll ask "what's that you're using?" It's pretty obvious if a guy's got a particularly good stick. It's not uncommon for players to change the stickers so they can use a brand other than the one they're being paid to endorse.

Batmaking is an ancient craft which takes a lot of skill and learning. Now they're mostly machine made on lathes. John Newbery worked at GN when they were hot and was regarded as a top batmaker. The pros all knew about him and followed his progress when he went solo.

In the mid-80s there was a big move towards heavy bats, which to some extent was a by-product of one-day cricket and the need to really give the ball a thump. Glenn Turner used a 3lb-plus bat which is a lot of bat for a small guy. The secret with heavy bats is getting the balance right: you can pick up bats weighing over 3lbs but they're so well balanced that they feel a lot lighter. Then it's a question of where the weight is – Martin Crowe used to use bottom heavy bats. There's no doubt that if you hit the ball with a 3.5lb bat, it stays hit. On the other hand it may take a fraction of a second more to move it and on bouncy wickets where you've got to get the bat up quickly, it can be pretty hard work. Viv Richards, Ian Botham, and Clive Lloyd all used very heavy bats and Lloyd also had six or seven rubbers on his handles.

In the past players definitely used much lighter bats and one of the things that Bob Simpson, who played in an era when bats were mostly 2lb 3oz/4oz, has done as Australian coach is to encourage his players to use lighter bats because they give you more dexterity. Allan Border for instance uses a lighter bat than he used to. It's not a bad idea on quicker wickets because they're certainly more manoeuvrable.

The way I bat – with an upright stance and playing pretty straight without a lot of wristy shots – I prefer a heavy bat. I use a 2lb 15oz/3lb bat. I used to use a 2lb 8oz bat when I stood more naturally and went back to a lighter one in the West Indies because I didn't fancy swivelling on the

A craftsman at work – Duncan Fearnley at his Worcestershire factory.

Swan Richards of Gray Nicolls.

end of a three pounder although compared to the amount of gear I was wearing, it seemed pretty light. When you're playing those blokes, your bat is probably the last thing you worry about.

They say the best bats have six or seven grains across the blade but I always liked to see very thin grains, a theory shared by Duncan Fearnley. And if it's got a little butterfly in the wood, it generally means it's a real good stick. Some guys aren't fussy but, whatever your attitude, it's important to have a bat that goes.

When the season starts I visit the maker. I'm contracted to GN Australia and when we're over there I go to their factory in Mordiallac, in Melbourne where Swan Richards is the maker. They've been tremendous to deal with over the years and keep some good sticks aside for us. Swan, who seems to know everyone from the Prime Minister to Allan Border, has lots of theories and is constantly experimenting and produces some amazingly shaped bats.

There's nothing worse than getting your bat shipment organised at the start of the season and then having them arrive to find they're not what you want. You never really know how good they are till you get out in the middle and hit the ball. On the other hand you can go out with a bat you're not happy with and scratch around and get a few runs. After a while it feels better and you wonder why you didn't like it in the first place. In the end it boils down to the person on the end of it but having a good one in your hands gives you confidence.

If they're not good enough you send them back to the maker, maybe to get them shaved. It's great to go to the factory because making a hand-made bat requires great skill and these people are real craftsmen who've been making bats for years. It's almost like making a musical instrument. Taking an ounce out of a bat is an awful lot and can change the whole feel of it.

They're making bats in India now and some of them are pretty good. The people involved are dedicated men: when we were there the Symonds man travelled 3,000 miles to present Andrew Jones and Mark Greatbatch, both Symonds users at that time, with a couple of bats each.

The tragedy with bats is that they wear out and players go to enormous lengths to make a bat last another innings or two. Ken Rutherford had a bat that was held together by tape and David Steele was known to staple them together but there was a rumour that he then gave them to tradesmen for services rendered. Some players modify their bats. I was in the West Indies when I found my bat was too heavy so I took it to a carpenter in Antigua to shave it down. I can't say he improved the bat much.

In India Bob Cunis was given a couple of Power Bats to use at fielding practice. He was very pleased with them and they were destined for the team gear of his club side in Northland. During the tour Danny Morrison started to use one of them in the nets and then used it in the middle. At the end of the tour Bob told Danny he could hang on to it for the Shell series and return it when we got back together for the tests against Pakistan. Both Bob and Danny are on the short side but Danny wanted an extra short handle so he lopped a bit off, turning it into a super-short handle which caused much hilarity in the team but some tension between the coach and his young charge.

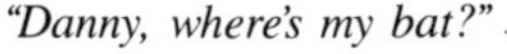

"Danny, where's my bat?"

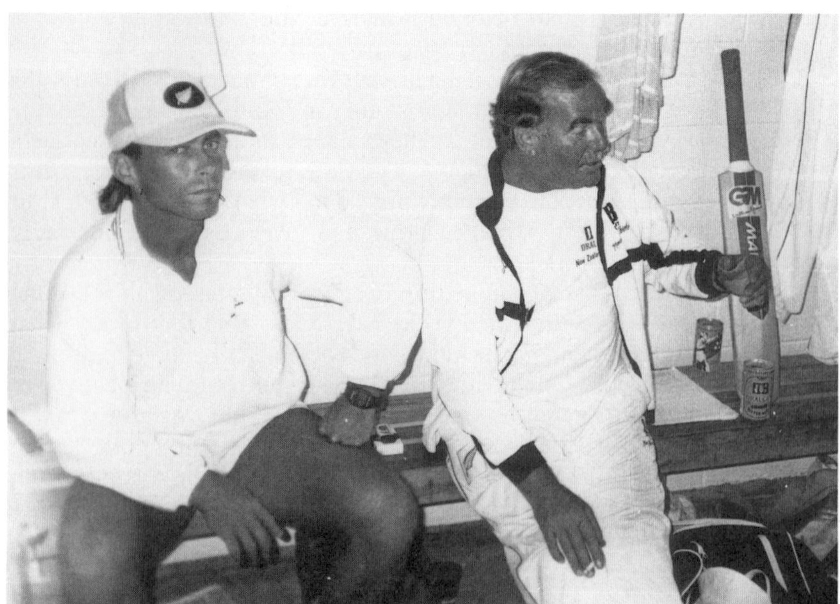

"It's the bat's fault."
J.G. BLACKWELL

"I'm not even slightly interested." Sneds' match-saving innings in Perth.
GREG PORTEOUS

If you've got a good stick, it pays to look after it. There's nothing worse than leaving your favourite bat by the nets and having someone pick it up and use it to hit long catches. If it's two days before a test and they take a chunk out of it, it doesn't do your build-up any good.

As you get older you learn the value of taking care of your gear. Bob Taylor and Richard Hadlee were both meticulous. Ritual and routine are important to performance. It's more psychological than anything else, a question of having the equipment that makes you feel confident. When I started I wasn't the greatest ironer of shirts and apparently there have been smarter turned out test cricketers.

Being fussy can have a point to it. Long-sleeved shirts protect your elbows when you dive in the field; some types of plastic thigh pads make a sound like a bat when the ball hits them; Glenn Turner pointed out to me that some bats creak which could confuse an umpire.

Some guys oil their bats and some don't. I don't because I like a hard bat and I put moisture into the blade by holding it over a steam kettle. In India they oil them and leave them in the sun to make them hard. Polyurethane is good because it protects them and keeps them hard.

It's ironic that the object of so much sanding and oiling and patching up and general tender loving care can also be the object of abuse. Many a bat has arrived in the changing room before its owner. When a player with a reputation as a bat thrower leaves the crease and heads for the changing room, there's usually an exodus from the area where the incoming player has his gear. Mark Burgess was notorious for it and that tradition has been maintained on suitable occasions in recent years by John Bracewell, Jeff Crowe, Ken Rutherford and Bert Vance. And sometimes myself.

Some will say it shows a lack of control but there are occasions when the frustration is such that the bat must fly. As you get older you tend to settle for unbuckling your pads, putting your head in your hands, and thinking about it. Generally the bat is flung when you've cocked it up but half an hour later you're inspecting it anxiously, hoping it didn't sustain any damage.

Players' bats tell you something about their owners. Ewen Chatfield had a GN double scoop which served him faithfully for years. He used it for knocking up and many significant and important innings for his country. It's got a great middle which Chats will admit to having used sparingly and the edge remains pristine. It's been used by the team for fielding practices for years and has become part of the Chatfield legend.

Lance Cairns' Excalibur bats were very heavy and with very thick handles. It was hard enough to wrap your hands around the handles let alone lift them. He had two: one for serious batmanship and one for the old heave-ho. No one ever knew what the difference between them was. He was a very dangerous man to give throw downs to because the ball came back at you so fast.

Jerry Coney was a great borrower of bats and therefore very adept at transferring logos. There were a number of Gray Nicolls users in the side – Bruce Edgar, Ian Smith, myself, and Jerry – so when we got a consignment of eight or nine bats, it was a case of making the correct decision early on because there were a couple that we all fancied. It's frustrating when a number 10, quite by chance, ends up with the best bat in the side. If that happens, a lot of intense negotiation takes place.

Barry Wood had a bat solely for warm-ups. It was three times the weight of a normal bat and felt like it was made of teak and, before he went in to bat, he'd pull it out and go through his repertoire of strokes. Then it would go back in his bag and he'd go out to bat with another stick. The Essex spinner and all-round cricket character Ray East had a bat which was flat front and back with the same logo on both sides so it looked the same to the keeper as it did to the bowler. The Derbyshire opener Tony Borrington was downright obsessive. He'd go to GN and try most of the bats in the factory. They'd just leave him there and let him get on with it.

Stephen Boock has had an interesting selection of bats which he always rated along with his skill as a batsman. One of them had an ad for his supermarket on it.

On many occasions in the nets Martin Snedden has launched into an attempted lofted drive for six or a pull for four only to see the ball just clear the nets or finish beside the bowler on his follow-through. Sned's bats now have the reputation of being particularly harmless. If the same thing happens to any player in the middle, the lads remark: "I see so-and-so has borrowed Sned's bat today."

The most useful man in our side is John Bracewell because he can put rubbers on bat handles. He carries an implement for the job in his bag and is an expert at the art. He took over from Cairnsy who sort of handed the mantle on to him.

A common practical joke in the New Zealand team is to put someone's bat in the pile of bats to be autographed which inevitably accumulates in the dressing room during a test match. The owner will come in to find his bat missing and eventually locate it in the pile with the autographs of the team on the blade, a situation which generally requires some work with sandpaper. In Sharjah Bruce Blair got so frustrated with his bats that he used one out of the to-be-autographed pile – real Victor Trumper stuff. It can't have been that good because he put it back afterwards.

One of the basic principles of cricket is that you should have a bat in your hands when you return to the pavilion. Mike Wright was trudging off after making a gutsy 50 for Northern Districts but the next player in was Stu Gillespie, who was a bit inexperienced at that stage and also liked using Mike's bat. So Stu went out without a bat and collected Mike's as they crossed, leaving Mike to acknowledge the ovation with a jaunty wave.

CHAPTER SEVEN

Out of the Spotlight

Scoring runs has always interested me but I was never one of those kids who go along to a cricket match with a scorebook and keep score. When I see boys doing that, I think they'll end up being very well-organised young gentlemen, probably accountants.

Every English county has a scorer. Carlin Beardmore was doing the (unpaid) job at Derbyshire when I arrived. He was a retired accountant and the club's treasurer, a very prim and proper English gent. He used to doze off on bus trips and we had a running contest to see who could tie his shoelaces together without waking him up. He'd come to life after a few drinks and I can remember him doing back rolls on a pub floor in Colchester one night.

His successor was Stan Tacey who'd served King and Country in India. Whenever we went out for a curry he'd stay behind because he'd made a vow never to eat curry again. Like most Derbyshire people he called a spade a spade which sometimes annoyed the players. The last thing you want when you're in the changing room reflecting bitterly on your dismissal is the scorer coming in and telling you what a lousy shot you played. None of our many captains responded positively to Stan telling them he couldn't understand a bowling change.

When things got boring on the field, we'd wave at Maurice the scoreboard operator, as if the numbers on the board were wrong. He'd come out looking flustered and start changing the numbers. There was a phone system between Maurice and the scorers which reminded me of a battlefront communication system during World War Two. When Kim Barnett became captain in his early 20s, Maurice used to sidle up to him on the first morning of a match and give him advice: "I've looked at the pitch and if I were you, I'd bat." Kim reckoned that if things went well, even if he'd done the opposite of what Maurice had suggested, Maurice would claim credit for it.

Most of the scorers had been on the circuit for a long time and were part and parcel of it. Jack Jennings at Northants was a clever magician and would play tricks for the players, and Clem at Essex was an integral part of the Essex bridge school. For a while Leicester had a bloke no one got

"There's something fishy here." Warwick Larkins and Jack Hill in the scorers' box at the Oval, 1978.

'Doc' Borrie, 'Matey' O'Sullivan and Lance Cairns the elusive first-five.

on with which was no fun if you had to share a box with him for three days. The scorers and umpires had lunch together and sometimes the scorers would be cross with the umpires because they couldn't understand their signals. They rated umpires on the way they signalled, something players never think about.

There were over-rate fines which could cost players individually up to a couple of hundred pounds each for falling behind the over rate. We'd come in at lunch with the opposition five down for 80 and Stan would have a long face because we were behind the required over rate. The scorers knew exactly how long a bowler was taking over his overs and someone like Stan Mortensen, who took his time, would get told off even if he'd got a bag of wickets. They were expert at sneaking in extra overs and if time was lost because of the weather, they'd be in to see the umpires, asking to have time deducted.

Like umpires and players, scorers have grounds they like and don't like, mainly because of the facilities. The Derby *Evening Telegraph* once likened the cramped score box tent at our ground at Heanor to a Punch and Judy show. At some grounds on a cold day, the scorers would emerge like ice blocks from the box.

Our scorer on the 1978 England tour was Warwick Larkins from Dunedin who paid most of his own way and contributed enormously to the team cause with his good humour. His Jacques Cousteau imitations were much appreciated by the team and he was also in charge of charades down the back of the bus along with Tube McIntyre, Jock Edwards and Steve Boock. A phantom leg spinner and middle order batsman, Warwick was actually called to his nation's colours for the game against Holland.

During the last tour match at Scarborough, Warwick took a punt on the cold fish starter at lunch. Shortly afterwards he received a blow to the abdomen during an impromptu wrestling match and the combination caused him intense stomach pains. An unsympathetic Brendon Bracewell suggested he might be the first person to die on a cricket tour since Dirty Dick on the Aboriginals tour of England last century. Finally someone drove him to the local hospital but lost their way and ended up at a crematorium, something Warwick didn't see the funny side of.

In 1983 the role was performed by John Patrick 'Matey' O'Sullivan, a Marist and Canterbury man, and enthusiastic performer of his own version of the Willie Away rugby move, known as Matey Away. It took place at the Ealing Cricket Club in London as we were waiting to get on the bus. A lineout was formed and Matey peeled off to collect an imaginary tap down. He then stormed round the end of the lineout and, in classic Pinetree Meads style, made a beeline for Lance Cairns, who was standing where an opposing first-five would be. As many British fly halves have done in this situation, Lance sidestepped the ball carrier and Matey drove forehead first into the brick wall Lance had been leaning against. He collapsed in a heap bleeding profusely, much to everyone's amusement, and had to be patched up on the way to Worcester by the team doctor, 'Doc' Borrie.

At that time Ewen Chatfield and I were engaged in a marathon game of 500 with Matey and Doc and we gave them an almighty thrashing on the way to Worcester. Matey was under heavy sedation which may have affected his judgment in the bidding department and a rift between him and his partner developed as the trip wore on.

That was an excellent tour for cards, although 1978 had been good. Jock Edwards and I got into a school with Cairnsy and Dick Brittenden. We had three days in Paris on our way to Holland and arrived at the hotel to find the staff were on strike so we were handed pillow cases and sheets along with our room keys. The rest of the team went out and took lots of photos while we settled in for some serious cards, emerging in the late afternoon for a visit to a nearby café for bread, pâté and red wine. The cards resumed first thing next morning. Jock played cards the way he batted and the kitty was like a short ball to him. Lance, on the other hand, played the way he bowled – very shrewdly – and we ended up losing £75, a tidy sum in those days. Perhaps we should've gone out and expanded our minds instead.

Like scorers, umpires are very much part of the English circuit. They get reasonably well paid plus expenses and some of them travel around in campervans to save on hotel costs. The umpiring standard is very high, although there's perhaps not quite the depth now as when I started. Umpiring all the time – they do 60 or 70 days a season – means that they're more relaxed and confident than their counterparts elsewhere in the world and many of them are ex-players so they know what it's all about.

Confidence is terribly important for an umpire. They've got to keep their composure even if they suspect they've made a mistake. Bad umpires lack self-confidence; if there's a negative reaction to their decisions, they get flustered and start making mistakes. When they make a mistake, instead of forgetting about it, they try to even things up which leads to payback decisions. English umpires are assessed over the season and if their marks aren't up to scratch, they're off the list and out of a job.

There's a sense of everyone being in the same industry which breaks down the barriers between players and umpires. There are also strict disciplinary standards which keep dissent and abuse under control. David Constant once reported me to Lord's for running on the wicket when I was batting. A lot of overseas bowlers get into trouble for running on the wicket when they start in county cricket.

Players generally walk in county cricket. I don't in New Zealand and no one does in tests but over there I felt a bit guilty if I didn't. Word gets around pretty quickly if you don't walk and you're labelled. David Steele loved batting so much he didn't walk. He once got a lot of glove on a delivery from the England fast bowler David Brown, stood there and was given not out. A few minutes later Brown saw him wringing his hand and blew his top. "Cramp, Brownie, cramp," said Steeley.

Of course there are always umpires you don't fancy or don't rate. In my first game I was given lbw and run out by Don Oslear and later that season he gave me lbw at the Oval when you could've heard the nick in the grandstand. I felt he had it in for me but next season I got plenty of runs whenever he was umpiring us.

Some of them are real characters. In my debut for the Derbyshire first team I encountered Cec Pepper, who had the disconcerting habit of breaking wind like a bus backfiring as the bowler was about to deliver. Cecil wasn't at all embarrassed. When I was the non-striker, he asked me, after yet another resounding blast: "Just kick that one to the boundary will you John?" Bill Alley used to call me 'Shirley Temple' because of my long, curly hair. Bill was not a man to get off-side with. One night in the bar he was heard sounding off about the Hampshire all-rounder Trevor Jesty: "I can't stick this Jesty," said Bill. "When he's hit on the pad, he's never out; when he hits someone on the pad, they're always plumb." Perhaps it was just coincidence that Bill gave Jesty lbw the next morning when he was a very long way forward.

Merv Kitchen was a bookie in the off season and I made a point of fielding at square leg when he was standing so we could chat about the horses. Nigel Plews was an ex-copper in the Fraud Squad and told amazing tales about scams and con men. One umpire enjoyed a drink and would have a couple of snorts at lunchtime to keep the chill out. Arthur Jepson was a great character and Dickie Bird is the best I've come across. They were blokes you could talk to over a beer and they'd tell you if you were doing something wrong, playing across the line, or whatever.

Towards the end of his career Arthur often seemed more interested in what was happening in the crowd than on the field. He also had a record of giving people out to the last ball of an over, often delivering his verdict on the way to square leg.

Dickie Bird has a flair for the dramatic. Seam bowler Keith Stevenson used to whirl his arms in his delivery stride and once clipped Dickie across the chops. Dickie reeled away clutching his jaw in theatrical style and moaning "he's broken me jaw, fetch a doctor". He made a swift recovery and, to show there were no hard feelings, gave Stevo an lbw decision next ball. He stood in a famous Derbyshire-Lancashire match at Buxton in the Peak District. Lancashire batted first on a very hot day and scored 470 for five; two of our bowlers, tired of watching their deliveries being smashed to the boundary, left the field saying they were suffering from oxygen debt. Next day Buxton was under several inches of snow but the sun returned for the third day. Lancashire declared and opening bowler Peter Lever's first ball pitched on a length and comfortably cleared Brian Bolus. Ashley Harvey-Walker, the other opener, promptly removed his false teeth and handed them to Dickie for safekeeping. Derbyshire was dismissed for 47 and 120 and the game became another nail in the coffin of the practice of leaving pitches uncovered over the course of a match.

English umpires do make mistakes of course and they have their weaknesses. Some of them give international players a better deal, as they do here, and there's one or two who very seldom give captains out. It may just be a coincidence that captains write umpiring reports. When games are drawing to a close, umpires who may face a bit of a drive home are keen to avoid rush hour traffic, and lower order batsmen can find themselves dispatched to the pavilion with few beg your pardons.

Fred Goodall was New Zealand's best umpire and early on he was pretty positive and confident in an abrupt way. You'd ask him from mid on how many balls were left in the over and he'd bellow the reply like a drill sergeant. This habit caused a sensation during his stint in England where they were used to umpires being a bit more under-stated. Fred copped a lot of stick from touring sides but he wasn't a bad umpire and you could have a few laughs with him. I'll always remember him describing a skinny fast bowler as being like an alsatian – "all ribs and cock" – a description as vivid as it was accurate.

It was very sad the way he was abused by the West Indies and Viv Richards in particular during the Eden Park test in 1986. In the end it got to him. It all went back to the Colin Croft incident and a few stories about Fred were blown out of all proportion and found their way back to the West Indies. I sometimes feel our umpires don't get the backing they deserve in these situations. Even at club level they get abused and there must be a small – and probably diminishing – number of people prepared to give up their Saturday afternoons for the privilege of being ranted and raved at. It doesn't happen in England and it's got to be stamped out here. I'm not usually an umpire abuser but sometimes they do have to be kept on their toes, even Pat Carrick, our first female umpire. I've never toned down an outburst because of her gender. She got a blast from one of the captains in a Shell Trophy match last season after botching a last over run-out decision: "Get back in the kitchen Pat, and stay there," he told her. I've got no problem with female umpires – some of our men umpires have been doing wonderful impressions of old women for years.

The longest, most detailed and most heartfelt tirade I've ever given an umpire was directed at the Pakistani who had sawn me off in both innings at Hyderabad in 1985. I even threw in some religious stuff because I thought that might get to him. He was the guy Boocky told: "You might as well sod off. You're only here to count the balls and we can do that ourselves." There's a joke about the Pakistani umpire who gets to heaven and finds two queues outside the Pearly Gates, one marked 'heroes' and one marked 'others'. He joins the heroes' queue and St Peter asks him how he qualifies. "I gave Javed Miandad out lbw on the front foot in a test match in Karachi" says the Pakistani. St Peter asks how come he hasn't heard of this impressive feat and is told: "I only did it two minutes ago."

Umpires have different ways of presenting the finger of doom. The Aussies have developed an elaborate method like a slow motion bowling action with the arm being raised in a dramatic sweep while some of the New Zealanders have their finger on about the angle they'd use for picking their nose. From mid on and mid off you sometimes see umpires start to give someone out, have second thoughts halfway through, and end up changing their mind as you watch their hands twitching behind their backs. A Pakistani Khizar Hayat who umpired in England for a while, had the fastest finger I ever saw. If he'd been a gunfighter, he'd have died in bed. There were times he had his finger up before you'd missed the ball.

The Sri Lankan, P.W. Vidanagamage, was unusual to say the least. He was a psychologist who seemed to think the best form of attack was defence. John Bracewell got a bit grumpy after he'd been clubbed over the top a couple of times and P.W. threw his hat on the pitch. P.W. was also the only person I've ever seen really rile Richard Hadlee.

The Aussie umpires are pretty relaxed and getting more professional but they've made some amazing decisions over the years like Robin Bailhache no-balling Lance Cairns for intimidatory bowling when Jim Higgs gloved a long hop. It was quite bizarre, especially in Australia where tailenders are expected to play bouncers, and considering Lance's pace, the slowness of the wicket, and the fact Higgs had been in for quite a time. Then there was Martin Snedden's disallowed catch. I thought Greg Chappell had a nerve to stand there but what was really baffling was the umpires conferring in the middle of the wicket. We wondered what on earth they were talking about.

At Christ's College we had Alex Knight who'd played for Otago. Once I came in to bat about number seven to join Rod Fulton, the captain, who was in the 90s. Alex insisted that I told Rod how many he'd got. I didn't want to and felt terrible when Rod got out on 98. Alex always used to tell me to put more weight on my defensive shots to try and score singles from them. I never took much notice of it but 20-odd years later I think it was probably a very good piece of advice. Years later Alex came to see me play in a test in Auckland wearing his Otago blazer and white flannels.

Another umpire we had at school was Jack Streeter. Jack used to give a lot of lbws, mostly to us. He wasn't as quick on the draw as Khyzar Hayat but he certainly didn't keep batsmen in suspense. We played a club side including an older guy who was a real identity in local cricket. Jack fired him but the bloke complained so much, he reversed the decision. We weren't too impressed but two overs later Jack dispatched him with what was possibly the worst lbw decision I've ever seen and this time he had to go.

I once did some umpiring in a Christchurch club game and reckon I made a couple of blues in a short space of time. It's a very difficult job and I don't envy them, particularly in this day and age of slow-motion replays and giant screens at the grounds. Not only do they get the treatment from some of the players – who are getting meaner all the time – and to some extent the media, but now the crowds are at them as well.

My favourite administrator would be Bruce Hosking who was president of Northern Districts and went on to be president of the NZCC. He was a big help in my career. We've done a bit of fishing together, the first time on the Manukau Harbour where Hosko's got a farm. It was very foggy and I was a shade apprehensive. He'd just finished telling me not to worry because he knew the harbour like the back of his hand when we ran aground, the first of two interludes on the sandbanks we had that day.

Hosko was on the players' wave length, a hands-on operator. He once took on Brian Hastings in a distance-for-age race and won. The ND team then nominated me to take him on and there was I, neck and neck with the association president in his singlet and underpants. I won but only because we made it a 110-yard race.

Bob Vance, former NZCC chairman, was a pretty straight shooter and decisive. He was doing a good job as manager in England in 1986 and I was sorry for him when ill-health forced him to come home and miss out on being part of our first series win there. Some of the funniest dressing room discussions I've ever heard involved Bob and Lance Cairns, both of whom had hearing problems.

Sometimes you wonder who the important people in the game are. During the rained-out first test against Pakistan in Dunedin in 1989, board members and assorted hangers-on had a fairly lavish lunch in the committee rooms under the grandstand while the players "huddled in their lavatorial dressing rooms", in the words of businessman Sir Robert Jones, a guest at the lunch. When Derbyshire played Worcester in a Natwest semi-final, the room where the players normally ate was turned into a reception room where the two committees had a sumptuous lunch while the players had fish and chips in the indoor nets.

There are dressing-room attendants at many English county grounds. Derbyshire couldn't afford one except for a brief time during the short but eventful captaincy of Brian Bolus. Harry Murgatroyd, a club stalwart in his 80s, was hired. He'd done a lot of umpiring at colts level, distinguished by a perceptible bias towards Derbyshire in tight situations and a habit of saying "Oh yes, you'll have to go" when giving someone out. Harry lasted only a few weeks before resigning in high dudgeon. He'd gone in at close play to take the drinks order but Bolus wanted the players' undivided attention as he berated them for their poor showing and ordered him from the dressing room. Harry made a dramatic exit, hurling the tin tray down on the cobbled floor, which left ear drums ringing within a 50-yard radius. Ted at the Oval, Taffie at Edgbaston, and Eddie at Worcester were dressing-room attendants I always looked forward to seeing and they were part of the appeal of playing at those grounds.

At Eden Park there's Mick, who looks more like a boxing manager than someone associated with cricket. He won Lotto a while ago and retired and now he comes back only for cricket tests. Graham Reddaway is the man in the big white hat who patrols the players' tunnel at Eden Park. An umpire himself and an active member of the Auckland umpires' association, he will be forever remembered for his comment, as details of Peter Plumley-Walker's bizarre death emerged during the trial, that "we can't go on losing umpires like this". Redds said Plumley-Walker was so enthusiastic, he even gladly umpired Hallyburton-Johnson women's cricket, an experience Redds described as "purgatory".

Gary Troup's father Basil, and his late sidekick Cliffie Humphries, were two of the unsung heroes of the Auckland cricket scene. They've been carting gear around for provincial and international teams for as long as I can remember; I first met them when I came to Auckland for a Brabin tournament at the age of 17. When we come home from a tour, whether we've done well and there's a crowd to meet us – even Mike Moore showed up when we came back from Australia in 1986 – or no one wants to know us, you can lay money on Bas being there. He's lugged gear in and out of changing rooms for touring teams who've been arrogant and treated him like the hired help and provincial teams with young blokes who're too big for their boots. Cliffie was a dreadful driver and the preferred arrangement was that Bas drove the players and Cliffie drove the gear.

Gatemen are people you can't ignore: Dave McLeod at Eden Park has turned away royalty and prime ministers for not having the correct ticketing but he does it in a genial way and he and the King of Tonga parted the best of mates. The gatemen at Lords behave as if they were recruited from Wormwood Scrubs and getting in is like breaking into Colditz, especially if you're not wearing a tie.

We have some great fans; Sir Ron Brierley has supported New Zealand cricket for years. Roger Bhatnagar flew to India to see Richard Hadlee take the record for test wickets. Roger, who owns a chain of electrical stores, often sponsors Auckland benefit games. There are so many TVs and videos sometimes it's like *Sale of the Century* without the questions. My greatest are undoubtedly Dion McCracken and his family of Dargaville. Dion has made scrapbooks for me for the last six or seven years, something I would never have got around to doing, and I'll treasure these scrapbooks in years to come. I see Dion and his family every year at the Eden Park test when they come down to Auckland for the weekend.

There's absolutely no contest for the title of number one fan of the New Zealand cricket team – that's hospital orderly Dennis Kidd from Hamilton. He's not only our greatest fan, he's Telecom's best customer. He sends telegrams to us wherever we are in the world – he spent well over $1000 on telegrams to the Emerging Players team in Zimbabwe and the side in India in 1987, all of them in his inimitable, short-and-to-the-point style, and nearly all ending with 'mate': "Well batted Wrighty, have a happy Christmas mate;" "Smithy, brilliant innings mate;" "Proud of you Kiwis". We really appreciate Dennis' messages and try to guess what they'll say. We're not often far off the mark.

With the media, I don't mind the guys who are there year in, year out, who've been around for a while and have some commitment to cricket: the likes of Dick Brittenden, Don Cameron, and Ron Palenski. Dick Brittenden was a total enthusiast and very fair. He used to get stick about being too much a Canterbury and High School Old Boys' man but he went through thick and thin with New Zealand teams and I enjoyed touring with him.

Bryan Waddle is a great supporter, always a New Zealander talking to other New Zealanders. He performs tremendous versions of 'Twist and Shout' and 'California Dreaming' and was such a hit in a Goa nightclub that they asked him back the next night. Bob Cunis was a big fan and would

"Any more bags?" Basil Troup.

A selection of telegrams from Dennis Kidd, our greatest fan.

JOHN WRIGHT AND THE NZ CRICKET TEAM
C/O THE AUCKLAND CRICKET ASSOCIATION
PRIVATE BAG
DOMINIONROAD

PROUD OF YOU KIWI'S
DENNIS KIDD

WRIGHTY
C/- AUCKLAND CRICKET ASSOCIATION

FINE HOME SEASON WRIGHTY. SOME BATTING MATE.
THANKS AGAIN FOR YOUR TIME AT SEDDON PARK.
DENNIS KIDD

SOME BATTING IN THE SECOND TEST WRIGHTY
DENNIS KIDD

FINE CENTURY WRIGHTY
SOME BATTING MATE.
DENNIS KIDD

CONGRATULATIONS ON GETTING YOUR HIGHEST
TEST SCORE MATE
DENNIS KIDD

stay to the bitter end to watch Wads doing his thing. Iain Gallaway is another good broadcaster and an excellent raconteur, and I used to enjoy Alan Richards – I grew up listening to him and I liked his voice.

I'm not keen on the fly-by-nighters who are only interested in headlines. I like to read about what's happened rather than get the journo's views. We all enjoy the praise when we do well and have to take it on the chin when we perform poorly but some media people aren't content to describe the game – what we get instead are their opinions. I think Television New Zealand's Peter Williams was the only bloke in the country who could read Abdul Qadir's googly and top spinner during the last Pakistan tour.

At times, the media seem to rate certain people and victimise others – Gren Alabaster, for instance, was heavily and unnecessarily criticised in Australia in 1987/88 – and there are times when you feel the media's reflex response is to be negative. I felt they got that way in 1989 when they were relentlessly critical of what they felt to be negative cricket. Draws are as much part of the game as wins and losses and I felt the Eden Park Pakistan test was a superb game of cricket.

The critics sometimes seem to want to have it all ways. I was criticised for not making a game of this year's Eden Park test and I can accept that – I shut the door on the Indians and the final day was a real anti-climax. I stand by my decision; you don't work like hell to win a series then throw it away at the last hurdle. Besides, the Eden Park pitch was so flat that bowling a side out in less than a day was never on, especially if we'd had to get the last few wickets once the shutters had gone up. The grounds for the criticism then was entertainment – I'd played safe and deprived the public of what could've been an enthralling finish – and they probably had a point. Then a couple of weeks later we lost a one-dayer to India by one run – you don't get many more exciting finishes – but all of a sudden the issue wasn't entertainment; it was that we made a few mistakes and lost the game. Players, and I believe most cricket fans, see the two types of cricket round the other way: test cricket is primarily about results while limited-overs cricket is more to do with entertainment.

I have a lot of time for the yachting broadcaster Peter Montgomery. I don't know the first thing about the sport but he makes it interesting. Yachting has become a monster sport in recent years and his tremendous enthusiasm has certainly been a factor. I think we need one or two more positive people like him in cricket because players, administrators and media all have their role in creating a positive image for cricket.

I get annoyed when I'm quoted out of context. In 1986 I was quoted as rubbishing the English attack and yet I'd never met, let alone spoken to, the guy who wrote the story. You can take part in a talkback programme and wake up the next morning to find that two or three sentences have been isolated and turned into a news story; taken out of context, the remarks might have a completely different tone. I could never get used to people, especially people I didn't know, ringing me at home and asking me questions out of the blue on issues I hadn't even thought about.

At times Kiwi journos bend over backwards to be nice to visitors. Some of them seemed infatuated with Imran Khan, for instance, and he escaped criticism for the allegedly boring cricket in that series but it takes two to tango and we didn't win the one-days 4-1 without being positive. The reverse of that is never giving the opposition credit for playing well, just caning us for playing badly.

Unless you've been there, you don't really understand; even those who have been there sometimes forget. These days it seems old cricketers don't fade away, they head for the commentary box. They can provide an insight which is good, but they shouldn't forget that they made mistakes too.

We might grizzle a bit but we're treated much better by our cricket media than Australian and English players are by theirs, who are pretty merciless. The English press has a lot to answer for in terms of what they've done to English cricket. After the English tour featuring the Ian Botham marijuana controversy, we went to Sri Lanka. An English journalist turned up there and just hung around our hotel for five days, presumably hoping to pick up some information. No one talked to him till one night he came into the team room for a beer. We asked him how he was enjoying his holiday.

Our first team doctor was Peter Borrie, known affectionately as 'Doc on Holiday' and noted for playing squash in protective glasses and being a terrible 500 player. During the Lord's test in 1983 back at our hotel, Bob Willis introduced Doc and me to Charlie Watts, the Rolling Stones drummer. Charlie looked as if he'd downed a few pints during the day and we got into this cross-conversation; he wanted to talk about cricket and we wanted to hear about sex, drugs and rock 'n roll. This continued well into the night, when Charlie realised he'd missed the last train back to his country estate. Doc had a spare bed in his room and thus gained the distinction of being the only New Zealand doctor, as far as we know, to have spent the night with a Rolling Stone. Doc asked Charlie to autograph a photo of his wife which he did, thanking her for letting him sleep with her husband.

Doc was a keen cricketer and when we were in Worcester, he went along to the Duncan Fernley factory and selected a new bat. He was very proud of his bat and wanted our seal of approval on it. A couple of us used it in the nets and said it was terrible, probably because its moisture content was too low. We actually talked him into wrapping it in glad wrap for several days to improve the moisture content.

He was followed by Richard Edmond, known as Doctor Doom, who zealously supervised our diets in Pakistan in 1984. When we arrived at a hotel, he'd hit the kitchens to check out the hygiene standards. Only a couple of blokes got sick and even then not for long.

Very few people in the touring party manage to wriggle out of giving me throw downs. At first Richard was frankly inadequate but many hours of unrelenting practice under the hot sun sorted him out. He didn't know much about cricket but soon learnt it wasn't a good idea to say "good ten John" when I returned to the dressing room less than satisfied with my performance.

Physios are probably more use than doctors on tours because of the number of muscular injuries. Before we took a physio on tour, getting treatment during a match was a real hassle – you'd find yourself having to go to the other side of London or Sydney for treatment. Graeme Ellison came to Australia early in the '80s. Known as 'PR' for the great public relations work he did for New Zealand, he distinguished himself by the speed with which he covered the ground to attend to an injury. When people complained about the air conditioning in hotels, he came out with the comment "open the window, they can't air condition the whole world".

In 1985 we had Graham Hayhow and Doug Edwards from the Institute of Sport. They'd been around sports teams a lot and were very professional. They took the warm-ups and stretching and put a lot of emphasis on suppleness, which hadn't previously been part of our preparation. Graham was hot on motivation. We'd come in at a break and he'd be waiting for us with his catchphrase: "the opposition are cracking – good value." When I batted he would keep telling me "endure, grind them into the ground, endure, endure!"

Mark Plummer, who's regarded as one of the lads, was marvellous in India, not only treating muscular complaints but sickness as well. He'd work day and night and whenever he sat down, someone would grab him for throwdowns which he did very well as you'd expect of a leading light of the Papatoetoe cricket club premier side. He worked harder than anyone and at the end of the tour he was exhausted. He's only slipped from his high standards once: he was giving me some physio when Mark Greatbatch came in and expressed revulsion at the sight of my toes. Plums agreed that they were the sort of toes you'd expect to see in a morgue, which made me feel a million dollars.

Before a test match everyone wants to know how the wicket's going to play. There are lots of theories flying about and the first thing captains do is ask the groundsman. Some of them don't have a clue and the wicket is likely to do exactly the opposite to what they predict. Groundsmen in India and Pakistan don't exactly overburden visiting captains with information.

It's not easy for groundsmen: batsmen want it flat, quicks want it green, spinners want something else, and the captain wants a surface his team can win on; he can expect flak from all of them if they don't get what they want. I felt very sorry for Gary Walklin, the Napier groundsman, after the test there this year. He did an enormous amount of work on the wicket but he lost the grass and it favoured batters too much. He got a real slating, including one from Martin Crowe who began a column by saying the Napier groundsman "should be shot".

Wes Armstrong at the Basin Reserve is my favourite New Zealand groundsman. He's a down-to-earth no-nonsense sort of bloke and has been preparing good wickets for years. Putting the covers on the wicket in a howling Wellington northerly would be a challenge in itself.

One of Wes's least favourite cricketers is Geoff Boycott. Boycott captained the English side that New Zealand beat at the Basin in 1978. Before the game Wes had a run-in with Boycott over the practice wickets, and during the match he was called on to repair the bowlers' footmarks while England were fielding. Wes arrived at the wicket carrying a gardening fork to be greeted by Boycott with: "What the bloody hell are you going to do with that fork?" Wes was about to tell him where he'd like to put it when umpire Bob Monteith diplomatically intervened.

Walter Goodyear was Derbyshire's groundsman for more than 30 years and became something of a local legend, even having a play written about him by Peter Gibbs, a former Derbyshire opening bat. Called 'Arthur's Hallowed Ground', it was performed on BBC television. Walter talked about the wicket as if it was his favourite son. The club wanted him to produce quick wickets and he used to say "it's so hard, it'll ring". Then Alan Ward and Mike Hendrick, our pair of international fast bowlers, would struggle to get it waist high. Batsmen would complain that it looked dangerously green only to be told "grass is always bloody green". When he thought he'd produced a belting batting wicket, he'd tell the openers "dip your beard in the gravy on that wicket, I've put it to sleep". If you weren't sure if you needed a helmet, a comment like that from Walter settled the issue.

The widow of Dennis Smith, a former Derbyshire player and coach, requested that Dennis's ashes be scattered on the wicket at Derbyshire County Cricket Ground. It was a windy day and the man from the undertakers didn't bother to wet his finger and test the wind before opening the casket with the result that the deceased's remains were blown into the faces of the small group of mourners positioned downwind. The group included Walter who returned to the club rooms in an agitated state. "Did you see that bloody idiot of an undertaker?" he demanded. "Look," he said, pointing to cuffs of his trousers, "I've got half of Dennis Smith in my turn-ups." Dennis himself was a character by all accounts. Peter Gibbs tells the story of being congratulated by Dennis on scoring his first century for Derbyshire. Anxious not to overdo the praise, Dennis added "but if you die tonight, we'll manage".

The groundsman's hut was a good place to go after a low score, a refuge where you could have a quiet smoke, get a bet on, and watch the races on their telly. In winter they'd be out there in the freezing cold, keeping an eye on the square and looking after the hockey fields while the committee members and officers would be up in the warm bar sinking pints.

Ces Renwick, groundsman at the Cornwall club in Auckland, apparently has soil samples from every test wicket in Australasia and soil analysis of many wickets around the world. Ces gave the Eden Park groundsman a hand before the Pakistan test in 1989. All the square needed to look like a stretch of Takapuna beach was a bit of driftwood and some seaweed. I saw the wicket a few days before the game and would have put my test fee on it being a raging bunsen – there was nothing holding it together. They literally glued the wicket together and Ces was adamant before the game that it would last the distance. Not only did it do that but we had an open wicket practice on it the day after the test finished and it played like a dream.

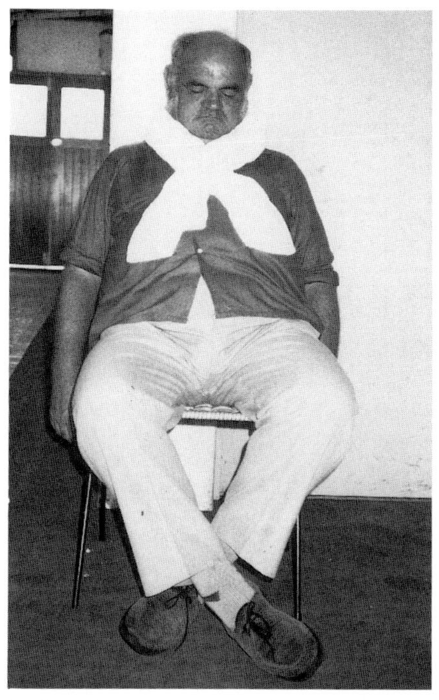

In the blue corner – Mick the changing-room attendant at Eden Park.

Thou shalt not pass – Dave McLeod, gateman at Eden Park.

Bomb-disposal experts at work! Fred Goodall and Steve Woodward. Geoff Howarth keeps his distance.

J.G. BLACKWELL

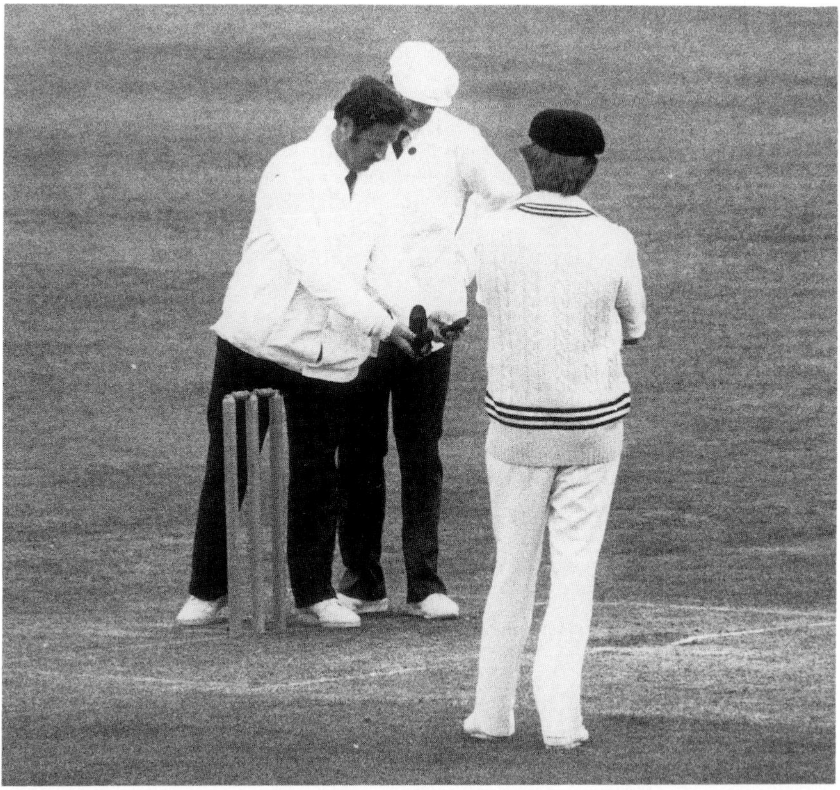

Lost for words – Radio NZ commentator Brian Waddle with Paddy Greatbatch.
MARGOT BUTCHER

Not just a pretty face – TV commentator Peter Williams on-driving during an impromptu innings at the Basin Reserve while New Zealand were playing Australia, 1990.
MARGOT BUTCHER

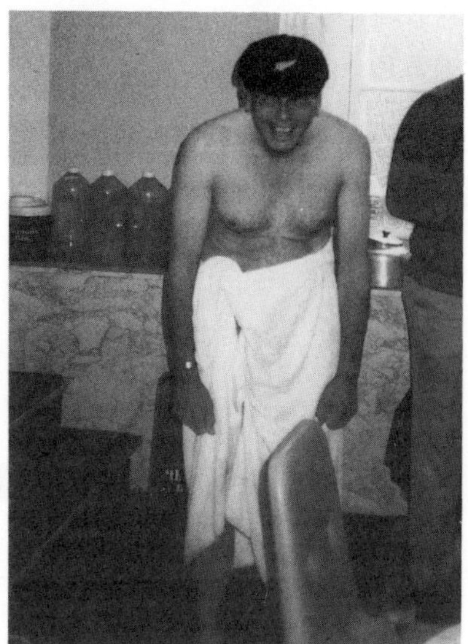

"Where's the sauna?" – umpire Dickie Bird.

Walter Goodyear, the Derbyshire groundsman.

Tools of the trade – Boycott has his bat, Wes has his garden fork.

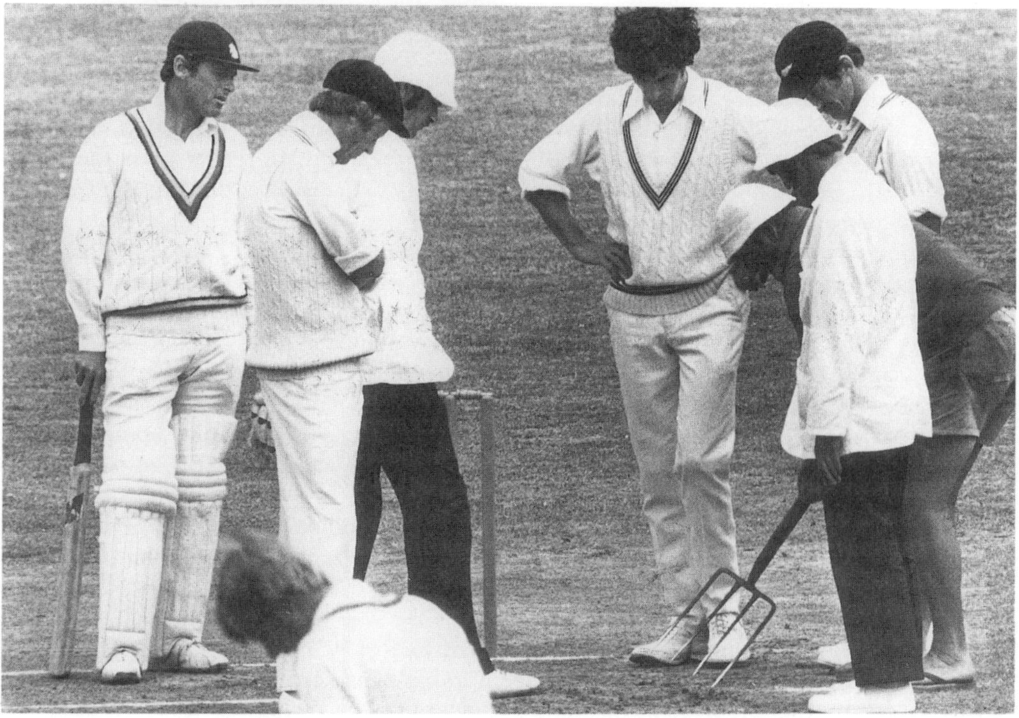

CHAPTER EIGHT

The big time

For me county cricket was a means to an end, which was to be a good test cricketer for New Zealand.

When I first played test cricket, the team had something of an inferiority complex towards the other countries – we doubted that we were good enough to knock them off. One of Geoff Howarth's greatest contributions was to instil in the side the belief that we were good enough to take on and beat all comers. Together with Richard Hadlee's magnificent achievements and the parts played by a number of very good, and in many cases under-rated, players, this change in attitude has made New Zealand into a very competitive team under all conditions and regardless of the opposition.

It's amazing how quickly people's expectations change. My first test match coincided with our first win against England. That was 1978. In those days a New Zealand victory was a major event. In recent years the focus seems to have switched from our results to the way we play the game and we've been criticised for not being entertaining enough. I understand the desirability of playing the sort of cricket that gets people through the gates; I also believe that having worked our bums off to lose the reputation for being international cricket's soft touch, we should think twice before we turn our backs on those attributes of gutsy competitiveness, doggedness, hanging in there and refusing to lie down which, prosaic though they may be, are our strengths and the foundations of our success. Our critics should bear in mind that if the international pecking order was determined purely on the basis of available natural talent, New Zealand could still be near the foot of the ladder.

Determined, resilient, resourceful; maybe plodding at times and a trifle dull; tough competitors and always proud as hell to represent our country: we've had our stars and our magic moments, but overall that's the way New Zealand cricket teams tend to be. Perhaps the way we are and the way we play says something about New Zealand and New Zealanders.

Recent English teams don't seem to have the same sense of national identity that other countries have. They're pros and whatever test cricket is to the rest of us, it's still a day's work to them. I think that attitude has probably become more pronounced over the years. I have a lot of sympathy for them because they play so much cricket: five or six home tests along with county cricket and three one-day competitions in their summer, then a winter tour with another five or six tests plus one-dayers. They're overworked, they get bored, and some of them have lost their mental and physical edge before they arrive on a tour.

English players are pretty good-mannered. We relate well to them and there's not much sledging or aggro. The players are good-humoured and play with a minimum of fuss and bother. When I first started in test cricket, they were confident playing New Zealand; they thought themselves to be superior and they were very professional – a good day's work was usually good enough against us.

They've suffered from bad administration, bad organisation and bad selection. The way that the media and selectors put players, especially youngsters, under pressure, has inhibited them. Inevitably the players they've stuck with have produced the goods but usually they stick with them too long and recent English teams have been marked by an establishment centred around the southern counties.

The England tour is a good one because you play so much cricket. It's not like the whistle-stop affairs in the other countries where you play a couple of first-class games, the tests, a few one-dayers then get out. The English are also the fairest public in the world and the game has such a wonderful tradition there; it really is part of the social fabric so the results of the national team matter far less than they do elsewhere: whether the England team is doing well or getting hammered, an incredible amount of cricket will still be played in villages, towns and cities up and down England and the game will retain its place in the nation's affections.

England is one of the few countries which doesn't doctor wickets to suit itself although that practice is now quite common in county cricket. During the 1989 Ashes series a cynic would have said that a groundsman ordered to doctor a pitch to suit England would have left it under a foot of water. But they're coming right – they have plenty of talent and a great nursery in county cricket.

I think it would be fair to say that Pakistan would be most people's pick as the least preferred nation to play against. The Pakistanis play to the limit of the law and in their country, all's fair in love, war and cricket: victory can be achieved by any means. It's a very harsh country and the cricket reflects the way of life.

There's more gamesmanship there than elsewhere – they're very hard competitors and quite nasty with it. They're very proud to be playing for Pakistan and they're scrappers, especially the successful ones. The mixture makes them very formidable, perhaps the most formidable, opponents.

Pakistan and umpiring rows have become synonymous, which is rather sad. If the umpiring standards in Pakistan's domestic cricket are as bad as the test umpiring we experienced on tour, it's no wonder they shout for everything: a decision is always on. To use an Australianism, there must be very few Pakistani cricketers who die wondering.

The crowds are very volatile: you're likely to have a small sack of rubbish lobbed on your head if you're fielding at fine leg. At Multan there was a riot which had to be suppressed with tear gas because some people couldn't get into the ground. The crowd was so big, a section of it moved in front of the sightscreen and couldn't be shifted. Then it was Pakistan's turn to bat and they mysteriously melted away. The crowds are more parochial than in India, where they give visitors some credit, but they're hard on their own players too. It's survival of the fittest and that's the way of life.

On the positive side, the players are extremely talented with the most wonderful hand/eye coordination, the crowds love their cricket and the wickets we played on were absolutely beautiful: Karachi would vie with Guyana in the West Indies as the best we've played tests on.

I enjoyed touring there more than anywhere else because it's so different. It's another world and it constantly spills over into the cricket: you can have a net and people will encroach on the net area so much that a bloke bowling off a long run has a gap a yard wide to run down; the batsman can be thrashing lofted drives straight into the crowd at enormous velocity and no one seems to mind; when you leave a ground the crowd will be milling around trying to touch you and has to be beaten back with sticks; when I dived to stop a ball on the boundary I couldn't get up because there were so many people pawing me.

The hospitality and care we received were second to none, so good that you sometimes forgot what hard beggers they are.

The West Indies cover a vast area and there are pronounced cultural differences between the different islands. Trinidad for instance is completely different from the others. They have an incredibly tough domestic competition because it's virtually different countries playing each other. Clive Lloyd's ability to mould them into a team by being a father figure to them was a critical factor in their consistent success. Now they seem very strong and together as a team which, along with their natural talent, makes them very formidable.

I know they felt very strongly that they were cheated over here in the 1980/81 series. The umpiring wasn't good but there were faults on their part which made it hard to have much sympathy for them. Their management was poor and their reaction in Christchurch, when they wouldn't come out at the start of a session, wasn't very sensible. Croft's barging Fred Goodall was idiotic and certainly didn't enhance their cause.

I've never been to a place where you're made so aware of the colour of your skin. You get called 'a white honky' when you're fielding on the boundary and you hear often, 'we're going to get you'. Individually they're good blokes and I have some mates among them, guys like Michael Holding and Desmond Haynes.

Their fast bowling is pretty awesome. Of all the nations, they've benefited most from access to English county cricket because every county

Senior rugby at university. I'm the Cossack, in the middle of the back row. Eight of these lads went on to play first-class rugby – unfortunately I didn't.

Off to practice, university days.

Back to university, hope we make it.

Backing up with Brian McKechnie at an under-20 tournament.

wants a fast bowler. They learn a lot over there, then they kick on. It will be interesting to see what happens if that dries up. Some of the test grounds in the West Indies aren't too flash, the outfields and stands are pretty rough, and the club grounds are obviously worse, but the wickets are generally excellent so bowlers have to do something to get results.

The crowds are effervescent and ebullient. When we played the one-dayer at Antigua, they had this massive stereo system and every time a West Indian hit a four, we'd get a blast of reggae at ferocious volume. There's always a buzz and a hum around the ground. They know all about you and they have an all-or-nothing attitude: a bouncer is applauded like a six.

It's amazing how casual and relaxed they are but when they pick up a bat or ball, it's like someone pulled a switch. They were born to play cricket like New Zealanders were born to play rugby and, like the All Blacks, the more professional and organised they get, the harder they will be to beat.

There's not a lot of subtlety to their game although you get graceful players like Holding, Lawrence Rowe and Jeff Dujon. It's based mostly on sheer power: they play it as it should be played – they bowl quick and hit the ball hard. They've certainly mastered the art of quick bowling and they do bowl to intimidate. It's a place where you want to get respect.

Cricket in India is almost timeless: teams have scored 800 and 900 runs in an innings in their first-class games. I always enjoyed playing against the Indians because they're the most sporting side. They have a serenity, a patience, and a grace about them although they can still hit the ball a mile. Their personalities are suited to spin bowling and spinners there have a greater acceptance of being whacked. They have so many spinners, kids bowling leggies and googlies – it's like quicks in the West Indies.

The crowds are very passionate and the top players are absolutely adored – they're regal, god-like figures although because of the vastness of the country and the parochialism, you can be hero-worshipped in Bombay and loathed in Calcutta. The north-south divide in England and inter-state rivalry in Australia is mild by comparison.

There are a lot of similarities with Pakistan but lots of differences too: Indians are just as volatile but less aggressive; charm is not a quality you readily associate with Pakistanis but India is full of it. They prepared the wickets to suit them when we toured but they also went out of their way to see we were well-treated. Like Pakistan, India is an experience in its own right, which makes the two countries the most interesting places to tour. Of the two, India gives the impression of being the more urban and westernised.

The crowd in Bombay was superb – harsh on the home team, generous to us and very knowledgeable. Men, women and children will go to terrific lengths to see cricketers and there were constant crowds outside the team hotels. Public interest is greater than anywhere else.

Australia means machismo, media hype, and nationalism. It's a man's place to play cricket. On my first tour there we struggled for the first half of the tour and played well in the second half. The Aussie players didn't want to know us when they were cleaning us up but when we started to compete, they'd have a beer after the game. In a way they're bad winners and good losers. Things were okay once we got their respect but they're pretty arrogant when they win. Maybe it's because everyone in Australia loves a winner, even losing Australian teams.

Victory was sweet there in 1985 and they found it a little hard to accept. We've always been slagged by their media as having little to offer. Just before Richard Hadlee cleaned them out at the Gabba, they were talking about our popgun attack. Some of the ex-players in the media still don't rate us and I don't think we'll ever go over there and start favourites.

They play it hard. I had a season of club cricket in Perth and there was more niggle than in our first-class cricket. You get sledged more there than anywhere. Guys like Rod Marsh and Dennis Lillee were hard to talk to at first but once you've got their respect, they're good company over a beer. There's always a bit of aggro when New Zealanders clash with Australians: both think the other lot have chips on their shoulders.

They have a great cricketing tradition which we lack and there's a lot of pride associated with pulling on the green baggy cap. When a player does that, big things are expected of him by the public, the media, and former players. If he doesn't come up with the goods, they don't want to know him. It would have been marvellous to have grown up and played cricket in Australia with conditions which are so conducive to good cricket, a tradition which ensures the game's place in society and is a source of inspiration to young players, and that aggressive attitude which I admire.

The organisation of cricket at state and national level is the best in the world. You've got grounds like the WACA in Perth where they've spent $A27 million and the facilities are superb. When you arrive, you get a typed letter of welcome setting out the conditions of the match and when and where you're to practise. In Adelaide they've just completed the $A9 million Sir Donald Bradman Stand which has been beautifully designed to harmonise with the ground's character and the practice wickets are fantastic. We could learn a lot from them.

We've got a good relationship with their players, built up over the last four or five years when Allan Border and Bobby Simpson have been in charge. In Perth in 1989 we went into their dressing room for a beer after each day's play. In many ways we've got a lot in common with them.

You can never underestimate them. They're great fighters and I respect them a lot and enjoy playing them because I would've liked to have played for Australia more than any other country outside New Zealand. The more we have to do with them and their cricket, the more we play them, the better it will be for us. Developing that relationship should be one of our top priorities.

Sri Lanka is the opposite in a number of respects, one of which is that I don't like playing there. Not because of the Sri Lankans – they're lovely people – but because it's so bloody hot! You're covered in sweat within minutes. You can wet your gear and have a shower but within four

"But I thought you were unavailable."

overs, you're completely dry. Then you start to sweat like a sow in a sauna. When you're batting, you're bathed in it. The sessions there from lunch to tea are the hottest I've ever experienced.

Like any young nation in any sport, they haven't yet learnt how to win. They have some very talented players but unfortunately the development of that talent is being held back by the internal strife. Unless they play regular home series, their development will be arrested.

They're nice people to play against. When they toured New Zealand, the two teams shared a Friendship flight from Napier to Auckland and we had a wonderful sing song. They have a humility about them, none of that superstar thing – some of them probably doubt that they're really good enough to be in the test arena. They're a little bit like the New Zealand teams was when I started: nice guys, and everybody knows where nice guys finish. Now we're a bit nasty and professional and tough. Give them time and the Sri Lankans will lose their innocence; then they won't be easybeats any more.

CHAPTER NINE

"If that's test cricket, you can stick it..."

By the beginning of the 1977/78 season, I was beginning to feel that it was a question of when, and not if, I would play for New Zealand. I'd had a season of county cricket and the move from Canterbury to Northern Districts had taken me from an environment where I felt people didn't rate me, to one in which people were starting to notice me. For ND in 1976/77 I'd opened with Glenn Turner and made 431 runs at average of 31. We'd played a three-day game against Australia which was regarded as a trial match. I got 14 and 47; if I'd done really well, I might have made it that season.

But it was far from cut and dried because both Bruce Edgar and Ian Rutherford – who'd been around for longer than both of us – were chasing the same spot. In 1976/77 Rutherford got 625 runs averaging 48 so he had the inside running. I've always been conscious of other players' performances because if you're going for a spot, you've got to out-perform the other guys who are also going for it and that's how it should be when you're picking sides. At Derbyshire they used to put on a plum voice and say: "If you've got two good players and one's a jolly nice fellow and the other's an utter wally, you pick the jolly nice fellow." They were taking off the Derbyshire secretary Major Carr but that sums up an aspect of England cricket.

Rutherford had played well for a few seasons. People used to say he was slow in the field but he could have been put in the slips and he was a hell of a good player. His performances for Otago definitely qualified him for test cricket. He was one of the tragedies of New Zealand cricket. He should have gone to England in 1978 which would have done a lot for his development. I always felt sorry for him – in the end Bruce Edgar and I got the nod but Ian had performed as well as us and I think missing out probably caused him to give the game away.

That season he'd moved from Otago to Central Districts which was probably a mistake, as his form fell away. It did mean though that he was opening with the test incumbent, Robert 'Jumbo' Anderson. Ian was very much the junior partner to Jumbo, who emphasised the fact by calling him 'Boy'. Once at a barbecue, Jumbo instructed Boy to fetch him a hot dog. Ian gave it to him and started running. Jumbo bit into it and took off as well – it contained a four-inch nail.

My English experience was a plus. England were touring that season and I'd played against them all. In that first season at Derbyshire, I'd got 1000 runs and topped the batting.

In the first game of the 1977/78 season I got 53 and 27 and 87 in the second. I was grinding away towards 100, batting against my old Canterbury mate Doug Bracewell, John's and Brendon's brother. His father was at the game and called out "Hurry up Wright, you even look like a Pom now." A few minutes later Doug caught and bowled me.

Our next game was at Wellington. I got one in the first dig then Bruce Edgar got 93 in his. We batted 100 behind and at one stage were 38 for four. I ended up with 115 and feeling that I had a real chance of making the side.

We were playing in Hamilton in the next round and the team was announced on the Sunday before the game started. Steve Boock and I were the new caps. I was pleased but not surprised. A couple of days later I was in Auckland and I went down to the park with a mate for a knock up. There I was, no pads or gloves, whacking the ball against a shed and thinking that in three days' time, I'd be playing in a test match.

We stayed at the St George Hotel in Wellington. It was cold and the net wickets were green. The chairman of selectors, Frank Cameron, did a lot of bowling in the nets with a roaring northerly behind him and seamed it all over the place. It was like his final inspection. The night before the test Jumbo Anderson and I completed our mental preparation by lobbing a few pears at a passersby from the hotel window. He nicknamed me 'Shake' because he reckoned I never ironed my gear, just threw it all into my bag and shook it up. Personally, I thought I looked pretty smart in the team photo. My father flew up from Canterbury for the game even though he hates flying.

On the first morning of the test I drove to the Basin Reserve with Jumbo and we got stuck in traffic. I was pretty apprehensive but very keen to do well. I'd always wanted to get a century in my first test. There's nothing like getting picked for your country for the first time – ask any sportsman, whether he's had a long career at the top or been a one-season wonder. There's something special about representing your country, especially this country. New Zealand is a tremendously sport-oriented country: a lot of people identify with sport and we have a proud international reputation. It's great to be able to say you played for New Zealand at the senior level. I'd made the under 20 and 23 teams but it had always seemed just a stepping stone.

The day was cold and overcast with a howling northerly. We went out and had a few throw-downs – there were no stretches or warm-ups in those days. The general opinion was that we had a pretty good chance of beating England for the first time ever because they didn't seem as strong as in the past. The wicket was hard and green and the English captain Geoff Boycott won the toss and put us in. We'd have done the same.

I walked out to bat with Jumbo, who generously allowed me to take first ball. I took two legs from Bob Monteith, then Bob Willis was racing in with the wind behind him. It was a good nut, pitching just short of a length on middle and leg and going across me, committing me to the shot. I got a faint touch and they all went up. I thought: "What a bloody disaster."

I knew no one walked in test cricket and the thought of it never entered my head. There wasn't much of a deviation and I didn't think Monteith could have heard the snick with the wind blowing down the pitch. There was nothing wrong with Willis's hearing though – he went spare and abused me roundly. I copped some from the slip cordon as well but it was fairly low-key stuff. My Derbyshire mate Bob Taylor was keeping and he didn't say anything and the others knew it was my first test. I'm sure they fancied their chances of getting me quickly anyway.

The next delivery was a very quick bouncer which cleared me easily and Bob Taylor by miles and went for four byes. There was another one like that in the over and a no ball so were were nine without loss after the first over without having officially laid bat on ball.

Mike Hendrick opened from the other end but couldn't get his rhythm into the wind and sprayed it everywhere. After a couple of overs Chris Old came on and Jumbo took 23 from his first three overs. Meanwhile Willis was really letting fly downwind, most of it fired outside off stump going away. That meant I didn't have to play many deliveries; it also meant I couldn't get away from facing him and down to the other end where they seemed to be playing a different and much less difficult game. Between overs Jumbo would tell me how well I was playing. I was thinking: "That's all very well for you mate, smashing it all over the park." All I wanted to do was to get down his end and he was just as keen to stay put. I got off the mark in the 52nd minute and changing ends so upset Jumbo that he was out for 28 in the 53rd. Our stand of 42 was the second highest of the innings.

By lunch I'd raced to 23. I went into the changing room and said, "If that's test cricket, you can stick it!"

The wicket was variable and Willis, Botham, Old and Hendrick were as accurate an attack as I've faced in test cricket. They really knew what they were doing. It was Boycott's second test as captain and his field settings were pretty defensive. Maybe he'd worked out it was going to be a low-scoring game. I got into a rut and just hung around, reaching 50 in 272 minutes. I really wanted a century but they just didn't give me a lot to hit. Play finished 30 minutes early because of bad light and we were 152 for three which we felt wasn't a bad effort in the circumstances. I'd made 55 in 340 minutes. I can still remember how hard it was batting in that wind: the ball came through much quicker downwind, the bat picked up like a

My first day in test cricket in windy Wellington. The England field placements look rather extraordinary.

feather at one end and like a crowbar at the other, and always the struggle to maintain balance.

That night Walter Hadlee congratulated me and suggested I should try to play on the front foot more. I've always appreciated Walter's remarks and have had some interesting chats with him because he's good on technique. Getting on the front foot to Willis that day though was easier said than done.

In fact it was really a bad start to a test career because it left the idea that that was how test cricket had to be played. I wish I could've started in different conditions.

The next day the wind had changed to a southerly and it was a bit brighter but I didn't have long to enjoy it. Bob Monteith gave me lbw to Botham in the first over. I was annoyed because I was sure it was going down leg side but I suppose under the circumstances I couldn't really complain. We went from 152 for three to 228 all out.

England were 89 for two at stumps and really ground it out on the second and third days. We had a good attack – Richard Hadlee, Richard 'Rock' Collinge, Boocky and Bevan Congdon whose figures were 17.4 overs, 11 maidens, two wickets for 14. That's invaluable bowling in test cricket because it gives the quickies a rest, apart from the wickets.

For me Congo was one of New Zealand's really great players. I'd always admired his attitude – he was known as a hard man by many who played under him. In one of my first games Congo gave me heaps and made a hell of a fuss because I'd whitened my pads before the innings and he reckoned the whitener was affecting the new ball. In England in 1978 I roomed with him once and he drew a line down the middle of the room and said "That's your half and this is mine." He was rather more meticulous than me. There was also quite an age difference – he was 40 and I was 24. The cultural divide between Congo and 18-year-old Brendon Bracewell was even more yawning and it couldn't be said that they established a rapport.

England were probably more defensive than we were: Boycott got 77 in 442 minutes. Together we must have really done a lot for Wellington cricket – there was a rumour they had to close the gates on the fourth morning because so many people wanted to see the two of us in action.

They were all out for 215 and at stumps on the third day we were 12 without loss. Jumbo and I put on 54, and at lunch on the fourth day we were 75 for one after another brisk session. After lunch Willis bowled bloody quick and the wicket was becoming really up and down. I was caught at slip for 19 and our last nine wickets went for 48 with Willis taking five wickets in seven overs in his second spell, ending with five for 32. We were all out for 123 and tea was taken at the close of our innings. I'd sat in a deck chair and watched the wickets tumble. Generally I didn't mind facing Bob Willis because he moved the ball across me to the off side but he was very quick when he got it together and always gave it 100 per cent. I got a century against England on a flat wicket at Eden Park in 1984 and he never stopped running in.

England needed 137 to win in eight hours. We were a bit downhearted but we still felt if we could get Boycott early, we were in with a chance. They didn't have a strong batting line-up with Geoff Miller, an all-rounder rather than a specialist batter, going in at three.

After tea Richard Collinge bowled from the northern, Cambridge Terrace, end. He pitched one up to Boycott, almost a yorker, on middle and leg. Boycott played across the line and was cleaned out – one for two. In his next over Rock got Miller and the one after that Randall. They were 18 for three wickets. Then Paddles started to bowl like the wind. In those days he sometimes needed a bit of a lift – like Rock getting Boycott – to get him revved up. One of the big things quickies have to learn is to go out and do it all the time. One of Paddles' deliveries to Brian Rose took off and smacked him on the arm and that was the end of him.

England had an excellent attack but a weak batting line-up: they didn't have the experienced players coming in in the middle order to steady the ship when the wicket was doing a bit. Botham came in and whacked a few – in those days we didn't know what sort of a player he was and he certainly took up the challenge – but Paddles bounced him out, caught on the hook. Boocky ran out Bob Taylor with a throw from side on. Suddenly the crowd was right behind us. It was a typical New Zealand thing which has happened a few other times: you get the momentum going and it just snowballs. At stumps England were 53 for eight. Seventeen wickets had fallen in the day for 164 runs.

The batting wasn't that great but it wasn't an easy wicket. We were more used to those conditions. In those days we often played tests in conditions we regarded as difficult but the opposition considered a mine field and I think it gave us a major psychological advantage over our opponents. You'd get shotmakers used to playing on true wickets coming over here and really struggling. Recently the wickets have been much flatter which doesn't suit us so much.

Jumbo and I had a couple of quiet ones that night. We were pretty happy about the situation but scared stiff it would rain. Monday was a rest day. We practised in the morning then had a quiet day.

Sometimes rest days are good and sometimes not. If you're not out it gives you a chance to have a breather and prepare but it also gives the bowlers a day to freshen up.

Tuesday was dark and overcast and the start was delayed for 40 minutes. England had only Old, Hendrick and Willis left, none of whom really had the capacity to pull it off, so it was just a matter of time and the rain keeping away. They were all out for 64 after three-quarters of an hour, giving us victory by 72 runs.

Richard Hadlee ended up with six wickets for 26 but in many respects it was those three wickets of Rock's which swung the game. They changed the attitude of the New Zealand team, the crowd and certainly the England team. If you're chasing a small total and you get away to a good start, it's a doddle but they lost a few quick wickets early and, all of a sudden, 137 was an awful lot to get.

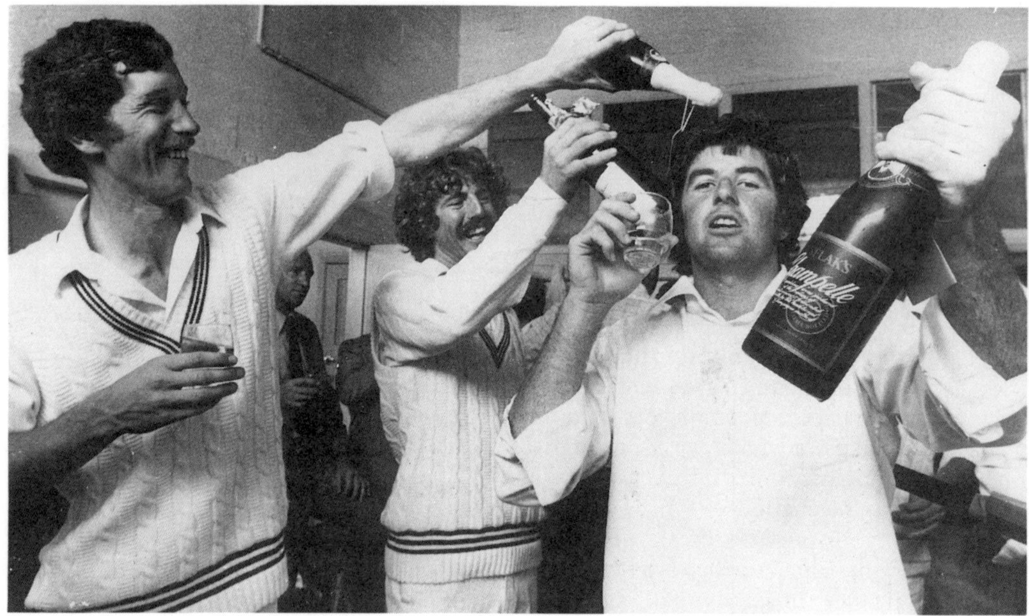

Debut boys – first test, first win. Boocky and me with 'Dag' Parker.
NZ HERALD

I got the batting award and champagne flowed in the dressing room. It was pretty special for the new boys, Boocky and me: our first test and New Zealand's first-ever win over England. Maybe we should have retired then and there, while we were ahead. It meant even more to guys like Congo, Mark Burgess, Rock and Dayle Hadlee who'd been around for a while and had a few near misses and a few hammerings from England. Frank Cameron was happy – he enjoyed our victories. We had a big night that night.

The next day I flew back to Gisborne where I was living and doing a bit of coaching. I wasn't a great flyer in those days and it was a bumpy flight made worse by my hangover. When the plane touched down I looked out the window and there were 50 or 60 primary school kids and a banner saying "Welcome home Wrighty". Journalists from radio and the local paper were there as well. I was almost too embarrassed to get off the plane.

The second test was in Christchurch and I went to get a haircut the day before. I was sitting in the barber's shop waiting my turn and the barber said to the guy in the chair: "What about the cricket then – wasn't that great stuff?" "Yeah", the bloke said, "but it was probably just a fluke." I thought: "What a negative attitude." As it turned out, I got nought and four and we got stuffed. Such is life: success and champagne one test; defeat and warm beer the next.

There was a postscript to my first test. When I returned to Derbyshire later that year, my teammates presented me with a memento of the occasion – a packet of Walker's potato chips.

Touch rugby at practice. Horne to Wright, while Gren Alabaster looks suspiciously offside.

Another net . . . I forgot my tracksuit pants!
J.G. BLACKWELL

CHAPTER TEN

Countdown

Preparation is essential when you come out of a New Zealand winter to go on tour. The team is sent to the Institute of Sport to be assessed and put on individual physical training programmes three months before the tour and at the same time you have to start working on your skills. When the tour starts, you're fit and you've done your homework. While overall fitness is important, the short Australian tour in 1989 showed there's no substitute for cricket fitness. Lack of it causes all the little niggly injuries, the strains and finger injuries, that happen because you're not used to playing cricket.

Once on tour it's essential that the lead-up games are used properly so that the team is really firing for the first test. Of course there are always players who perform in the lead-up games and flop in the test and others who do the opposite – Mark Greatbatch in India in 1988 and Australia in 1989 for instance. It's the tests that count.

Before the series, you assess the pre-test phase and the test venues. When Pakistan were here in 1989, it was obvious the result wicket was at Carisbrook. When England toured in 1984, we knew it would be Lancaster Park. I'd always heard the wickets were good in India but those at Bangalore and Bombay had been prepared to turn square and it was obvious there'd be a result.

By the time you reach the first test on tour, you will have sorted out who's going to play except for one or two positions. It's very important that the batters are in form so you organise things to give them the best possible chance of getting into the groove. With the bowlers, selection will often be dictated by conditions at the venue. New Zealand conditions are pretty hard on spinners because they generally favour seamers – you'll probably have a spinner in the 12 but he's often in line for the 12th man spot.

The first test is the toughest in many ways: the players may be new to each other, you may not know some of the opposition, and winning the first test gives you an enormous psychological advantage. It's important that you go into test matches with a positive attitude, aiming to win, although realistically if you're one up with one to play, a draw is a good result.

We were in that situation against England at the Oval in 1986, never having won a series there. We went in to win but we weren't broken-hearted when it rained on the last day. It was similar when we went to Eden Park in 1984 with the chance of our first-ever series win against England. The wicket was so flat that a result was always unlikely, especially after we won the toss and batted for two and a half days.

At home the team is picked when we arrive at the venue so everyone knows where they stand except the candidates for 12th man. On tour there's a party of 15 or 16 and although everyone may have a fair idea of what the side will be, it's not finalised. There can be two or three players who are going to sit out the series which is hard. They've got to be positive towards the team despite their own disappointments. They're part of the dressing room and that in itself creates problems as some dressing rooms are too small for 12 let alone 15 or 16.

We gather at the venue or arrive there two or three days before the game which gives two full days to prepare. As test time draws closer, people start getting a bit tense, less tolerant, a little niggly. I certainly get more introverted and guys like Andrew Jones, Stockley Smith and Braces get a bit toey. Everything goes up a notch: people can't be late for anything, training can't be bad. More bite comes into the whole set-up and things have just got to be right: the team has got to be hardening up, sharpening up.

Before the first home test or at the start of a tour, the ground rules have to be laid down: you're in the New Zealand team and certain standards are expected of you – you have a tradition to live up to. This is an area in which we've really improved. The captain and the coach spell it out: no time for fooling around, do it well, do it right, quality counts. It's also important that individuals have done their homework and preparation although some players have the ability to coast through the build-up and lift themselves for the tests. Jerry Coney went up a notch for tests and Geoff Howarth wasn't a heavy practiser although he'd have a net or two before a test.

At the hotel, all sorts of superstitions and personal preferences come into play. Guys who've been successful when they've roomed together in the past want to be together again. The standard of the hotel can affect players' frames of mind. In Hyderabad in Pakistan we stayed at the Fataz (known as the Fatarse) which wouldn't have rated a mention in the Michelin guide to the world's leading hotels. It had been opened three months previously by General Zia but from the state it was in, you'd think the honours had been done by the last viceroy. For most of us the first look at the restaurant was the last. The rooms had strange names: there were Superior A and B, one of which was occupied by manager Ian Taylor and the other by Paul McEwan and Chats. They became our meeting places for a few quiet ones and our dining room where we set up the microwave. It was also the TV room where we set up a video and gave *Cat Ballou* and *Tootsie* a thorough airing. Some guys watched them five times in five days. On the rest day we had an all-day movie session beginning at 9 a.m. and finishing at three the next morning.

The card room was Silver Lining B and Mr and Mrs Wright occupied the bridal suite. In Pakistan orange is the colour for marriage and everything in the room was vivid orange, which took a lot of living with over nine days. Boocky and John Reid were in Rosie A. Steve got nine wickets in the game and Reido a century so they were very keen to room together for the next test. Martin Crowe and Mark Greatbatch are good mates and like to room together. You also tend to put guys who aren't in the test side together so they can have a night out without disturbing the team. Every morning we were woken up at five by the calls to the faithful to pray to Mecca, broadcast through loudspeakers. I thought it was quite mystical but not everyone shared my view.

The Fataz was actually the scene of a fiercely contested T-shirt ripping contest on the night of the rest day initiated by Martin Snedden and culminating in irreparable damage to Lance Cairns' favourite T-shirt. The way Cairns dealt with the ripper brought this game to an abrupt conclusion. That same night Jeff Crowe woke from a troubled sleep and looked at himself in the mirror to find himself a whiter shade of pale from head to foot after the application of a large quantity of talcum powder while he slept. It gave him a hell of a fright.

After that test match we went to a massive reception attended by everyone who was anyone in Hyderabad. It was a blazer and tie affair and the Pakistan team were all smiles because they'd just won the series. The smiles weren't for us because that afternoon Jerry had gone on television and virtually accused them of cheating. There was a gigantic spread but because it was a meatless day, it was all salads and that sort of thing and our team doctor gave it the once over, then rushed around telling us not to eat anything. The mayor got very concerned when he saw we weren't partaking; unfortunately he chose the wrong person to ask why not. Braces hadn't had a great test: he'd got a pair and been the object of Cairnsy's wrath in the affair of the torn T-shirt. Braces' explanation was short and to the point: "It's cold and it's poop."

I have a fixation about traffic noise so if I find myself on the fourth floor overlooking a motorway, I won't be happy. I like good sleeps and my need for a quiet room supersedes everything else. Others are bothered if they're cramped for space. Modern cricketers are probably pretty spoilt in terms of accommodation compared to their predecessors and the calibre of hotel New Zealand teams get has certainly improved since we've become a force to be reckoned with in test cricket.

Sometimes we have a chat the night we arrive to run through what's happening over the next two days and next morning is generally practice. If there's only one practice facility and two teams wanting to practise, you can have problems because most teams like to practise in the morning, especially the day before the game.

The standard of practice facilities is very important. In England and places like Adelaide, Perth and Bombay, they're very good but one of the worst aspects of New Zealand cricket has been the poor standard of practice

"Come on, lads" – Bob Cunis, Braces and Franko at practice.

Loosening up at Lord's – "That's the last time we eat at that restaurant, Lance."

wickets. They've been good at Eden Park the last couple of seasons but for three or four years before that, they were atrocious. Quite often in New Zealand we've turned up for pre-test practice and found the facilities inadequate, which is very frustrating. Ther've not very good in the West Indies either. Practice is important especially for guys who are out of nick and want to bat. It's hopeless when net wickets are poor or nothing like what you're actually going to play on – you wouldn't find Becker practising for Wimbledon on a slow clay court – but you've just got to make the best of it.

We leave the hotel about 9 a.m. The communications system is generally a notice on the manager's door, posted before 10 or 11 p.m. Some of the messages which have gone up after 10 p.m. have been a bit wobbly.

Some grounds I walk into and like straight away. You get a feel for them and a sense that you're going to do well. It's chicken and egg because that feeling is often associated with past success there. I like the Oval, Eden Park, Bombay, the Melbourne Cricket Ground. I like the Adelaide Oval although I've never done particularly well there, but I've never felt comfortable at Lord's.

Players have their favourite spots in the home dressing rooms – Richard Hadlee has sat in the same place at Lancaster Park for 15 years – and certain players like to change next to each other. Generally it's just superstition, trying to recreate the procedure you followed when you had success, but these rituals are important. If you're new to the ground, you just grab the best spot you can.

We start with a warm up and looseners. It used to be taken by the player in charge of physical fitness – Bruce Edgar or Ian Smith – but now our physio Mark Plummer does it: a couple of laps of the ground and some stretching. Then the cricket manager announces the batting order. If he's really well organised he'll have a few of the ground staff doing some bowling. There's 15 guys wanting a bat and only seven or eight bowlers and you don't want to knacker your test bowlers. Usually a batter and a bowler bat together so the bowlers get a rest. If we get to the ground early and the groundsman hasn't got the wickets ready, we have fielding first.

You bat for 15 or 20 minutes and have to be pretty focused. Some guys like to go in and play strokes, feel the bat on ball; others like to play like they play in the middle. What you don't want is guys going in and having a thrash. You can't afford to waste practice time.

If you practise well before a game, it seems to flow through. I had two really good nets before the Oval test in 1986 when I got a century. I just concentrated on leaving the ball. I hadn't had a good series up till then and didn't feel very confident when I got out in the middle but because I'd practised well, it seemed to flow through.

It can go the other way of course; you can have a terrible net then play well. Some guys have the superstition that a bad net is a good sign, like the theatrical superstition about poor dress rehearsals. But batters don't like having their poles knocked over in the nets and when it happens, the ones left standing might get whacked over with the bat. Everyone's starting to get pretty intense. Bob Cunis likes to see signs of the boys getting edgy before a test, like Braces abusing Bert Vance for smacking him over his head in the nets before the Perth test in 1989. He'll say "they're getting ready for it, I've got this feeling."

Practice has got to be fairly realistic. With someone like Hadlee, you leave him to do his own thing. He'll probably want to bowl a couple of spells at top speed to make sure everything is in working order but the younger guys need a bit more work to get their line and length. Chats liked a lot of bowling. You like to come out of the last practice before a test feeling prepared, thinking "I'm ready, my game is ready, I'm set to go." We generally finish with some fielding and the slips work very specifically, getting their spacing right and so on.

We have that afternoon off and a second practice the following morning. You've got to be careful, particularly bowlers, that you don't leave it all on the training field, especially in hot countries.

After the final practice I leave my gear in the changing room ready for the next day. I hate to be rushed on the day of a test. I'm not going to bat in a rushed way so I like to slow everything down. Some of the guys like to play golf in the afternoon but I couldn't stand all that walking or going to the beach either. I like to stay in my room, thinking about it and watching TV. At this stage the physio's being kept busy with players wanting some attention before the game and the niggling injuries needing treatment.

By this time you should be really into the mental side of your preparation, working out how you're going to play it, what your job in the side is, what you want to achieve. This is where the reminders pasted to the coffins, the self-hypnosis, the visualisation and relaxation come in. Some guys lie on their beds and play an innings in their minds.

We have the team talk either immediately after the final practice or that evening. It lasts 45 minutes to an hour and we go through what we want to achieve, what we're there for. It's a bit of a pep talk. We talk about representing New Zealand, reinforce people's confidence, go through the opposition again. We'll be doing that right through the game, trying to work out what they're trying to do, how they're looking to bowl at us.

Glenn Turner's analysis of individual players was one of his great strengths; he analysed the Australians very well in 1985. The Aussie coach Bobby Simpson is extremely analytical; he's been a coach for a long time and now it's paying dividends. I talked to him in 1987 and although I'd been playing for 11 years, he pointed out things I'd never even thought about like 'stopping' the ball when you're looking to take short singles because the shot that goes to the fieldsman is more likely to produce a run out than the one the fieldsman has to come to. Simpson was certainly a big factor in Australia winning the World Cup in 1987: he'd taught the Australian batsmen how to work the ball around and their running between the wickets and fielding was terrific. I think he's a superb example of a cricket manager although he has his critics in Australia.

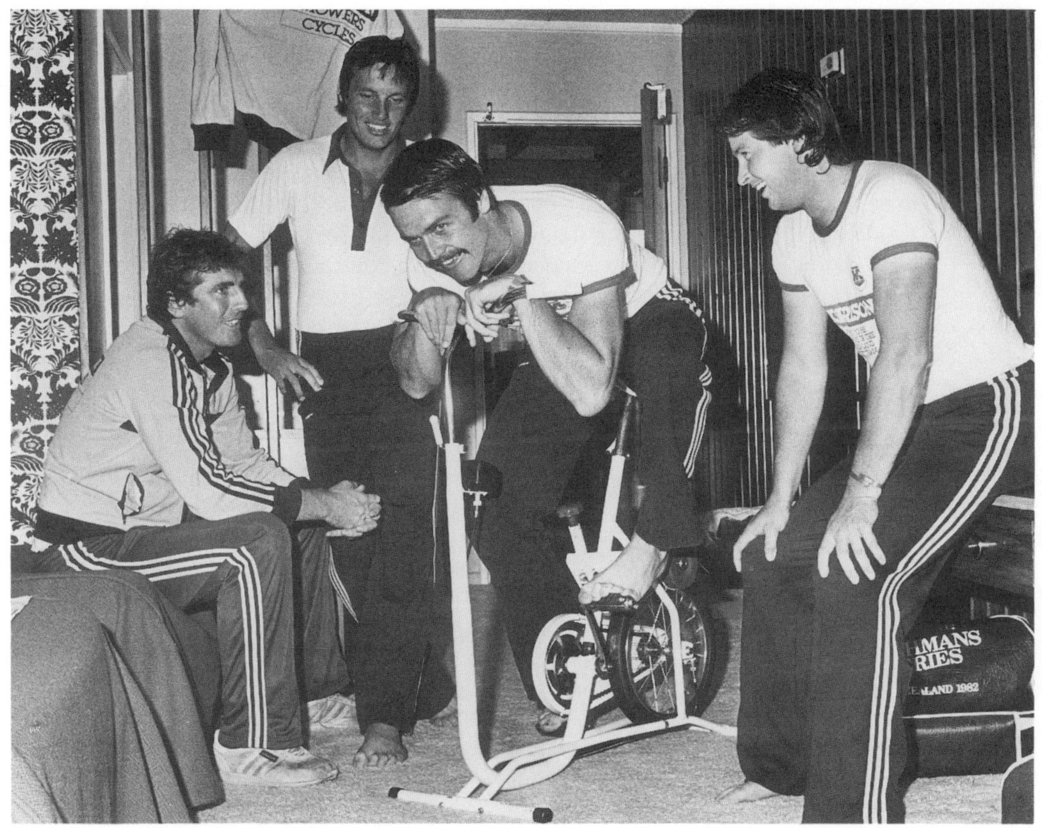

A team of experts observe Gary Troup's fitness test.

We talk about how different bowlers make life difficult for certain batsmen: Hadlee for Gatting, Cairns for Gower, Bracewell for Border. We make plans for individual batsmen. But these plans of attack and individual field placings ultimately depend on the bowlers. You can stack the slip and gully area for a guy who has a weakness outside off stump but if the bowlers give him half volleys on leg stump, the planning has been a waste of time.

We keep coming back to basics: playing straight, leaving the ball outside off stump, bowling in the right area, playing in sessions, building partnerships. At these meetings there's a feeling of pulling together. Frank Cameron was very good with bowlers whereas Bob Cunis's strength is in motivation and positive reinforcement. He's a straight talker and people know where they stand.

We'll talk about conditions, about playing for five days, being organised. It's not like rugby, a short, sharp burst. Over five days you go through the highs and lows and have to hang in there. One of New Zealand's great strengths has been against the West Indies in Wellington in 1987 and Australia in Perth in 1989, for instance. Performances like those reflect inner resolve.

We've backed ourselves to go out and compete and when the wheels have fallen off in the previous game, we've been able to start again. I admire that resilience in New Zealand teams.

It's also important at these meetings to make sure the guys' feet are back on the ground if we've won the previous test. Some of our greatest disasters have followed triumphs: in 1981 we beat the Aussies at Eden Park then went to Christchurch and got stuffed; we lost at Christchurch against England in 1978 after that first-ever win against them in Wellington; we blew out in England in 1983 after beating them at Headingley. By this stage a lot of pressure is coming on and players have to learn to take the pressure off themselves so they can perform. I like to emphasise positive reinforcement and people working for each other.

On tour the test team will be announced at this meeting. At home the selectors come to the meetings and sometimes make a contribution. It's a collective effort. Perhaps the captain doesn't have the best analytical mind in the team. There may be people who are better in this regard or who have spotted something he hasn't thought of. On the other hand you can't let it get out of control with so many points of view coming forward that the meeting loses its direction and focus.

That happened after we'd lost a test we should have won at Sydney in 1985. We knew the wicket was going to turn and that Bob Holland's leg spin would be a threat. Glenn Turner had hammered away on the theme of not sweeping leg spin and then a number of players had got out doing exactly that, which seemed to prove Glenn's point. But some of the guys felt Glenn had gone on about it so much that he'd created mental blocks; when they had tried to sweep, they'd made a mess of it whereas if they hadn't been thinking about it so much, they'd have played the shot successfully. This argument was backed up by John Bracewell who'd joined the team just before the game, missed out on the team talk and went in and swept his way to 80. The team meeting before the next test ended up with two factions holding non-negotiable positions but something positive must have come out of it because we won the game.

We've sometimes had pre-match dinners, which the English team always has. I don't like them at all. I think at that stage people should be able to do what they want, eat when and where they want, and go to bed when they want. A two-hour sit-down meal in a restaurant takes away those freedoms. I generally get an early night. At test time players have little rituals, reminders of past success. They're important and it's vital not to interrupt them: it could be rooming with the same guy, sitting in the same spot in the dressing room, or going to a certain restaurant. You can't get in the way of those things. We don't impose curfews because they don't work.

On the morning of the game people are pretty nervous, especially the openers. Everybody's psyched up. The ones playing in their first test are really feeling the pressure. It's very important at this stage to feel part of a team in which everyone is wanting their team mates to do well. Under some managements and leaderships that hasn't been the case: there's been the perception that the people running the show are just interested in themselves and couldn't care about how others do.

The team comes down to breakfast in dribs and drabs. The bus trip to the ground is pretty quiet and the not knowing whether we'll be batting or fielding is the hardest part. Most of the guys will be listening to walkmans – I like to listen to Mark Knopfler's Local Hero; Hadlee's tastes are pretty conventional – John Denver, the Dubliners; Blainy's into hard rock – Bryan Adams, Def Leppard.

In the West Indies the bus would be scheduled to leave the hotel at 9 a.m. and it would turn up about 9.20 because the driver was operating on West Indian time. Although that would normally drive you mad, one of the nice things about playing there or in India and Pakistan is that things are less regimented. At Lord's you have to wear full whites in the nets; there you wear shorts and t-shirts. Driving to the ground in some parts of the world you might see things that put it all in perspective and make you realise that there are worse things in life than making a duck in a test match.

At the ground we do our warm ups and have a net. At 10.30 the captains toss and then you know what you're doing. If we're batting, I can concentrate totally on the job. There's a release of tension if we're in the field because from the moment I woke up, I've been geared up to batting. There are times when you want to bat and times when the wicket looks green and juicy and you'd love to field first. On the first day of a series you sometimes feel like fielding so you can have a good look at things. You can want to bat and not want to bat at the same time, even going as far as to pad up while superstitiously hoping it'll somehow go the other way.

In very hot conditions you worry about whether you'll have to bat on the fifth day and what sort of shape you'll be in. In Adelaide in 1987 I got 40 on the first day then had to wait till the fifth day for the second dig. There was nothing on the game and I was knackered and didn't perform well.

Once I know I'm batting, I might have a few moments on the loo – some players have been known to throw up – then I put on batting trousers and shoes, get padded up, have a hamstring stretch. Then I sit and calm myself. The changing room will be very quiet, the other guys letting the batters prepare in their own way. If we're fielding there's a lot of noise, a lot of geeing up, a lot of team interaction, guys practising catches, and a chat before we go out. As the openers prepare, there are just a few quiet "good lucks," "what do you want at the drinks break?" "see you at lunch".

The other guy is doing his own thing. Bruce Edgar and I are similar personalities and went through similar routines. As the two of you walk out to the middle, you exchange encouragement and a "let's get stuck in". Then it's those familiar thoughts: still head, play straight. Now all the preparation and all the bullshit that's been flying around doesn't count for anything. All that matters is performance.

CHAPTER ELEVEN

Under pressure

I've been a nervous cricketer since I was at primary school. I played only one year of organised cricket out in the country but I can remember not being able to sleep the night before the North Canterbury primary school trials.

I've tried to analyse why I get nervous because I've always thought it would be great to play clinically, like a surgeon, cutting your emotions off completely. But I'm not made that way temperamentally; I have batted clinically a few times, usually after I've been in a fair while.

I wanted so much to succeed in test cricket that, without knowing it, I was putting a lot of pressure on myself and getting more nervous than normal. In many ways that intense desire for success made tests a bigger ordeal than they would normally be. In the first test at the Oval in 1978 I found I was still quite nervous even after I'd got established which was a new dimension of anxiety. I started to wonder how I could approach it in a more clinical manner.

In 1981 it occurred to me that I'd spent five years of my life playing professional cricket and a good deal of time before that playing in New Zealand and an awful lot of time practising and working on my technique in both hemispheres and no one had ever taught me or even discussed the mental side of batting apart from telling me to watch the ball. I'd seen Len Hutton quoted as saying that batting is 70-80 percent in the mind and been aware that I hadn't really given any thought to planning my mental approach. I'd always known too that I was my own worst enemy – most people are, really. Bob Willis had been in touch with a Sydney doctor, Arthur Jackson, who was a world authority on hypnotherapy and had worked with Bob on the mental side of his game. I wrote to Arthur, who replied with a tape, the first of several. For a few years I played the hypnosis tapes before a game to relax and get into the right mental habits and by and large they've helped; I've definitely become less keyed up about playing.

Improved mental habits are largely common sense and there is a danger of getting too precious and complicated about it. However, cricketers are becoming much more aware of using good mental habits and mental

To duck or to jump? That is the question. Willis to Wright.
PATRICK EAGAR

preparation to reach peak performance. It's not uncommon these days to see guys with their objectives, motivations, rules and patterns sellotaped to their coffin lids. We've all read books on the subject – one or two have read quite a few. I'm sure players before us have done this type of thing but there's a lot more awareness now. Richard Hadlee is pretty relaxed these days but he's talked about the attitude and motivation problems he had a few years ago and how important goal setting has been in the latter, and highly successful, phase of his career. Martin Crowe certainly places a lot of emphasis on mental attitude and organisation.

John Heslop, a Dunedin surgeon, managed us in the West Indies in 1985 and he tried hypnotherapy at a couple of team talks. At one stage John made Geoff Howarth straighten his arm under hypnosis and then Geoff couldn't bend it. We were staying at a hotel on the beach in Antigua and he got us together in this octagonal hut with no windows for a session. The American tourists on the beach were assailed by John booming out "you are relaxed, you will play the West Indian quicks with consummate ease tomorrow". Later Derek Stirling was going around saying in this horror movie voice, "You are getting sleepy, very sleepy. Tomorrow you'll play Garner off the front foot."

Most of the pressure that test cricketers are under is self-imposed: they're so desperately keen to succeed; they have certain expectations of themselves and people have certain expectations of them – team mates, family in some cases although never in mine, fans, media, which they allow to become a burden of pressure. My parents never put pressure on me to perform. They were keen for me to play a team game and enjoy it. "How'd you get on today?" was the usual comment from them. They were very wise parents.

Obviously the significance of the occasion is a factor – if there wasn't so much at stake, and if it wasn't televised and played in front of large crowds, test cricket would be the same as club cricket: players are doing exactly the same things. The secret is to work out how to take that pressure off yourself and create a relaxed environment. To do that, you must learn to deal with failure and the fear of failure. When I was younger, I wouldn't speak for a day after being dismissed but the harder you are on yourself over failure, the more you come to fear it.

In India in 1988 Bert Vance missed the first tour match so had only one game to win his competition with Trevor Franklin for the second test opener's spot. He didn't get runs and wasn't picked. Then he had one game before the second test to stake his claim. There was pressure on him but he was so determined to succeed, he put a lot of extra pressure on himself. When he got out for not too many in his second game, he was a frustrated cricketer. That's when touring can be quite hard – you get limited opportunities so you have to take them.

In a way New Zealanders are lucky that we don't have great player depth: we seldom have more than about 20 players of test quality compared with 30 or 140 in England so there's not quite so much pressure on in the sense that you know you're likely to get a good run if you get picked. English players seem to be playing for their places half the time, which creates uncertainty. If I'd been English, I doubt that I'd have had the extended run at the start of my test career and it takes time to adjust to the mental side of test cricket.

A batsman knows that one mistake and it could be all over. You don't get another go to redeem yourself. It would be nice to play a game in which you always had a second chance. Sometimes when you're dropped, it almost takes the pressure off. You think: "I could be out now but I'm not so why get worked up about it." It doesn't seem so serious any more.

I may be wrong but I always envied bowlers. A bowler can have a bad spell or session and come back and do really well because unlike batting, you can make a mistake, or several mistakes, and still come back. Batters can make a mistake and get away with it but they can't assume that will happen. Bowling is physically harder but mentally easier although there are situations in limited-over cricket, particularly bowling at the death, when there's a lot of pressure on.

One-day cricket is interesting because everything happens in a shorter time which puts more pressure on people. You have to score quickly, bowl tighter. But more risks are taken and, when all's said and done, it's not the real thing. It doesn't have the importance of test cricket nor do you have to live with your mistakes over five days.

I think all players feel pressure, especially at test level. Test cricket in many ways is the pinnacle – you're playing with the best against the best. It's very unusual for a player not to worry about it and I can't think of a New Zealand player who didn't worry about it at all. Some guys just disguise it better. Geoff Howarth came across as a cool customer but he used to get as uptight as anyone – he was sometimes ill through nervousness. Lance Cairns was pretty relaxed most of the time and he used to get frustrated with me because he felt I played negatively because I was nervous. We played together for Northern Districts and he knew what I was capable of. He was trying to be positive.

You get up on the morning of a test and it starts to hit you, that nervous feeling of "here we go again". At that stage I sometimes feel like giving up test cricket. Some guys can't eat, some are violently ill. I'm pretty tense before I bat and like to have plenty of time and to be left alone. You definitely don't want hassles and this is where management is important: you don't want Joe Bloggs coming into the dressing room. Captaincy changes things because you don't have that inner-directed time.

It was really through chats with Jackson and reading the odd book that I developed a method which has helped me. Over the years I've learnt from him that experience is not only about playing conditions and the technicalities of the game but what you learn about yourself, your weaknesses, and how to cope with them. My method involves a few ground rules. First off, I'm my own toughest opponent: winning against myself is the hardest thing; if I'm in control of myself, I'm in control of my destiny and can go out and give it my best shot. It starts with training, having the discipline to put in the work on my game. Secondly, I always accept that I made the mistake and that I can't blame other people. You've got to look.inward, not outward. You might have got a bad lbw decision but should you have played the shot in the first place? Sometimes you don't have control over what happens but generally you have to be accountable to yourself.

You've got to have confidence in your own ability. Botham is very confident; Miandad looks so comfortable with a bat in his hands, he could be sitting on the couch in his front room. Hadlee in the latter part of his career has been supremely confident; Greg Chappell radiated confidence. Body language has a lot to do with it: Dean Jones has confident body language but perhaps he's not quite that confident inside. Allan Border probably gets nervous but he's got a great temperament.

I've always had the attitude that if I hang in and keep going, I'll succeed over the long term – I'm confident in my ability and am happy with my changed stance of the 1990 season which feels more natural. Against Australia at the Basin my innings of 117 not out was very satisfying. To play positively under pressure and to beat the Aussies at home gave me a tremendous thrill. It seemed a culmination of years of hard work and certainly made up for some of the disappointments over the years.

You do see players with tremendous ability who don't make the most of it and others with limited ability who make themselves into tremendous players because of their mental skills. Then there's the third category: talented players who made themselves even more formidable by being tough competitors. In the first category I think of Jock Edwards who had ability but could've been better organised and John Morris at Derbyshire who on talent should stroll into the England team. Collis King was a player of incredible natural talent who just never made the most of it, Bernard Julien another.

Then you have guys like David Steele and Ewen Chatfield who've made the most of their ability through their attitude, Boycott who was really together mentally at the wicket, Bob Willis who always ran in, and Lillee who was an amazing competitor. Allan Border is as tough as old boots, a great competitor. I admire him more than anyone in that respect. When the going gets tough, he gets tougher. He's had a lot of pressure on him as captain and whether or not he's been a good captain – in many ways he has – his batting's been superb.

Tough competitors respond well to pressure, they rise to the occasion, and vice versa. It's interesting to see how players perform when the pressure's on and a game's winnable compared to when the cause is hopeless and there's absolutely nothing to lose. A lot of players produce their best performances in that situation because it's almost pressure-free.

Being relaxed is the ideal mental state for a good performance. It's no coincidence that a lot of my test centuries have come in the third test of a series. Playing Australia in 1981 I had scores of 34, 0, 4, and 13 going into the last innings and I was pretty relaxed. I thought "damn it, I've had a bad series. I've got nothing to lose, I'll just go out and give it my best shot." That showed in the way I played – probably as well as I ever have. That's the ideal performance state: relaxed but highly motivated.

I love batting after I've got a hundred. It's almost pressure-free because you can afford to fail, which perhaps isn't the best attitude. In county cricket there were times when I was lazy, I felt I'd done enough. But I did get runs in that state. I often felt it would be great to bat and not worry about how many runs you have, which isn't easy when you've got a huge scoreboard staring you in the face.

The great skill, one I've never mastered completely, is to focus completely on the present. It's the only thing a batsman can control. It's amazing how complicated batting can become if you start thinking about the shot you've just played, the ball that nearly knocked your block off, the guy who's warming up at fine leg who's a bit quicker than the one you've been facing, how many runs you've got, how your hands don't feel right, how you're not moving your feet.

When the bowler comes in to bowl, you've got to narrow the focus right down, eliminating the peripheral things, and really zero in on the ball he's about to deliver. Focusing on the moment is really what it's all about. Bob Simpson says I over-concentrate because I start when the bowler begins

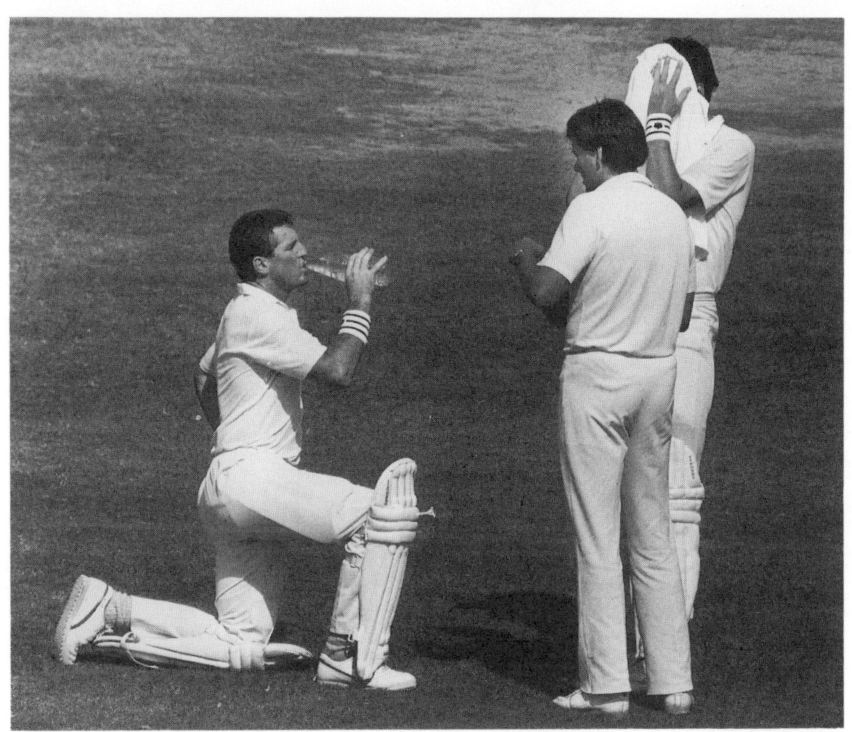

Drinks courtesy of good old Sneds. Franko, in only his seventh test, is still a bit shy.

J.G. BLACKWELL

"It's all over now, baby blue."

his run-up. He argues that you can't maintain absolute concentration for more than three or four seconds so you shouldn't switch on until the bowler is a few yards from the wicket.

I concentrate on two key thoughts: keeping a still head and focusing on the ball I'm about to receive. Obviously there are technical things you have to remember but they just happen if you're concentrating on the moment. Then you try to do it over and over again. If you're not relaxed, you take risks and wrong options and start to focus on other things. Negative thoughts are a problem. Greg Chappell said that he tried not to think about failure because that creates pressure. Failure means you might be dropped, you'll look like a wally, that your opponents won't rate you.

A great mental strength is having the ability to go on, not stop because you've done enough. The New Zealand team talks about this a lot and Glenn Turner was big on it. When Martin Crowe got 106 at Lords in 1986, Turner was critical of him for not carrying on to a really big score. There's a tendency to reach a comfort zone where you're happy with your performance; because you won't feel as if you've failed if you get out at that score, you don't force yourself to concentrate and push on. Turner had that ability. Crowe is striving for it now.

When you're really concentrating well and not worried about peripheral things, it's amazing how quickly time goes. All of a sudden drinks have arrived. You're really into what you're doing. You get the feeling, one I really enjoy, of applying your whole being. And when it becomes routine and you're doing it over and over, automatically, then you're there, you've achieved that state of clinical detachment. When I got my first test century, I played ball by ball, over by over, just trying to last the over. It was the same against the West Indies at Wellington.

There are lots of things you can do to prepare yourself for batting. I use a lot of mental imagery, play the innings in my mind. You might be going to face a particular bowler and you imagine playing him, practising your shots, working out where your feet are going to go. You walk out onto the ground and look at the blank scoreboard imagining your name in the batting slot with a big score beside it. You're conditioning yourself, programming your mind, creating a good attitude and habits of thought. You get a good, positive attitude by continually working on having good habits in your thinking. Sometimes I struggle because I have too many negative thoughts – keeping them out of my mind isn't easy.

Some people are more together mentally, more organised, than others. I often smile when I read in programmes that I have a good temperament. I know how to handle myself in that area, I can survive, but early in my career I could have been better. I think teaching people to think about the game will be a big development in the next few years. But there are limits to how far you can take this stuff because it's only a game. I've often thought after I've got a low score that there aren't going to be too many people in China worrying about it.

It does affect the way people treat you. I guess it's the old human instinct

A familiar position after a few too many.
J.G. BLACKWELL

"How's your father?"
J.G. BLACKWELL

Lance trying to hit another six – this time over the keeper's head.
J.G. BLACKWELL

"Well left, Chats."
J.G. BLACKWELL

– people like winners. It even happens with players and administrators: they'll walk into the dressing room after a day's play and gravitate to the guys who've done well. It's certainly easier to talk to the heroes – I'm not the best conversationalist in the world after a duck.

I don't think the public realises what pressure players put themselves under to get the best out of themselves. It's easy to be a knocker and play it from the sideline but being in the game, you can see how hard a guy has worked and what he's put himself through. That brings out great camaraderie and team spirit. When a bloke's having a bad run, the rest of the team really wants him to succeed.

I notice it now with rugby. Having played senior club rugby for three years and even marked the odd All Black, I've become a sideline expert now that I'm watching it. It's easy to make judgments but unless you get out and do it yourself, you don't understand. The average sports fan must be curious about what makes sportsmen tick because they see only the final performance and there's a hell of a lot that goes into it beforehand, particularly on the mental side.

Once you get out there, it's survival of the fittest. When you go up a level, the big adjustment is mental. The standard of test cricket is certainly higher than first class but the mental step is a lot bigger and some handle it better than others. It's particularly important to have success early.

Martin Crowe had to succeed after his early failures against Australia and doing it gave him mental strength and confidence. Ken Rutherford was pushed too far too soon and it made it hard for him to come back. Andrew Jones and Mark Greatbatch had early success and have gone on from that platform. I found it hard because I didn't get a hundred till my 14th test and was averaging poorly although I'd had a good first test.

It helps young guys to come into a team containing players who've got it right mentally and to be surrounded by guys who've achieved and are successful. Howarth started that process and these days the team is more confident as a unit. To be able to communicate and help guys through is one of the big things about team unity but the true champions draw their confidence and mental strength from within.

The way to win is to perform. If you strive for performance level, winning follows. It's like the All Blacks and the perfect game – winning comes as a result of continually lifting your sights to a higher performance level. To be a really good performer you've got to love what you're doing: that feeling of joy is very important. I couldn't say I've enjoyed batting or playing cricket all the time. It's just a bad mental habit because it's another way of putting pressure on myself. I really wanted to succeed and the flip side of that is that I dreaded failure. Because of that, I got less enjoyment from actually playing and in some ways it hasn't helped my performance. I haven't been as aggressive as often as I should have been in tests because I've stuck to my method of hanging around, believing I was more likely to be successful that way. Having said that, the wickets in New Zealand were pretty sporting early on and I don't know if I had the ability to go out and smack the world's best bowlers around on a green top.

The job of an opener is to hang around till lunch but there are guys like Gordon Greenidge, Kris Srikkanth, and Keith Stackpole who go out and cream it. I wish I played that way more often but there always seems to be a good reason to play safe. The first day often sets the tone for the match and seeing off the new ball poses questions and creates an internal conflict. There's a split-second decision between hitting the ball and leaving it; you can get in position then watch a half volley go by or belt it. Although you've got to survive, and I've always backed my technique and patience to enable me to do that, you've got to be positive too.

Howarth said I didn't have a middle game: I was either too aggressive or too defensive. I don't move the ball around enough and I haven't allowed my ability as much scope as I should have. I never regarded myself as a player of outstanding natural ability but it's a hard thing to judge. In county cricket I always played well going for it and I should have carried that more regularly into the test arena. Mind you, the English attack in my first six tests – Willis, Old, Hendrick and Botham – was probably the best I've faced outside the West Indies. They didn't give you much.

Players are always trying to put pressure on their opponents in all sorts of ways. Some bowlers don't mind being worked but can't handle being attacked. Quite a few English county bowlers can't stand being smacked. The West Indians, on the other hand, hate batsmen leaving balls all the time; they like you to take them on because, at their pace, that's a high-risk approach. The quicks of course have plenty of firepower of their own and bouncers aren't their only means of intimidation. Andy Roberts gave you a very cold, hard stare, certainly not of the 'come and have a beer' variety. When Ian Smith got runs at Guyana, Malcolm Marshall told him afterwards how much he was looking forward to bowling at him in Barbados where he would 'kill' him. It's not a nice thing to have on your mind all the way from Guyana to Barbados.

The Aussies have traditionally led the way in sledging but aren't always as tough as they pretend to be. They were for real in 1980/81 but in 1985 they didn't have quite the bravado. I enjoyed facing Lillee, because he was such a clever bowler but by then he wasn't as quick as he'd been, more a Hadlee type. He didn't sledge me a lot; we were good mates. Michael Whitney did. He came in for the third test in 1988 all fired up and said to me, "you've been playing all these years and still you're nicking them", which wasn't the most penetrating analysis I've ever heard. Then he proceeded to bowl a load of half volleys which spoilt the big, bad fast bowler routine a bit.

Greg Chappell was a very tough competitor and would have a word from time to time. He was also very tough on his team. This can go too far: Viv Richards lost his cool completely and ranted at Jeff Dujon when he dropped me in Wellington.

I get involved from time to time. John Bracewell and I tend to tangle when we're on different sides. In his first season of Shell cricket he had a go at me because he thought I'd nicked one. I told him he was "nothing but a f....ing curly-haired golliwog", not exactly Oscar Wilde but it kept him quiet for a while. Braces seems to like getting stuck into captains – Dilip Vengsarkar in India, Graeme Wood at Western Australia, even in his first series he managed to get right up Greg Chappell's nose by calling him 'Mr' Chappell – but he'll have a crack at anyone. When Mike Velletta was struggling against Danny Morrison at Perth in 1989 he managed, after a slow period, to hook one off the splice that just cleared short leg. Braces called out: "That's six." Braces is a compulsive competitor and I admire that attitude enormously.

The best way to respond to sledging is to ignore it and pretend it's not bothering you. Being able to take anything they throw at you is part of the game. The West Indies don't go in for it a lot but their actions probably speak louder than words. The Pakistanis yap away like vicious fox terriers. You don't know what they're saying but it's safe to assume they're not inviting you round to meet their sister. They're very sharp and particularly good at pressurising umpires with their orchestrated appeals and synchronised running down the pitch towards the umpire. After a while it must have a psychological effect and they keep the pressure up off the field with constant criticism. Sledging isn't at all subtle and in fact it's the least of your worries – if you get upset by it, you're knackered.

Glenn Turner found it distasteful, not really part of the English way of playing the game. He found it difficult to accept that someone could sledge you on the field and have a beer with you afterwards and he's right if it goes over the limit. Some players like to keep their distance from the opposition during a series – they feel that if you get too familiar, you can't go out and 'hate' them on the field. I've never really worked on that basis myself: if anything, the more you know about the opposition, the better. You try to learn a lot without giving much away but in the end the game is played in the middle. These days social contact between the teams is limited and you can't have a beer with the Pakistanis in Pakistan anyway. Teams generally keep to themselves but friendships develop outside that.

The English pros use the old tricks: let one go outside off stump and they'll throw their arms in the air as if it just missed. You end up having to ask your batting partner how close it was. Or they work on the umpire – stifled appeals followed by "sorry ump, that obviously wasn't out". Then after a few of those to give the impression that they're fair and reasonable men who'll go up only for certainties, they'll have a really big shout.

I don't mind my team sledging as long as they're not losing control of themselves in the process, which sometimes happens. There are times when a fast bowler is sledging you when you feel you're frustrating him, winning the battle. No one felt like that when Andy Roberts gave them his stare.

Now and again you come across a bowler who really seems to be taking it personally. Personalities do come into it and if a quickie doesn't like someone, he'll probably bowl quicker at him; likewise if he doesn't rate

Butterflies – Willie Watson waiting to bat.

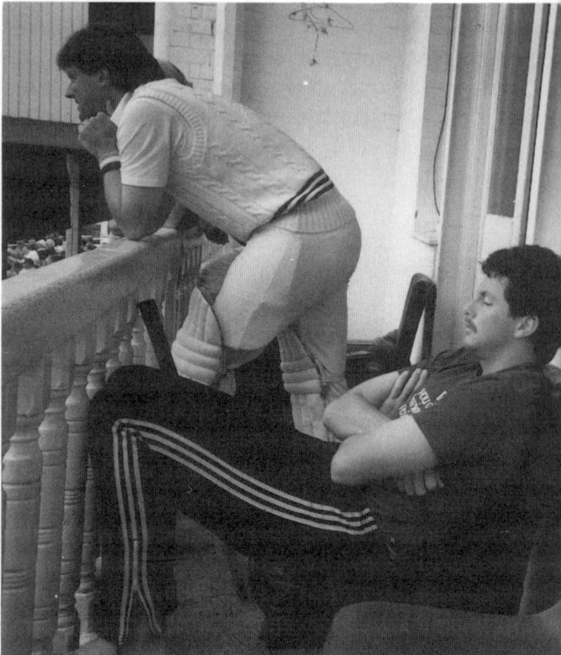

"I have complete faith in you, Ev." 'Billy' Stirling and Evan Gray on the balcony at Trent Bridge, second test, 1986.

a batsman or thinks he's chicken, he'll go up a notch. That's why you don't want to send the wrong signals; it's important to appear calm and in control even if you're quaking inside.

As if the pressure created by the occasion, the opposition, and your own fears, ambitions, and expectations isn't enough, it can come in other forms – running out your team mates for example. It's a horrible feeling: you've not only let your team down but you've ruined that bloke's chances of performing. You've got to pick yourself up and get it out of your mind as soon as possible. Either you get out or you knuckle down and make up for it. I've been involved in a number of run outs – I once ran Geoff Howarth and Jeff Crowe out in the same innings at Headingley – so I know how it feels.

Or dropped catches: I remember dropping David Hookes off Jerry Coney in a one-dayer. It wasn't that hard – I just muffed it. If looks could kill, ten Kiwi cricketers would've committed murder. Every run he gets after you've dropped him is another turn of the screw. You've just got to accept the fact that it happens – after all, no one tries to drop a catch – and not let it affect your performance. But it's worse than getting a duck.

Or crowds: One of the hardest things to accept is a knocking remark from your home crowd. You get fruit and veg well past its sell-by date thrown at you in Pakistan, racist abuse in the West Indies, and called a wanker and worse in Australia, so you hope for something better at home. After I hadn't made runs in the Wellington test in Pakistan in 1989, I was hitting up in front of the stand at Eden Park before the last test when someone yelled out "bet you $10 you don't get 5." I felt like ramming the bat down his throat. Some fans don't like you and some do. Probably half think I'm a good player and half don't. You're more aware of the crowd in one-dayers because you get abused, especially in Australia. Most of it is good natured and if it's not, it's so boorish and mindless that it's not worth worrying about. Generally people like that have got more problems than you have.

Or umpires: in Hyderabad in 1985 I was given out caught behind in both innings and didn't even get close to either of them. I thought I was going nuts when it happened a second time. All you can do is get your batting partner to confirm that it happened the way you thought it did but sometimes they can't.

Or the media: I trained like hell for the 1986 tour of England. I'd broken a bone in my hand and I did strengthening exercises, then scored a lot of runs in the lead-up games. I was mentally and physically prepared to do well – it was important to me to succeed in a series in England. Then I got a duck in the first innings of the first test. They put us in, in the second innings just to try and knock a few of us over and score psychological points and I bagged a pair. It was so disheartening, an absolute disaster. I felt utterly deflated after all that preparation. The next test innings was the toughest of my life. On the day before the match I gave an interview to Radio New Zealand and said that I thought the fact that England had quite a young bowling line-up was to our advantage. An English tabloid took it up and a story appeared under the headline "Wright doesn't rate England attack". It's not what you want to say when you're sitting on a pair and in danger of doing the treble.

It's frustrating when a writer hasn't grasped the subtleties of what's happening because he doesn't know the game well enough. The public's view is influenced, probably in many cases determined, by what is written in newspapers and said over the airwaves; cricket followers can make up their own minds from what they see but many of them, aware of their limitations in terms of knowledge and understanding of the game, defer to the judgment of the pundits. If the public only knew. Some cricket writing bears out the axiom that a little knowledge is a dangerous thing.

Quite often a batsman will be criticised for playing a loose stroke or not moving his feet; no credit is given to the bowler who defeated him; another batsman gets a bad decision and reads the next day that he played an undisciplined shot. People read the story and don't realise he was sharked out. You hope it shows up clearly on TV but there's a strange reluctance among commentators to come out and say so when umpires get it wrong. How often do we see replays of an obviously mistaken umpiring decision and hear the commentators hide behind cop-out comments like "viewers can make up your own minds" or "the umpire's a lot closer to the action than we are"? It's hypocritical for commentators to pretend the umpire hasn't made a mistake when he obviously has and doubly so when they're very quick to talk about players' screw ups.

I can be reasonably sensitive and some players get hurt when they get a slagging in the press. Although England has the best cricket writers, it also has the worst and some of the things the tabloids do are shocking and have very little to do with cricket. In New Zealand we're generally pretty well treated and you've got to be realistic: you can't expect to be patted on the back if you play a bad shot and let the team down. But it would be good to get more constructive criticism instead of the negative stuff all the time. I think a good journalist describes more than he analyses.

But it's no good making a fuss, because players can't win – the press always has the last word. Never read the paper if you've had a bad day is a sound rule. In England I got *Sporting Life* which just has the scores; the rest of it is racing. Furthermore you can't worry about umpiring mistakes or crowds picking on you or getting criticised in the media. If any of it starts getting to you, you need a rest. To the hard-minded players, the tough competitors, it's just water off a duck's back.

But despite it all, you're still out there where lots of others would love to be. To be under that type of pressure, to test your mettle in the hottest flame, to push yourself to the limit, to enjoy the absolute thrill of getting a hundred or suffer the total disappointment of failing is a great experience and one of the wonderful things about playing sport at top level. It's all a question of how you handle yourself.

I'm a middle category player – I haven't had as much success as some but I could've filled a few scrapbooks in my time. I've also learnt things about myself which are a help in areas outside the game. I have Rudyard Kipling's poem 'If', with the lines about meeting the two imposters, triumph and disaster, and treating them just the same, in my motivation book. I re-read it several times after the first day's play at Perth in 1989: the Aussies were 290 for two after I'd won the toss and inserted them in what was a borderline decision.

And in the end you've got to remember that it's a game. It's all very well worrying about facing the West Indies but it's easier than jumping out of a trench with a gun in your hand, wondering which one's got your name on it.

CHAPTER TWELVE

Leave 'er be, Levi

One of the best comments on slow batting I've read was about an old Derbyshire player Charlie Lee, who was not renowned for his dazzling stroke play. After a run chase had been rained off, a journalist wrote that it would have been interesting to watch Lee batting "against the clock rather than the sun dial".

David Lloyd, the former England opener and these days a much-in-demand after-dinner speaker, reckoned he was so painful to watch that once, when he was having a bit of a hit on his front lawn, his wife pulled the curtains. Spectators sometimes come out with something more original than "have a go, ya mug". When Derbyshire was playing at Old Trafford, where trains run past the ground, a barracker told Bud Hill to hurry up because "the trains are ahead 4-1".

When I was a kid I smacked it around like everyone else and I generally still do except in test matches. I can think of certain incidents in my career, starting at secondary school, which have influenced the sort of player I became. When I got into the Christ's College 1st XI, I found that the only shot I could play against the spinners was the sweep, a shot I don't play at all now, because I didn't feel strong enough to thump it all over the park. In the sixth form I started opening and the coach, an Englishman called Johnny Baxter, instructed me that my job was to go out and survive the first session, then bat for as long as I could. That's what I did.

In my first test I took 50 minutes to get off the mark and Bob Willis remarked that I'd never die of a stroke. The experience left an indelible impression of the way test cricket is played.

County cricket teaches you to be an accumulator. After a particular painful innings against Leicestershire, I was moaning to Ray Illingworth in the bar when he came out with the old pros' maxim: "You can't get them in the pavilion".

When I look back, I wish I had tried to belt it round more, but I always had a survival instinct. I don't like having to 'unbuckle them and think about it'. I often felt like Brian Bolus, a Yorkshireman who played once or twice for England, who was sometimes heard to mutter ruefully over a pint: "I

"Leave 'er be, Levi." Peter Kirsten doing just that. It's nice when you're 150 odd and their nasty fasty, who's been running in at you all day, bowls a delivery that you leave as it narrowly misses off stump – then you look up and smile at him.

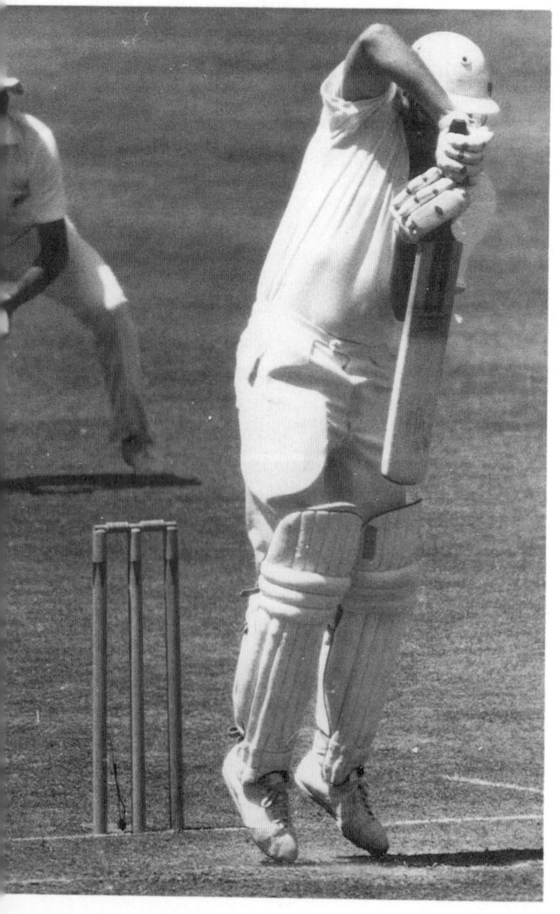

Down ...

J.G. BLACKWELL

... back ...

J.G. BLACKWELL

almost played well today". There's no getting away from the fact that slow batting is boring and I always make a point of watching players like Richard Hadlee, Ian Smith and Lance Cairns bat, although I probably wouldn't like to be the next man in. There's always something happening with these guys.

In county cricket I had no trouble scoring quickly and used to hit a lot of boundaries, but I didn't move the ball around much. I was more a two-speed player: either collecting or trying to take the attack apart, either going too slowly or going berserk. You've got to be very careful when the shots are flowing because the adrenalin starts to pump and you can find yourself going for shots that aren't really on.

One of the secrets of New Zealand's success is that we've had batsmen who've hung around for a long time and made slow 30s and 40s. We've had guys who valued their wicket and Frank Cameron, when he was chairman of the selectors, emphasised that. The opposition have always known that they've got to prise us out, which has paid dividends, particularly against the West Indies. It's probably in our nature as Kiwis: we're competitors, extremely resourceful.

For an opener, the prime objective is to get through to the first break – drinks on the first morning, for instance – especially if you're chasing a big total. Basically you're denting the opposition, getting the shine off the ball, and that's what I've endeavoured to do. In the first test against the West Indies in 1987, I'd made six by drinks. I've always batted with the knowledge that the longer I'm there, the easier it gets. There can be easy runs on offer for openers because there are gaps in the field but if you're looking to leave as many balls as possible, you limit your options.

. . . and forward.
J.G. BLACKWELL

"Leave 'er be, Levi," David Steele used to say. It's a great feeling to know where your off stump is and I get immense satisfaction out of watching the ball pitch, knowing where my off stump is and that the ball will seam outside it, and letting it go. You see the anguish on the bowler's face change to annoyance as he realises you knew what you were doing. The slips and keeper will ooh and aah and make out it missed by an inch but they're trying to con you. It's a great art for an opener, especially when the ball's moving around and you want to play as little as possible. If you can watch it go by, you're getting a feel for the pace of the wicket, how it's playing, how quick the bowler is. There's nothing better than going out there and having to present the bat to only one ball an over.

Early on I struggled to know where my off stump was but I became a pretty good judge of it. Some bowlers have the ability to move the ball both ways and then you must be careful or you'll shoulder arms and find your off pole cartwheeling or be lbw without playing a shot. John Lever was very difficult for me because being a left hander bowling to a left hander, he was able to swing it both ways.

Chats is one of the great leavers. He plays with half his bat then withdraws so only the edge is facing the bowler. He misses a few but he has a wonderful ability to block the ones on the stumps. Bowlers who move the ball away from him aren't in the hunt.

In a test match you might have faced 30 balls and let 23 go. Assuming your partner's faced as many, ten overs have been bowled which is almost drinks. If you've only got three or four to your name there's a tendency to think "Cripes, if I get the unplayable ball now, it won't look good in the scorebook". It could be a technically perfect, classic opener's four but it's still four. That's when patience becomes important because there's a temptation to have a whack.

When drinks arrive and you're still in single figures, you're probably wishing you were a Greenidge or a Srikkanth who could go out and give it stick; or that you could come in at number six when the bowlers are knackered. You tend to feel that way late in the day if someone down the order has got a quick 30 and you've grafted for the best part of two hours for 16. They're just numbers in the book so it can be frustrating.

Going under the first bouncer is another good feeling. You know the quicks are going to let you have it and avoiding the short ball has become an important part of the game. Helmets are a blessing although they have encouraged intimidatory bowling because the consequences of hitting someone on the head aren't so fearful. Despite that it would be foolish to bat in the West Indies without one.

The key in avoiding bouncers is watching the ball. If you do that, you'll instinctively get your head out of the way of it. Every time I've been hit, apart from once by Rumesh Ratnayake who completely beat me for pace, it was because I took my eyes off the ball.

The second thing is to keep your body weight forward so you're in a position to duck. Martin Crowe has sorted his technique out and avoids

Smithy clips another to the boundary through point.
J.G. BLACKWELL

The Jones boy displays a flourishing cut.
J.G. BLACKWELL

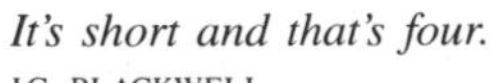

It's short and that's four.
J.G. BLACKWELL

very well whereas Hadlee gets into some amazing positions, using his bat as a periscope and playing his self-protective hook. Somehow he always manages to either miss it or hit it safely. The helmet's been a big help to him. In 1978 Ian Botham really worked him over with bouncers and his batting wasn't very productive. Jerry Coney had his jump defensive shot which was effective in New Zealand but not in the West Indies where the ball just comes after you off the hard wickets. There you have to duck and Jerry adjusted well.

Ken Rutherford had a lot of difficulty in the West Indies because he'd never been exposed to anything like it before. There's no gutsier player around but it doesn't do your confidence any good when you're facing a continual barrage and you know you're not getting into quite the right position to avoid the ball. Playing the hook only encourages them to put fielders out and bounce you some more. You have to wait till they're knackered and the ball's soft.

In Barbados Marshall softened up Stirling with a couple of quick bouncers which he managed to avoid without entirely maintaining his composure. Then he pitched one up a bit but Billy was expecting another bouncer and ducked. The result was reminiscent of Ian Rush lunging forward at the near post to nod home a low cross: the ball cannoned off the peak of Billy's helmet onto the stumps. It was a tense situation and a case of any excuse for a laugh and that certainly produced one. The incident was subsequently referred to as '1-0'.

Pad play frustrates spin bowlers. Dilip Doshi got very annoyed with me when I got my first test century at Eden Park in 1980. He kept pitching a foot outside my off stump and I kept thrusting my right pad forward and going through the motions of playing a forward defensive. Doshi kept telling the umpire I was only pretending to play a shot. He was one of the mildest mannered men ever to play cricket, but after several hours of watching the ball bounce off my knee roll, he resorted to vulgar abuse. John Bracewell is also infuriated by pad play but is somewhat quicker to make his feelings known. Daffy O'Sullivan, the Central Districts and New Zealand left-arm spinner, having bowled a particularly frustrating over to Peter Coman, the Canterbury opener, yelled down the wicket: "Coman you're nothing but a cowboy!" Peter responded, using his bat as a imaginary rifle, with: "Bang, bang, you're dead."

I often feel spinners get a raw deal when they hit the pads: what would be considered an exceptionally good shout from a medium pacer is regarded by umpires all over the world as outrageous coming from a spinner. I don't think you'd last long trying to sweep medium pacers off middle stump but batsmen seem to get away with it against spinners.

Pad play not only frustrates the bowler but sometimes tests the umpire's patience. Now and again you get the feeling the bloke down there in the white coat has had enough. This is particularly true in England where they give a lot more lbws. I use my pads a lot because I have a long reach and can get well down the track but you have to make sure you keep the bat behind the pad because you've got to play a shot. Or at least pretend to.

I've developed a steady technique against spin but I wish I'd learnt to use my feet. It's really a confidence thing and I'd encourage all young players to do it; it gives you so many more attacking options. The Indian and Pakistani players like Javed Miandad, Mohammed Azharuddin, Asif Iqbal, Sunil Gavaskar, and Zaheer Abbas use their feet superbly and are fantastic to watch, by far the best players of spin. Miandad plays the turning ball brilliantly: he not only goes up and down the wicket but across it as well, and he plays the ball very late. Allan Border is very good, an excellent sweeper and uses his feet well. Viv Richards can murder the slows but is more of a power player.

The West Indies have got a reputation of having a weakness against spin which means they've lost a few games on turning wickets like everyone else. There's a certain logic to it because they're not going to lose many on quick wickets. Their approach to playing spin can be summarised this way: plan A is to hit the ball over the fence; plan B is to hit it out of the ground; plan C is to hit it onto the next island.

There was an obvious difference between what people saw me do in county cricket and first class here and what they saw in tests where I might've tried too hard and been too concerned with playing safe. People like Geoff Howarth, and Hadlee, Lance Cairns and Bob Taylor at Derbyshire would tell me I was a better player when I went for my shots. Certainly the test centuries I've enjoyed most – against Australia in 1981 and Pakistan when I got 80 out of 100 scored in a session, and last season my 117 not out against Australia and 113 against India at Napier – were attacking innings.

Early in my career it was a rarity for the side winning the toss in a test in New Zealand to bat. The ball seamed a lot, we often played seamers, and in quite a few of our home test wins we won the toss and put the opposition in. It's difficult to play shots when the ball's moving around and you always tend to think it'll be easier after lunch. Quite a few stroke players have come here and struggled in the conditions – Gavaskar, Kim Hughes, Clive Lloyd, Zaheer, Alvin Kallicharan, David Gower – because of the seam and uneven bounce.

Whatever the conditions, you have to decide how you're going to play: either you back yourself to take them on or you back yourself to hang around and play the percentage game. Generally I've done the latter. That was basically what the team expected from Bruce Edgar and me. Bruce made a conscious decision to play that way and I suspect one of the reasons he gave up test cricket early was that he felt the responsibility of getting the innings off to a sound start was shackling his ability. Without that pressure on him, he's played a lot of shots representing Wellington. I've often gone out saying to myself that I'm going to smack it but not had the guts or conviction to carry it through. The decision is made before you realise it. The bowling is also up a notch in test cricket. You get a lot fewer loose balls and those that you do get are generally on the protected side of the wicket.

Once you get into that mode it becomes very hard to change the tempo of your batting. Bruce got an 80 at Lord's in 1986 and batted for a long time. Then Martin Crowe came in and outscored him. Bruce had done the hard work and restricted himself to certain shots, whereas if he'd gone for it, he probably would've got a hundred. I got 99 at Melbourne in 1987 and Peter Sleep bowled me some awful rubbish when I was in the 60s. I should've whacked him over the top but I played him defensively and the scoring opportunities I let go by cost me a century.

Against Pakistan here in 1985 I decided I was going to go for it in the last two tests. I got 60 in the only innings at Eden Park and 30 at Carisbrook playing really well. I got out hitting the ball through midwicket in the air when normally I'd have played it with less freedom. There's a great ability in being able to temper attack with defence. So often you decide a shot's on then make a split-second decision to hold back and it's the difference between a one-bounce four and holing out; it's also the difference between the great players and the good ones.

Cricket is all about timing and if you start to force it, you get problems. There's no point in being aggressive on your attacking shots and not in your defensive shots because you stop using your feet. If you're not in an attacking frame of mind, you stop using your feet and a couple of inches makes the difference between being able to hit the ball through the covers and not being quite there and having to pat it back to the bowler.

At Perth in 1989 Mark Greatbatch gave an absolutely magnificent display of positive defensive batting. He was positive when he blocked the ball and positive when he left it and when he played a shot, he went through with it. It was one of the best innings of its type I've seen and a good example that when you're batting slowly, you must be positive in your own mind.

I'd love to be a really good cutter and then just pick them up through the on side. As a left hander opening the innings, you get a lot of short wide stuff outside off stump. If they know that stuff will get caned, they've got to bowl at the stumps and then you can work it through the on side. To play the cut you need consistent bounce, and not many New Zealand wickets provide that. Of Kiwis, Bevan Congdon would be the best cutter I've seen and Andrew Jones is very good but generally the best cutters are Australians and West Indians because their pitches encourage square of the wicket shots. Ian Smith is a great cutter but he has to concentrate on playing straight because if he's not thinking about it, he'll try to cut good length balls on middle stump.

Test cricket takes a lot of time. There're not the issues of bonus points and declarations you get in Shell Trophy cricket and you're not often under time pressure. Openers are rarely expected to score quick runs. In tests an innings of 30 in two or three hours can be extremely valuable but there's rarely a need for it in a three-day game.

For an opener, getting 30 in 40 minutes and then getting out is nothing to be proud of because the new batter has to face bowlers who are still fresh, a ball that's still relatively new, and, if there was anything in the wicket, a wicket that still has some juice in it. Ask Martin Crowe if he'd rather come in at 30 for two after half an hour or 30 for two after an hour and a half. The state of the wicket is very important. If it's doing a lot then every run counts but if it's flat, you've got to pick the pace up.

In my first test as captain, against England at the Basin in 1988, I opened with Trevor Franklin and Bert Vance, who was playing in his first test, was at three: we didn't have a lot of experience. I batted too slowly to get 30 and that night we were 190 for three, 40 to 50 runs short of what we should've been on that wicket. That meant that despite batting well the next day, we had to bat into the third day instead of getting them in before stumps on day two – the 200-run follow-on means you need at least 450. On the other hand I batted all day for 55 in my first test on a very different wicket and it helped us win the game.

Against Sri Lanka in 1983, we were one up in a three-match series going into the final day of the second test. Howarth went early, then Reid went first ball so we were 15 for two after 20 minutes. Then Martin Crowe and I just blocked it to death for most of the rest of the day although we had a theoretical chance of winning. There was grumbling from one or two of the team who felt we should've gone for it and Coney and Cairns

That wonderful feeling, a test hundred. At Eden Park against England, 1988.
J.G. BLACKWELL

in fact thumped it around late in the day when it was all academic. Bob Vance, then chairman of the NZCC, was there and he wasn't too impressed either.

I considered that a bloody good innings. We drew the game and won the third to take the series 2-0. Later that year when the Sri Lankans were in England I saw their cricket manager interviewed on TV and he said that the way we played that day taught his players what test cricket was all about.

Howarth had a similar decision to make in the third test against India at Eden Park in 1981. We went for the runs early then closed up, which upset some of the crowd. A spectator came out to the middle and abused us. But we were 1-0 up in the series and series wins are important. If winning doesn't matter, why keep the score?

You do see examples of players disregarding the team's requirements and batting for their averages. Botham supposedly ran out Geoff Boycott at Christchurch in 1978 when the England dressing room considered Boycs wasn't pushing it along towards a declaration. Botham claims that he took it upon himself to give the skipper the "yes, no, sorry mate" call. Boycs copped a lot of criticism for batting too slowly at Yorkshire. Sometimes it was justified but he certainly didn't do Yorkshire's chances any harm with the runs he got against Derbyshire. And he was a superb five-day player.

The best slow innings I've ever played was against the Windies at the Basin Reserve in 1987 – 138 in a couple of minutes short of 10 hours. It wasn't pretty. I got to the stage where I was existing at the wicket. But it helped our cause: we drew the series. Then there was the one in Sri Lanka, my first test, and the Oval in 1986 when we were playing for a draw – we couldn't win and a draw would give us our first-ever series in England. I was 70 overnight and Turner told me I had to bat as long as I could.

Sometimes you think you're batting too slowly and you go in at the break saying "sorry lads, I can't hit it off the square". They'll tell you you're doing a good job, keep hanging in there. The only time dogged innings aren't appreciated are when there's a specific, attainable target to go for or in limited-overs games – then there are no excuses for not going for it. Slow batting is using up the balls to be faced and depriving team mates of balls they could be dispatching to all parts of the ground.

All of us have been guilty of it. The dilemma of one-day cricket is that you can only justify taking 60 balls to get 30 if you kick on and get your next 30 in 20 balls. Andrew Jones is a good example of that. He takes a little time to establish his innings and then he picks it up. Batting for a long time for not many, then getting out is unforgivable. Every now and then it happens but you can't let it happen consistently. It's easy to get a safe 35, especially opening the innings, and reduce the opportunities for the guys coming in lower down.

The decision you have to make is whether you just carry on, on the basis that your innings will naturally accelerate, or whether you start trying to hit it out of sight. The sensible player sees this situation arising in advance and realises he's going too slowly: you can have a look at it for 15 or 20

"That felt good."

M. BAKER

"Everything's under control, Chief."
J.G. BLACKWELL

"Chief, we may have a slight problem here."
J.G. BLACKWELL

balls; after that you have to deliver. It's all about options: if you're going to hit it over the top, don't go to a spot where you have to clear a deep fielder.

My one-day record isn't very good. I've tried to analyse it: sometimes I've over-attacked and many times I haven't pushed on from reasonable scores. I've got only one international one-day hundred. I've never been a very good worker of the ball for ones and twos which is the basis of limited-over cricket: you've got to get bat on ball and move it around. Miandad is the best I've ever seen at it. Glenn Turner is New Zealand's best exponent of one-day batting.

Martin Crowe has found limited-over cricket frustrating. I think he's starting to come to terms with it and he'll certainly have to do that when he takes over the captaincy. He's a natural one-day player in that he possesses all the skills – he can move the ball around and play the big shots – but I think he went through a stage when he found it frustrating because he's a perfectionist and there's no place for perfectionism in one-day cricket. He was also required to do some bowling which I don't think he enjoyed.

The structure of tours these days is such that one-dayers become ten-a-penny and they almost lose their significance. In the West Indies we played a one-day international three days before a test and it's difficult not to put it low down your list of priorities. In India we played five in eight days. In Australia you play two teams five times and it becomes tedious. You're being flown vast distances to play in front of huge crowds who treat it like a rugby test and enjoy hurling abuse at you. It's all done for financial reasons and from the players' viewpoint, it's hard to believe you need ten games to decide because everyone takes part and you're just there for the one-day cricket.

I've often thought New Zealand should put more time and energy towards succeeding in limited-overs cricket. We should go into a camp set-up like India and Pakistan and train and select specifically for the one-day game. Success in one-day cricket is very important because it attracts crowds, and gate receipts play a significant role in determining the financial success of any tour.

I quite like the situation where you just have to go out and bat for hours. It makes things less complicated, defines what you have to do. I keep saying "all day" and let everything become repetitive, take on a rhythm. You can lose that when you have a break but the longer you go on, the quicker you're back in the groove. Things just happen. The first 30 takes ages then you have a spurt, get a couple of boundaries, and suddenly you've got 50. Then you struggle along for a while and you find you're on 86 or so. You're never tired when you're getting runs but you notice it afterwards: I chew gum and my jaws ache after a long bat. You get off the field and realise how worn out you are and you're stiff the next day. I wish I'd felt that way more often.

I'm sure there a lot of spectators who've watched me bat, thinking "I wish Wright would get out" but I've never had much sympathy for that point of view.

CHAPTER THIRTEEN

Picking winners

The only time I've ever been dropped from the New Zealand team was on the 1985 tour of Australia. I was averaging about 20 in the one-day series and although my two previous scores had been 60 and 20, I wasn't hitting the ball well. We needed to beat India in Launceston to make the finals. I was really keen to play and felt I should've played because of my experience and because it was a crunch game.

At the selection meeting – Turner, Coney, Hadlee and myself – we were going through the team, various names were mentioned, and I suddenly realised my name wasn't being bandied about. It was reported, presumably with one of the other selectors as the source, that I'd dropped myself but that wasn't true. Nothing was said so I finally said "I guess I'm not in the team" and left. At the team meeting Martin Crowe questioned the wisdom of my non-selection, the only time I can remember that happening. Of course I was biased but I thought "good on you". Martin's temerity earned him a stern rebuke from the management. Perhaps I didn't push my own case hard enough – a frequent predicament for a tour selector – but there wasn't a lot I could do about it: you can't knock your head against a brick wall. I'm sure Turns and Jerry came to the meeting with their side worked out and maybe Richard fancied opening. That wouldn't have been a bad idea because no one made any runs and we lost the game. As it turned out, I ended up captaining the side in the field because Jerry came off with a migraine.

There were times when I could've been dropped and times when I wouldn't have minded missing a one-dayer but on this occasion I was amazed that I had to reach the conclusion myself – no one actually said anything and there was no discussion of the reasons. I must've come close to being dropped other times, especially early on, and there have been times when my one-day form hasn't been all that special. In New Zealand there aren't as many guys pushing you for the place as in other countries but I'm the type that's always looking over his shoulder to see what's around. You can't afford to be complacent.

In another country my results after ten tests would have had me out of the team and having to fight my way back. It may even have been a good thing in that I probably needed a break to get my confidence back. I felt I wasn't getting the results and the more you feel that, the harder it is, and it becomes a real barrier. I think that happened to Ken Rutherford.

I've been a tour selector since 1984 and at times I've felt that we were two or three players short of being a really good side. It's always the last two places that are the problem, either because of injury or guys not performing or because the depth simply isn't there. It used to aggravate me but when I became captain, I got a lot more philosophical about it. You just pick the best side from whoever's fit and available and get on with the job. It does get difficult when players have 'grey area' injuries and it's a toss-up whether or not they'll be fit to play; you want them to play but deep inside, they've already made the decision that they won't.

When I started, there wasn't a coach so selection was a bigger issue. The manager was always involved but not in a cricket sense. You get managers who consider themselves experts in this area – some were a help, some a hindrance, and some were absolutely confusing. In England there are plenty of games outside the tests so everyone gets a chance; the first-class games are really just for build-up and practice. You're representing New Zealand and you want to win but teams are being picked to give players an opportunity to play their way into the test side. On other tours there might be no more than a couple of warm-up games before the tests or one-day internationals which makes it very hard for the borderline cases. It's something players have to accept but some find it very hard: they've trained for two months, they're keen to make the side, they get on the tour and find opportunities are limited. That's when selection can be a thankless task.

Before the era of the coach, the selection panel was generally the captain, vice-captain and senior pro. We had four in the West Indies where Frank Cameron was assistant manager but really there, it seemed to me, as a selector. A panel of three – captain, vice-captain and coach – is enough. Being a selector on tour can be a nuisance when you have selection meetings on a day off: they may be over in 20 minutes or they may drag on. Either way, you'd rather be by the pool.

My hardest selection decisions were those involving Bruce Edgar. Bruce didn't have a particularly good home series against England in 1983 and John Reid had come into the side for the tour of Sri Lanka which meant someone had to miss out. We knew Reid could play well in those conditions – he was a fine player particularly of spin and medium pace, as his record shows. If we played both of them, there was no place for Geoff Howarth. It was pretty tough on Bruce who'd faced the music against the other countries only to miss out against Sri Lanka. He was pretty disillusioned and who could blame him?

Reido didn't get runs in the first two tests and we had to make the decision in the third test. It was a dilemma for me: as a matter of principle I thought Bruce and I should always open the batting; we were great mates, opening partners, and I wanted the guy to play. But Reido had played the cricket and Bruce hadn't. That's the way it is these days – you go from one test to the next and changing the team means bringing in someone who's been watching rather than playing and hasn't got in through performing on the field. Howarth and I went for Reid and Coney for Edgar. Reid got 180. Bruce also got the rough end of the deal on the 1985 tour to Pakistan. He had a reasonable tour, got sawn off a couple of times, then he was dropped and Geoff moved up to open. I felt that was wrong because Howarth was never an opener.

I've enjoyed selecting on tour but it's not easy. Very rarely has anyone made a fuss. When a player doesn't say anything but it shows in his face, when he's not particularly keen to catch your eye when you walk past, you know they're hurting but to their eternal credit, they keep their mouths shut and get on with the job. It's also hard when you've backed a player but lost out on the vote. Hadlee wouldn't have gone to many team talks wondering if he's going to be in the team. People like Evan Gray and Wally Lees have had a hard go but in New Zealand you generally get picked if you're consistently impressive, which isn't always the case in other countries.

I feel strongly that at the end of the day, the captain's views should prevail. He should definitely be consulted at home as well – he has a say but it's not the final say and that's gone against me over the composition of a touring side and a test side. It always boils down to one or two places but I feel the captain should have the guys he wants. I was desperately keen that John Bracewell should play at Eden Park against the Indians last season but I lost the vote.

Once the team's picked someone has to tell the ones who've missed out. That's never an easy job and I think it's important the captain does it. Some players find non-selection harder to accept than others. When you're on the committee but not captain or vice-captain, guys can bail you up and try to find out what happened but you can't divulge what went on in the meeting. It's also important players know what the team is before anyone else. There has been the odd occasion when the final team selection was released to suit newspaper deadlines; when journalists know before the players it can lead to all sorts of problems.

In the 1978 World Cup we arrived at Old Trafford for the semi-final keyed up and ready to go. They'd picked a squad but the side hadn't been officially announced. We had a session in the nets; at that stage Gary Troup didn't think he was playing and Ewen Chatfield thought he was. Troupy was disappointed but being a good guy, he raced in like the wind to give the batters a stern work-out. After the net I walked back with Mystery Morrison and he asked who was in the side. I said I thought it was the same as for the last game and just then an announcement to that effect came over the PA. With half an hour to go, Troupy was heading for the showers and Chats was getting ready to play when Glenn Turner said to Mark Burgess that he'd better make sure everyone knew what the team was. It was then Troupy found out he was playing and Chats discovered he wasn't. It was the only time I've seen Chats visibly angry and understandably so. For the rest of that tour the answer to the question "who's in the side?" was "the first eleven in the bus".

One-day teams are difficult to select because you've always got to have five bowlers, preferably six. Sometimes a batsman might be getting runs and media write-ups but his runs aren't being scored quickly enough and other guys are being forced to sacrifice. Someone else might have had a string of failures through no fault of his own, having had to throw his wicket away. I think one-day selection will get more specialised as there's more recognition that a good test cricketer doesn't necessarily make a good one-day cricketer. Paul McEwan is an example of a player who should've played a lot more one-day internationals because on his day he can tear attacks apart. In India we didn't have the right balance for the limited-overs game but the side was picked to play tests.

Some people like to know exactly where they stand the night before, whether they're in or out. It's understandable if they're in line to be 12th man and if it's clear-cut, fine. But you rarely know exactly what the wicket's going to be like and you can't let people relax too much. Because of the health problems in India we sometimes had to delay naming the side till the morning of the game when we knew who was fit. In India and Pakistan you can spend three or four hours sorting our your side then find out in the morning that half the team is down with a virus. On those tours you're in with a chance till the team walks on the field.

In Sri Lanka 'Billy' Stirling played in the first two games then spent the rest of the tour watching cricket and drinking copious quantities of coke. The practice facilities weren't good so he couldn't even do much training. He wasn't picked for the one-day series at the end of the tour because of his lack of cricket. The venue for the second game, which we had to win to wrap up the series, was about 50 minutes from Colombo. The Sri Lankan wickets were brown and flat although they used to seam a bit first thing which didn't amuse me. But when we got to this ground, we found the wicket was as green as a Taranaki dairy paddock so we decided to play all the seamers. Billy had left his boots at the hotel so someone had to get in the Morris Minor taxis they have in Sri Lanka and rush back to get them.

It was at least 100 degrees and horribly humid. Billy was psyched up – mustard keen because he hadn't had a game for four weeks. He ran in like Carl Lewis for his first over which included three no-balls; a nine-ball over off the long run in that heat was pretty draining and the coke and cigarettes were catching up with him. One delivery was dispatched into the next door cow paddock which didn't help. The same thing happened in his second over: he started out charging in, bowled a couple of no-balls, and by the end of the over he was drenched with sweat and his gait was starting to resemble that of a marathon runner who's hit the wall. By halfway through the third over he was off his short run and it ended up being a tough day for him.

It's quite interesting when you canvass team mates' opinions: there's often a wide variety of opinion and you get to know whose judgments you respect. Hadlee is an imaginative selector – he'll produce things out of the blue that you've never thought of. There'll be some very interesting choices if he ever becomes a national selector. Cairns had his theories, most of them like his batting – straightforward and attacking – and Snedden was very good in India.

Frank Cameron was one of the great selectors. The first time I met him was when I turned up for my first test, in Wellington in 1978. He bowled to us in the nets and he was just about the best bowler on show. At his team talks he generally had the opposition out for 50-odd with us bowling inswingers and outswingers – as he talked, he acted it all out, with his wrist snapping away and fingers flicking – and we'd get 500. We called him Chung because he used that expression – 'chung!' – when he talked about the ball zipping off the pitch. At dinner he was always either smashing one through the covers or bowling the unplayable delivery.

He really wanted the guys he'd picked to do well. You felt he was behind you but he never got too close to the players. He was always telling me how well Edgar and Ian Rutherford were playing. He'd tell Ian Smith how well Wally Lees was keeping and vice versa. I think he found the tests harder than the players did. He had favourite spots around the ground where he'd been sitting when the opposition had lost wickets and he'd keep returning to them. After a session in the field, he'd come in mopping his brow with a handkerchief, saying, "By God that was hard". When we had to get 120 to beat the West Indies at Dunedin in 1980, he couldn't take it and left the ground, drove up to the top of a hill, and listened to it on a transistor.

Once we were dismissed in a one-dayer against Australia for 74 runs – I was out first ball and the game was over by 4.20 p.m. Bob Vance, the NZCC chairman, addressed the players and Frank pointing out that we had let down not only ourselves but also the cricketing public, and we'd better get our act together. As soon as Vance left the room Frank got up and told us if we kept playing that way, HE'D get the chop. Then he paused and added: "But rest assured, some of you will go before I do!"

I sometimes felt spinners weren't encouraged much under his panel and Howarth's captaincy although we did play on a lot of seamers wickets. He was very consistent and loyal but you didn't want to cross him. He had cricket at heart and was loyal to the players who performed for him but was severe on those that didn't. He was from the hard school – as a bowler he was as tight as a bull's arse in fly season – and he sorted people out reasonably quickly and knew what test cricket was all about. He made his mistakes, notably keeping Chats out of it for so long, and I didn't think sending Kenny Rutherford to the West Indies was not a great idea.

Glenn Turner had very black and white ideas about certain players – he didn't think Trevor Franklin's technique was up to it for instance – so he was certainly consistent. He was very technically oriented – there was a right way and wrong way of doing things – and he had much the same attitude tactically. But he knew the game inside out and if he had the time to be a selector, he'd make a reasonable job of it.

In England in 1986 he liked picking five bowlers. I thought this was a luxury and that Jerry should have bowled more but Evan Gray played which I felt left us a little short of batting: I prefer six specialist batters. Events proved Turner right. He was generally very sound in his selections but set in his ways.

Don Neely is very theoretical, sometimes too much so. He has great knowledge of players' performance statistics, works very hard, tries like hell and is very keen on the game. He's given tremendous service to New Zealand cricket. He's definitely the best-dressed selector we've ever had, with his double-breasted suits and blazer and shirt combinations.

I rated Gren Alabaster highly. I don't know if he enjoyed Australia – there was a lot of media pressure and some of the press, especially the New Zealand ones – got into him. We didn't practise the day before the test in Brisbane because he thought we were prepared – that's never happened before or since. At the team dinner the night before he said we were 'cherry ripe'. We were – for the picking.

Bruce Taylor is an enthusiast and likes selecting everything. I think some of his most difficult decisions have involved race horses – he always has his copy of *Best Bets* and a transistor at test matches. Fortunately, Tails

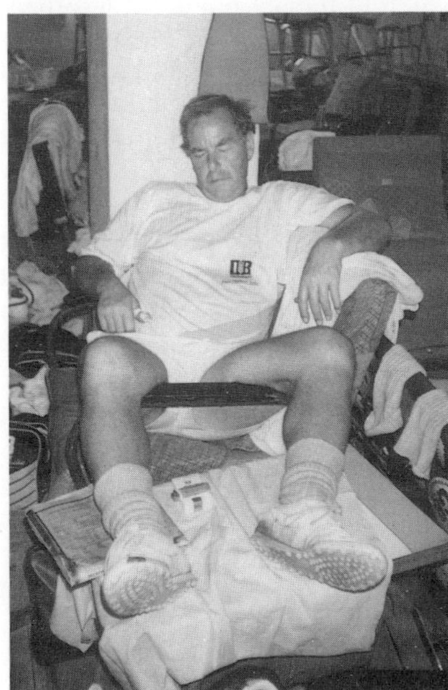

A worried man – selector and coach Bob Cunis.

"Name and telephone number please." Convenor of selectors Don Neely recruiting on the boundary.

J.G. BLACKWELL

hasn't yet taken a boxed trifecta of Wright, Rutherford and Jones in the second leg of the double at Oamaru.

John Guy had a lot to do with my career because he was Northern Districts convenor when I moved up and they picked me. Not surprisingly I felt he was a good selector. He was absolutely besotted with the game – ate, slept and breathed it.

I was very pleased when Bob Cunis got on the panel. He knows the game, is a good judge of a player, and has the great strength that he can select and still relate to players. He can drop players but they still find it hard not to have a beer with him. He has great communication skills.

He always has his team organised. At practice in India he'd tell Sneds and I to get our teams organised and we'd see him in his room later and sort it out over a cup of tea. In Perth in 1989 Bob believed that some of our players were too psychologically brittle to practise alongside the Aussies so we had to practise when they weren't there. I thought that was a bit over the top.

In India I told him he wasn't watching enough batting and that comment had come through from the players. It didn't thrill him but he agreed to it. That day at warm-ups he bent down to do up a lace and his back went so he had to watch from a deck chair, which in India seem to be designed for maximum discomfort. It was a one-dayer and when we came in after fielding he said "Okay, I'll watch but as a New Zealand selector, not as the coach."

At times Bob has had trouble hitting high catches. He blames his bat and this problem has been the subject of some heated discussions between us. After a pretty intense practice on the short Australian tour, I banished him to the dressing room and took over the task. I kept the boys at it in the heat for quite a while, hitting a succession of what are known as 'high changers'. Bob sympathised with the lads in the dressing room afterwards, telling them I was turning into a martinet. "Did you see poor Willie?" he ranted, "he was dry retching." Willie Watson had to gently inform Bob that he'd actually swallowed a fly.

Bob's always been a good source of advice, for batsmen as well as bowlers. In my first season at Northern Districts I asked him what an opening bowler looks for in a batsman and I probably learned more from him in that season than I've ever learned from a lot of batting coaches. Bowlers have their thoughts on what's sound and what's not sound and batsmen sometimes aren't aware of what they're actually doing.

Bob made me square up a little bit, pointing out that when a left hander plays a forward defensive shot and the ball goes to gully, he hasn't got the angles right. When the bowler is coming right arm over to me and I'm playing straight, the ball should go straight back on his side of the wicket, my on side. Bob said he used to hate left handers who hit the ball straight back to him. It was simple, solid advice.

He was a hard man on the field. Glenn Turner once hit him for three fours in a row. The light wasn't very good and Bob told him "Do that again

The selection panel – Derby Day at Epsom.

"It's a nice fit but do you have any other colours?"

Party time.

Eye-catching – 'Billy' Stirling and Evan Gray.

"Thanks, Matey, I love ice cream." Celebrating New Zealand's first-ever test win in England, at Headingley, 1983.

A load of hot air – birthday boys Martin Snedden and Merv Hughes.
MARGOT BUTCHER

and I'll beam you." Glenn knew he meant it and was a little more circumspect from then on. I played against him in a Hawke Cup match, Poverty Bay against Bay of Plenty. Bay of Plenty had a useful side with him opening the bowling with Hira Unka. We got in the second afternoon and went through to tea without problems. After tea the ball swung everywhere. I found out later that Bob had swapped the Kookaburra ball for a Steeden and that dark red ball really moved around.

Towards the end of his career he played for Bay of Plenty against Fiji. He got a bit of stick in the first innings, which he wasn't too happy about, but in the second he had two wickets after two balls. He walked down the pitch and told his team mates, "this is how you bowl to these guys". His third nut disappeared out of the park and he finished the over with two for 14.

It's important that the provincial teams are well selected by people who know what they're doing. The better the selectors are, the better the chances of the right players coming through and in New Zealand we haven't got the depth to afford mistakes.

There was a one-month gap between me leaving Canterbury because I couldn't get into the squad and playing for Northern Districts. Within 18 months I was playing county cricket and three years later I was playing in a test. There have been some terrible selection mistakes – Hedley Howarth being dropped from the Auckland team; Rod Redmond's treatment on the 1973 England tour; Eric Gillott coming back from that same tour and not being able to make the ND side; Wally Lees and Ewen Chatfield's omission from the 1978 tour to England.

Evan Gray has had a rough ride – he's a hard guy to fit into a side sometimes but it must have been heartbreaking missing out on some of those games and tours. Playing four seamers has often worked for us but there've been times when Boocky and Braces haven't been picked for games on wickets that did turn.

There's a great art in bringing in new blood to avoid the situation of having a top side for a long time which then suddenly breaks up because of retirements or guys going over the hill leaving you with a team of novices, as happened in Canterbury. You've got to keep bringing in young guys.

Selectors are amateurs and they spend a lot of time watching cricket, giving up their holidays, and they cop a lot of stick for their trouble, unlike administrators. No one hears about it when they make good picks but you sure hear about it when they make bad ones. Quite often they make the right selection but the guy's not in the right frame of mind, but over a period of time they should sort themselves out, demonstrate consistency and work to an overall plan.

Selectors have a tendency to make the best player, or more specifically the best batsman, captain. It doesn't necessarily work that way – captaincy is a separate issue – but it is very important that the captain is picked from among those players who are absolutely sure of their place.

I found it very hard to understand why I was passed over as captain and, as often happens with players who are dropped, it's made harder by the fact it's never explained to you. I was vice-captain under Geoff Howarth but then Jerry got the job when Geoff was unavailable for the tour of Pakistan. He didn't have a good tour and afterwards said the captaincy didn't suit him. But then when Howarth retired, Coney got the job again, but he was vice-captain then so it wasn't unexpected. I felt that I was unlucky and I was desperately keen to have a crack at it. On the other hand I probably got the vice-captain's job too early and didn't put enough effort into it. In fact it probably would've been better if I'd never had the job at all. I finally cornered Cameron and asked him what the story was. He said I'd had some bad managerial reports, which I thought was bull.

There's a lot of communication now and the selectors are much closer to the players than they were in Frank Cameron's day. They get to know them and find out what makes them tick. But there's a danger in getting too close to the players: not too long ago a selector had half the New Zealand team around to his place for dinner. He didn't seem to worry about what the other half thought of it.

Frank used to write out about five different combinations and Cunis does that too. Then you go through them. It's not just a matter of getting the right players, it's getting the right balance, particularly when selecting a touring party.

One of the worst selected teams I can remember was England in 1986 when they had Derek Pringle as number six batsman. Two of their specialist batsmen were inexperienced and they had a keeper who wasn't much of a batsman. We had one real strike bowler and the idea should have been to have enough batting to have seen him off. But after Lords they dropped Peter Willey who is a really good batter and a great competitor and brought in Pringle whose batting isn't good enough to qualify him as a genuine all-rounder at test level.

I've sat in on a few selection meetings and been impressed with the thoroughness, the amount of homework that's been done, and the effort that goes into getting the best side out. Then a player they've picked doesn't play well and they get rubbished by people who are always wiser after the event.

At least we seem to be past the days when players could get picked on the basis of their performance at net practice before a tour as happened with Dave Gallop and Graham Vivian before the 1965 tour of India and England. They had to bowl their leg spinners in front of the selectors who then decided which of them went on the tour. As anyone who's played a bit of cricket knows, there are a lot of good net players around.

I've always enjoyed the way selectors walk around the ground, usually in a group with their hands in their pockets or behind their backs, walking much slower than everyone else and trying to look incredibly knowledgeable about what's going on. You can pick them from 200 yards away.

At team talks the selectors inevitably tell us they've picked us because we're the best players in New Zealand. I've always thought that was stating the obvious. There'd be something seriously wrong if we weren't.

CHAPTER FOURTEEN

The fastest guns in the west

Fear, whether butterflies-in-the stomach nervousness or full-on, loose-bowelled terror at the prospect of facing fast bowling, is the most basic emotion in cricket. Every cricketer has felt it at one time or another.

At all levels of cricket, people want to know if the other side has anyone quick; from a dismissed batsman, the comment "cripes he's quick" says it all. If there's some fiery stuff being sent down, it's not unknown for the next man in to have to answer an urgent call of nature which necessitates being locked in the toilet until there's a bowling change.

The effect a fast bowler can have on a team is illustrated by a story told by my old Derbyshire mate Bud Hill. This happened a few seasons before I arrived at Derbyshire, when the skipper was an excitable Yorkshireman called Brian Bolus, and concerns their first encounter with the South African whirlwind, Mike Proctor. The lads had heard a lot about Proccie, mostly about how he started his run-up in the next county and thought the object of the game was knocking over batsmen rather than stumps.

Gloucestershire batted first and declared shortly before stumps for 360-odd, leaving just enough time for Proctor to have a bit of a dart before close of play. There was a tense silence in the Derbyshire dressing room as Bud and Tony Borrington padded up and, as they headed for the door, they were stopped in their tracks by a scream of "Just a minute!" and turned to confront Bolus who wanted to give them some last-minute encouragement. "I don't want you to think Proctor's quick," thundered Bolus. "**He is quick!!!** – but don't think about it." Bud recalls that by the time he got to the wicket after Bolus's pep talk, his knees were knocking so badly, he could scarcely take guard.

When there's a quick operating from one end and something friendlier at the other, it can have a dramatic effect on the running between the wickets. The batter facing the music will run like hell for singles and threes and jog what should be two hoping to turn it into one. Or else he'll take off for a single like Ben Johnson after a doctor's appointment only to have his invitation declined by his partner who'll then proceed to block hell out of the gentle stuff he should be flogging to all parts of the ground.

If an English pro hears a new overseas signing to the county circuit is a really good bowler, that's one thing. If he hears the new bloke is 'really quick', – or a 'nasty fasty' as they are known in the trade – he'll be thinking "Oh no, not another one."

Playing against Northants used to be a lovely little game in the days when their overseas player was the Pakistani medium pacer Safraz Nawaz and even better when they had Roger Harper, that rarest of cricketing species, a West Indian spinner. Then they signed Winston Davis and later Curtly Ambrose and the fixture ceased to bear any resemblance to a fun game.

For a time Northants had both Harper and Davis on their books but under the rules governing overseas players in county cricket, they couldn't play both of them in the same game. You could arrive at Northampton, where the wicket's normally flat and fairly slow, expecting they'd play Harper. Then you find the wicket's a green seamer, Winston's in the side, he's fresh and raring to go, and what you expected to be just another day at the office becomes an exercise in survival. I'm sure the other teams had similarly unpleasant surprises when Michael Holding and I were taking turnabout with Derbyshire. The Somerset and England allrounder Vic Marks was always highly delighted to see me when Somerset met Derbyshire because it meant Michael Holding wasn't playing.

Every cricketer would secretly like to be a fast bowler. It takes hold early – all kids try to bowl as fast as they can. I certainly did. I can remember a particularly rapid spell for Malvern vs Ashley at Dudley Park, Rangiora, with a howling Canterbury nor'wester up my backside when I was 11.

I'd give my eye teeth to be able to bowl quick – I mean really quick; let's face it, I mean absolutely lethally quick – even for just one afternoon and I think a lot of opening batsmen have the same desire. I'd want to bowl at a few nominated adversaries, maybe fast bowlers with whom I have a few scores to settle or just cricketers who've annoyed me. If this wish came true, I'd work methodically in the waist to the top of the head region with a few toe-crushing yorkers thrown in to keep them honest.

Unfortunately I've never really been able to bowl. It requires suppleness and from an early age my attempts to touch my toes ended just below my knees. They tried to teach me at Derbyshire but eventually gave up.

Once you reach that really top speed, you have the whip hand, the power, the ability to put people in their place and settle scores. Faster bowlers are cricket's macho men, the fastest guns in the west. They usually have the last word: you can take them on, hook them, and they can put out a backward square leg and move fine leg squarer and let you have another short one. You have to be exceptional to hook successfully against the real quick stuff.

You could never say you enjoy it but in a funny sort of way I do like it. When you face quick bowling, you concentrate harder and the clarity of mind you achieve is almost sublime. Isn't there a saying about imminent death concentrating the mind wonderfully?

For an opening bat, facing the quicks is what it's all about. There are players who are known in cricket circles not to fancy them, not to handle them well. These guys are known as being better 'below the waist', good players when the ball's not bouncing. Not too many of them open the batting. When you go out to face it, you're thinking "hell, this will be heavy going". It's a real battle with yourself. You know that the bowlers are trying to intimidate you, that they'll hit you if they possibly can. People talk about restricting the number of bouncers – it's fair enough that you can't bowl six out of six but two or three an over are part of the game. If too many are being bowled it should be controlled by good umpires backed up by strong administrators. But as an opener, you expect a few early on. It's part of the softening-up process.

The pace of the wicket is a key element. If you're playing somewhere like Eden Park No 2 where you know the wicket won't be quick and it's not going to bounce, you don't mind who's bowling. But wickets like the Basin in the old days or Perth are a different matter. The bowlers respond to that a lot more than people realise and it becomes a different game when there's something in the wicket for them.

A lot of factors determine the precise nature of the ordeal: the wicket, how the bowlers are feeling, the state of the game. If it all goes a certain way, you can find yourself in the wrong place at the wrong time. That happens to openers more than other players.

You psych yourself up for it. You know they're going to let you have it and frankly, you're not looking forward to the experience. Then all of a sudden it's okay, you're seeing it and handling it. I always loved to go under the first bouncer – it's like the first tackle in rugby. You know if they do drop it short, you can get out of the way. Then you can get down to business knowing you're going to be all right.

You've got to get behind the ball and keep your head really still. Michael Holding rated Peter Willey and Ian Chappell as the two best players of pace he bowled to. Both had exaggerated open stances, almost chest-on to the bowler, which obviously put them right behind the line of the ball.

You've got to lean forward whether you're playing forward or back. People say you shouldn't play the quicks off the front foot but I believe you should be moving into the ball whether you're playing off the back or front foot so you can get yourself out of the way of the ball. A good quick bowler will move you around the crease, get you coming forward, then drop in a short one; get you going back, then fire one up to you. I always try to play going into the ball so that if you miss it, it hits you in the chest.

If you start playing away from your body, you're gone. You know you're going to get the short stuff but you can't let that worry you. If you're anticipating it, you'll be on the back foot before you've picked up the length which makes you vulnerable to lbws and prevents you from driving in the unlikely event of the delivery being pitched up.

The two quickest – Michael Holding and Jeff Thomson. Differing styles, same result.

GEORGE HERRINGSHAW & TONY EDENDEN

If you've got reasonable reactions and you watch the ball, your reflexes will automatically get you out of the way. When you see guys ducking into balls that are just short of a length, it means they've taken their eye off the ball. I've been hit only once when I've kept my eye on the ball, by a Sri Lankan.

Bruce Edgar and I used to practise lobbing the ball at each other's heads and moving our heads out of the way. You spend time with the bowling machine just avoiding the ball. You don't have to move much to get out of the way and it's a great feeling when you move in a controlled way and it just misses your visor and the bowler knows you knew what you were doing. It's a bit like sparring without being able to hit back. You try to stay out of trouble, keep your wicket intact, and pick up the runs when you can: get a bit of a bat on it here and it flies past gully, flick it down the legside there. You don't get to play too many glory shots.

I wish I'd been a better cutter and really gone for the cut because left handers get so much short stuff outside off stump. Of course it's a waste of time trying to cut a bloke like Garner because the ball's always climbing on you. I tried it twice and got dropped twice. I admire Gordon Greenidge because he really takes the bowlers on: if they drop it short, he hooks. In this country there's so much said about not hooking, not cutting – altogether too much 'you mustn't'.

To play those shots you need true wickets which is why I hooked a lot more in the West Indies – the wickets were more predictable. In New Zealand we need good, quick wickets. We've got lots of strong athletic guys and there's absolutely no substitute for pace: it's the cricketing equivalent of a big, strong, mean forward pack.

Danny Morrison has quickened up a lot since he first made the New Zealand team. Early in the 1989/90 Shell Trophy series Auckland played Central Districts on a greenish Eden Park number two and he bowled the fastest deliveries I've seen from a New Zealander at the CD opener Scotty Briasco. After Scotty had chested one off and snicked a couple over the slips, he said to me as I passed him between overs: "Wrighty, I wonder what the beach is like this time of year."

Although I admire the guys who take on the quicks, I'm sure the reason for our comparative success against the West Indies is that we hang in there and wear them down. You need a lot of staying power against them. With four of them, it means they can always have someone reasonably fresh to fire away. If a wicket falls, they've got a couple rested and ready to be unleashed at the new batsman.

The danger with taking them on is that they're so quick, it's very hard to control the hook shot and they can put a couple of guys out to catch the uncontrolled hook. It unsettles me when they put blokes out because you start thinking "he's going to let me have a short one" and as soon as you start thinking about the ball in advance, you're in trouble. The other problem with hooking is that not every bouncer has the same steepness of bounce or the same pace. Andy Roberts had two bouncers, a slow one and really quick one and a lot of people, Colin Cowdrey for one, having handled Mark-1 comfortably enough, were just getting started on their hook shot when the Mark-2 version arrived with bone-crushing velocity.

On the 1985 tour, we played the West Indies Under 23 at St Kitts. The wicket was a little damp and their attack was Walsh, Gray and Merrick, who were all sharp. I opened with Ronnie Hart, who was competing for a test spot and hadn't got any runs in the first game. The wicket was doing a bit and at lunch, after two hours' hard labour, we were 64 without loss. Ron was on four.

As we walked out after lunch Ronnie said "Wrighty, I think I might take it to them a bit." I said "fair enough, Ron". The third nut after lunch from Walsh was a screamer, rearing off a good length. It hit Ron on the chest and glove just below the chin and lobbed to short leg. As he walked off he said to me, "I should've bloody hooked it."

Some bowlers' actions make it harder to pick the ball up. Jeff Thomson was a slinger who brought the ball up from behind his back; Malcolm Marshall and Wasim Akram have very fast arm actions and 'run through' their deliveries whereas bowlers with high, classic actions like Dennis Lillee and Joel Garner show you the ball and make it easier to get a sight of it.

Facing these fellows has been the ultimate challenge and I get more satisfaction out of playing them well than anything else; not necessarily scoring but hanging in there and taking what they can throw at you. The day you start shuffling out of the line, not getting in behind it, is the day you put your gear in the attic and head for the bowling club.

The best innings I ever played was for Derbyshire against West Indies at Chesterfield in 1980. We played most of our home games at Derby, which was one of the slowest wickets in England while Chesterfield was one of the quickest. I'd just played them in New Zealand and hung around without getting big scores which was disappointing and I felt that maybe they didn't rate me.

I was in reasonable nick. Before the game I was reading the press release put out by the Derbyshire secretary which said the wicket would be hard and green "which would suit our seam attack". That consisted of Mike Hendrick, John Walters, who was military medium and Barry Wood, who wasn't even that. I couldn't help feeling that if the secretary had thought things through, he'd have concluded that the conditions would suit the Windies a hell of a lot more. I took comfort in the thought that he couldn't tell a cricket wicket from astroturf but when I got to the ground, I discovered to my horror that it really was hard and green. They won the toss and put us in and I was absolutely delighted that Mike Holding wasn't playing. Unfortunately Andy Roberts, Garner and Marshall were.

Roberts hadn't been in great form and the word was his test place was in danger which was motivation we could have done without. The Windies were also on a big win bonus if they won all their county games so they meant business. As Barry Wood and I prepared to go out, we were asked – perhaps facetiously – what we wanted at the drinks break. I said a glass of champagne. Woody, ever confident, said he'd want his white floppy hat. The last ball of Roberts' first over took off and smashed his helmet flap into his ear and Woody departed bleeding profusely. As it turned out he did need his white floppy – to stem the flow of blood. When we fielded Walters broke down and Woody had to do a lot of bowling and he didn't feel up to opening in the second innings.

Peter Kirsten didn't last long. Marshall, then the young up-and-comer, was bowling at the other end and he was pretty nippy. I worked a few off my pads and took a few thumps on the legs. I felt pretty calm. I wanted to do well because I didn't think I had their respect; I wanted them to think there was a bit of substance to me, that I'd front up to whatever they threw at me. They might get me out but they'd know I wouldn't back off just because they were quick.

David Steele came in. He'd been a good player of fast bowling, very much a front foot player. I took my eye off one from Roberts and it hit me in the side of the visor. When you make a mistake against the quicks, and I've made a few, there's a very short space of time between your awareness that you've ballsed it up and the consequence of the balls-up. I went down feeling like the gong in a bell. The first thing I did was check everything was still there. I hate to think what would've happened if I hadn't been wearing a helmet; as it was I could hardly move my jaw for four days. I got hit by Roberts again, then by Collis King who was barely medium pace. Steeley asked Roberts if he'd mind taking it easy because he, Steeley, had only a couple of years left in the game and had a wife and two children at home.

"Come watch the red ball fly!" Garner to Dujon via Wright.
BROOKS-LA TOUCHE

Wearing everything but a mattress – Ruds and I go out to open at Trinidad.

Roberts choked back the tears of remorse and continued to bowl with the same disregard for our well-being as before. I was a bit put out by the implication that single childless batsmen were fair game.

Steeley got hit in the bollocks and crawled to square leg grunting and groaning. It was a bit like the punch line in a play and everyone cracked up laughing. In the end he got out to King which hacked him off, after he'd taken the medicine from the others. In the second innings he wore a helmet for the first time in his career.

At lunch we were 86 for one and Geoff Miller seriously considered declaring because he felt the wicket was so dangerous. The fact that he was next in might have had something to do with it too. I got 96 that day which meant an awful lot to me.

I opened the bowling when the Windies went in to bat needing seven or eight in their second innings and bounced out Faoud Bacchus first ball. Perhaps that says more about the pitch than anything else.

In the fourth test in Jamaica on the 1985 tour, we had to bat after a rain storm. They really stuck it on us and it was the quickest concerted barrage I've faced. The rain had absolutely bucketed down and for a while there didn't seem any chance of play. The wicket was reasonably quick anyway but the rain really juiced it up. Their attack was Marshall, Garner, Davis and Walsh.

Marshall's first ball, a loosener, zinged over my head and Dujon had to jump to pull it down. Dessie Haynes at short leg gave me a grin and said "Good afternoon John". As an opening batsman he knew exactly what was going through my mind, which was "Hell, this wicket's pretty quick."

I got 55 out of a total of 138. It wasn't the sort of innings you get big headlines for but I liked it a lot. I got a smack on the visor from Davis and spent more time on my backside than on my feet. In a way it was the purest form of cricket in that your actual physical well-being was at stake.

The West Indians are ruthlessly professional and they had us on the ropes. We'd had two flat tracks – and got two draws – at Guyana and Trinidad and their attitude was "Welcome to the real world". Their tactics came in for criticism from our camp – that was the innings in which Jerry Coney got a broken arm – but I never expected anything else. They have got away with too much at times but any team with their attack would do exactly the same. The main problem is that the bouncers don't give the batsman much of a chance to play the ball and that's what the lawmakers must address.

A staggering number of West Indians can bowl fast. You go to the nets there and there'll be three or four club bowlers who are really sharp. Michael Holding used to talk about guys who play beach cricket who were really quick. It's a way of life and they get conditioned to it. The former West Indies opener Roy Fredericks was called 'Concrete Head' because of the number of times he'd been crusted without any apparent damage. The most frightening batting they have to do is probably in the nets although Jamaica against Barbados games are meant to be pretty lively affairs.

John 'Mystery' Morrison tells the story of going on one of Ken Sandford's Ambassadors tours and running into Andy Roberts, then 18 years old and unknown outside his little island of Antigua. Mystery's opening partner didn't last long and a bloke called Crash Aldridge came in. Crash wasn't seen to move his bat from the blockhole as a couple of deliveries from Andy whistled past into the keeper's gloves. At the end of the over Crash wandered down the wicket and said: "We haven't got anyone like him on the coast."

In county cricket there's a great reliance on West Indian fast bowlers to knock the top and tail off the innings. Almost every county has one so you get plenty of exposure to them. Some of the names wouldn't mean a thing to New Zealanders but they're all very quick: George Ferris, Hartley Alleyne, Ezra Moseley, Sylvester Clarke. Clarke was one of the nastiest of all: very sharp and very awkward. I once made the mistake of not walking after I snicked one off him. There was nothing on the game and I hadn't got many so I thought "oh well". It seemed to dwell on his mind for a couple of years afterwards. He bowled big inswingers, like Lance Cairns, but three times as quick.

The West Indian crowds love fast bowling, and they get really involved. Each time there's a bouncer and the batsman gets sat on his bum, there's a great roar. It was fun while it lasted but I'm in no hurry to go back there. You get conditioned to it and it's remarkable how slow other bowlers seemed when I went back to county cricket. There aren't too many quick bowlers in New Zealand so it's hard to get conditioning and practice against them. Bowling machines can simulate it, even using tennis balls.

With the West Indies' four quicks you get no let-up from the barrage and it's a wearing-down process. One of the quality things about their attack is the way they bowl with the old ball. There's a real art to keeping the ball in good nick and Pakistan are particularly good at it. It's no accident you see quite a few greasy-haired quicks around and sometimes the amount a ball swings is directly related to the amount of cream in mid off's hair. Essex are another side renowned for their care of the ball.

Speed is relative. After a while you find there are your common or garden quick bowlers, guys who are pretty nippy. You come across those all the time. Some of them hit the track hard and make pace off the wicket, seamers like Hendrick, Garner, and Botham in his early years. With the genuine speed merchants, you face three or four balls without too much bother, then they'll whip one past you. In terms of miles per hour, it's probably not that much quicker but it seems three yards quicker. With the first category, you have to be careful; with the real quick guys, they put in a bit of extra effort and it's past you. That's the difference.

The guy who sticks out in that context is Jeff Thomson. Early on the 1981 tour we played Queensland and in the first innings he was pretty sharp for three or four overs. He wasn't picked for the Aussie side and in the second innings he must have decided it was time he got down to business and he was incredibly quick. When he wasn't quite right, he was sharp; when he got it right, he was like lightning. He bowled a similar spell in the first innings of the third test in Christchurch in 1982. He must have been absolute dynamite before he damaged his shoulder.

During the 1979 World Cup, we played the West Indies in a group match and Michael Holding bowled four very fast overs. It was a really flat wicket but he was as quick as anyone I'd faced at that stage. The time between him letting the ball go and it arriving seemed unbelievably short. He had the ability to bowl the really quick delivery when he wanted. At Trinidad in 1985 he was going along smoothly, bowling within himself, and then he let go a lightning bouncer. How I got out of the road of it is still a mystery to me.

If they look quick on TV then they're really quick because television slows everything down. I remember being in Perth and watching the West Indies on TV and they looked rapid. I think I changed the channel.

The wickets in India and Pakistan have nothing in them for the quicks and batting there is very different from playing in the Caribbean. It's very difficult for the quicks to bowl fast right through an English season because there are just too many overs to bowl. You can face Malcolm Marshall on a flat wicket at Basingstoke without too much trouble. Then a few weeks later, you run into him at Chesterfield where it's green and bouncy and he's transformed. However, Malcolm, in his first few years in county cricket, ran in whether the wicket was flat or not. Colin Croft, in contrast, would only bowl quick when the conditions were in his favour. Some of them need the motivation of the big occasion. In 1978 I faced John Snow in a Gillette Cup quarter final at Hove and he was nasty. He had the reputation of never turning it on in county games, just lifting it for test cricket.

It's all very well being quick but you still have to bowl it in the right place. Of course if you're really quick, you only have to put three out of six anywhere near the target and you're going to achieve something. A good test for a bowler is coming back for a second spell with the old ball. Derbyshire's Devon Malcolm, who made the England team last year, could bowl like the bloody wind with the new ball but was a different proposition with the old one.

Line's a big thing. I never liked guys who pitched outside my leg stump and came on to me. Thommo bowled from wide of the crease and came into your chest from outside leg stump. If it comes down straightish and it's over middle and off or even middle you can sway out of the way but it's much harder against that line. Courtenay Walsh, Clarke, Winston Davis and Mike Proctor all did the same thing, aimed into the rib cage. I found that more difficult than Marshall coming round the wicket and angling it in from outside off when you could get inside the line and maybe hook.

Then there's a guy like Andy Roberts who you felt could hit you anytime he liked because he was so accurate. Thankfully when he came to New Zealand he'd lost a little pace and the wickets were slow but he cleaned me out a couple of times in England.

Apart from Thommo, the Windies are in a class of their own when it comes to pace although I didn't face Lillee at the height of his powers.

Bowler and batsman bend their backs. Kapil Dev bounces Andrew Jones.
J.G. BLACKWELL

"Where on earth did that one come from?"

"It's all right, you can come out now, he's finished his spell."
J.G. BLACKWELL

Malcolm Marshall greets me at Trinidad.
J.G. BLACKWELL

When I faced him he was still a great bowler and pretty nippy but more a Hadlee type of bowler. Imran was pretty quick, Bob Willis was a great trier and Botham was, early on. Like batsmen too, they all have their days.

On the odd occasions when a nasty fasty knows he's got a batsman scared, he'll try to keep him on to prolong his agony. He won't do it to a specialist batsman but someone like Sylvester Clarke would do it to a tailender just for the sheer hell of it.

There are players who bring the best out of quicks because they simply don't like them. Tony Greig's comment in 1976, delivered in his unmistakable South African accent, about making the West Indies grovel certainly spurred them on. Peter Kirsten, in the course of scoring a hundred in each innings against Surrey on a very flat wicket, had an altercation with Sylvester Clarke. The term 'garden boy' was allegedly used by Kirsten, once again articulated in the accent of the high veldt. Sylvester, who had a memory like a mainframe computer for lesser provocations than this, later went on the rebel tour of South Africa and went up three notches whenever Kirsie was down the other end. Kirsie discovered the hard way that Clarke preferred to express himself with a cricket ball than to say it with flowers.

It's always amazed me how the meanest, most competitive, players in New Zealand were spinners: Braces and Stephen Boock who also had the verbal prowess to go with their meanness. They are both much meaner than Hadlee and Danny Morrison for instance although Brendon Bracewell was very competitive as a young man so it may be in the blood.

I've always been a bit of a wimp in that I make the effort to exchange a pleasantry or two: "Morning Malcolm, how are the kids, man you're bowling well today." But of course in test cricket, it doesn't make a blind bit of difference. On the other hand, needless provocation is just asking for it. Hartley Alleyne was quick as anyone when he got it right and every time he pitched it up to Woody in this particular Derbyshire v Worcestershire game, Woody would play a perfect forward defensive shot, holding the pose as if he was having his photo taken for a coaching manual, and smile smugly down the wicket at Hartley who was absolutely infuriated by this routine and bowled faster and faster. I went down the wicket and said to Woody "For heaven's sake, stop smiling at him. Apart from anything else, you look bloody awful with your teeth out."

All sorts of things can get them going. In a one-dayer against ND at Seddon Park, Thommo was going through the motions, just having a gentle work-out, until the umpire, the late Bruce Bricknell, no-balled him four times in an over. Thommo went wild and started swearing at the batsmen and the umpire and suddenly he'd gone from rolling them down at a nice leisurely 70 mph to the genuine blink-and-you've-missed-it article. I was thinking "I don't care if he bowls from three feet past the crease, just stop no-balling him".

I don't mind number elevens getting one or two short ones if they've hung around for a while but it hacks me off to see someone like Chats getting bounced as a matter of course. It's so thick and macho. It's pretty pitiful if they don't even try to get the rabbits out without resorting to bouncers although in test cricket you've got to expect it if you hang around. Of course there's no quarter given by the West Indies; they simply don't give a toss whether the batsman can handle himself or not and most of their quicks can bat a bit.

On the other side of the coin it's very discomforting watching your bowlers giving their quickies a peppering. Early on I used to think "Oh we're for it now" but I came to realise it didn't matter what happened: they were still going to let us have it.

I haven't got a lot of time for the quicks who dish it out then come out to bat looking at their toes and wearing four chest protectors or the ones who bounce everyone but the quick bowlers. There are certainly some guys who don't get as many bouncers as they deserve but I'm speaking here from an opening batsman's point of view.

Michael Holding doesn't like hitting people. He had his moments in his younger days but he's an example of a fearsomely fast bowler with a conscience. Andy Roberts never smiled, never said anything, just gave you the big stare. He didn't really have to do anything else but, although he was scary, he was a nice fellow off the field. Thommo would be at you in all sorts of ways and Lenny Pascoe had plenty to say, mostly on the theme of what pleasure it would give him to pin your head to the sightscreen when he got you on a fast wicket, but again good company off the field.

Beamers are despicable. They're frightening because you simply don't pick them up. In 1976 England sent Brian Close and John Edrich, both of them well into their 40s, out to open against the Windies and they got a few beamers from Wayne Daniel but he just didn't know where the ball was going. Croft, who did know where it was going, bowled one at Coney in Christchurch in 1980 which was completely in character.

Some quicks walk straight back to their marks when they've hit someone. I understand why they do it: I suppose it adds to the image, another notch on the gun, but I can't say I admire it.

The really good bowlers are the clinical ones, the ones who don't lose their cool. They might get quicker when they're annoyed but they don't rant and rave and lose their composure. When a bowler starts waving his arms and setting his own fields, you know you're getting somewhere. The good ones also go up a notch when a partnership is broken and a new batter comes in.

How do they rate? For pace Holding and Thomson first, followed by Marshall; for meanness, Roberts, Clarke and Marshall; for skill, Hadlee and Lillee on their own, then Imran, Holding, Roberts, Marshall and Garner. I didn't face Lillee and Roberts at their absolute peaks when they must've been awesome and as I say Thomson must have been something else before his shoulder injury.

The accent on relentlessly hostile fast bowling in the modern game has literally changed the face of cricket in the form of the batting helmet. After the first test against Sri Lanka in 1983/84, I decided I wouldn't need my visor during the rest of the series so I left it under my bed. About four days later I came to the conclusion I'd made a silly mistake as a surgeon tried to straighten my nose. Rumesh Ratanayake was one of those slightly suspicious bowlers whose full-length balls are a lot slower than their short ones. He just did me for pace: it came so quickly off the wicket and just kept climbing. I realised late in the piece that it was going to climb over my bat and was heading straight for my face. I would have been okay if I'd worn my visor. Needless to say I have done ever since.

I wouldn't say Rumesh was a chucker but there are bowlers who bend the arm when they put in a quick one and he might've come into that category. He's clipped quite a few guys and once hit three West Indians in a one-day game at Melbourne which must have amused the hell out of his team mates.

I know a lot of old timers disapprove of helmets but I wouldn't like to play the quicks without one although I accept they've given bowlers much more licence. I've been hit on the head 15 times or so and I think I watch the ball as well as anyone. But I've made mistakes and with a helmet I know the consequences aren't going to be really serious. I can't see the sense in being able to protect your private parts but not your brain. Over the course of a lifetime I figure I'll get more use out of my brain than my balls.

Jack and the Beanstalk. 'Big Bird' Joel Garner in his delivery stride alongside umpire Steve Woodward.
FOTOPACIFIC

"Hey you, slow down."
J.G. BLACKWELL

"Thanks a lot, Merv!"
J.G. BLACKWELL

The slower ball.
PETER BUSH

CHAPTER FIFTEEN

Bats out of hell

The object of batting is to make runs. The great accumulators, the Boycotts and Borders of this world, who consistently produce the goods may not please the purist who wants poetry in motion or the one-day fan who just wants to see the ball blasted out of sight, but runs are the bottom line. Great batsmen score runs in massive quantities; some are pretty to watch, some aren't. It can be argued that the attacking batsman, the scorer of two-hour centuries, is a match-winner and therefore should be rated more highly than the accumulator. But the long-innings player can save games which may be just as important over a series; he can negotiate the innings through early danger when the ball is new and the pitch juicy, creating a platform for the attacking player to come in later and dominate. One thing I admire about Allan Border and Geoff Boycott is their ability to score runs on bad wickets.

In county cricket you may get three or four bats a week. Sometimes you strike a great player in top form on an absolutely flat wicket on a small ground. Because he knows that, come what may, he'll get another bat tomorrow, the shackles of caution are loosed and he plays with more freedom than he normally would, particularly in a test match. In those circumstances the great players bat as if they're from another planet. Those players and those innings left lasting impressions on me.

I always hoped that I could play that way but eventually realised that I might match them now and again, but I couldn't do it all the time. Some of those incredibly gifted players aren't so hot when it's whizzing around the nose – Zaheer Abbas for instance – but the true greats don't care how high the ball's bouncing.

Sometimes in county cricket I felt I attained perfection in my terms. I even did it a few times in tests: against Australia at Christchurch in 1981 when I was 90 not out overnight and went on to 141 hitting ten boundaries, and at the Basin Reserve 1990, or at Karachi when I got 80 out of 113. In those innings and various county knocks I felt I batted as well as I was capable of doing.

But I was nowhere near greatness. I tried but I lacked that edge which the greats have. It's made up of a combination of qualities, physical and mental attributes, some learned and some innate. They have technical skills, some of which club cricketers possess to a degree; the greats master them and in some cases, refine them to perfection giving themselves a speciality on which they can base their game and on which they can fall back if the other elements are out of sorts – Border's fierce cutting, for instance, or Viv Richard's on-side play. The three who stand out as having strengths in every department are the South African Barry Richards, Greg Chappell and Javed Miandad.

No matter how good you are, you must be able to do the basics well: the bat must come through straight and you must present the full face of it at the moment of contact. It doesn't matter whether the bat is picked up straight or towards gully – it's the way it comes down which counts. People say Andrew Jones isn't correct but I think he's one of the most technically correct players around because at the point of contact, everything is right: his head is over the ball and he plays with the full face of the bat.

Great players strike the ball with extraordinary timing, dismissing it from their presence with a waft of the bat. Viv Richards hits sixes into the 15th row of the stand with the economy of movement of an Aussie bushman discouraging a fly. He once hit a straight drive off Mike Hendrick that was little more than a forward defence. If the ball hadn't hit the pavilion, it would've ended up in the neighbouring county. They time their strokes to get maximum energy from the ball and the most out of their body weight; their muscles are relaxed so the bat swings smoothly through the line of the ball instead of being jerked fractionally off line. The greats all have tremendous balance and a still head – their feet move to bring the head into line. They have completely different styles but do the basics the same way.

Most of them were well-coached when they were young, perhaps because they came from cricketing households like the Chappells and the Crowes. But whether they learnt the game in the back streets of a shanty town or at a private school, they got into good habits early on and when these were combined with their natural gifts of athleticism and hand-eye coordination, exceptional performance was the result. Batting isn't a natural activity – the natural way to hit a moving ball is to club it with a horizontal bat. Furthermore to hit a deviating, bouncing ball with a straight bat, you have to move your feet: compare cricket to games like softball and baseball. Some of my musician mates are dead-keen on the game and play social cricket but they find it hard because they were never taught the basics.

Top players see the ball early and hit it late. They have the ability to pick up the ball early, read the length of the delivery, which gives them time to get into the right position to deal with it. It's an ability which is more apparent against the quicks when a batsman appears to be less hurried than others and what's happening at 90mph looks as if it's in slow motion; but great players of spin like Javed and Zaheer get into position early then play the ball late using their dexterity with the bat handle. Playing late gives you more angles off the face of the bat with which to defeat field settings.

The greats are strong mentally: they have total determination combined with self-confidence which feeds on their success and becomes absolute. It shows in their body language: Greg Chappell marched onto the ground like a duke surveying his estates; Viv Richards struts and flexes like a prizefighter awaiting the bell; Sunny Gavaskar was serene; Miandad is completely relaxed, chattering and gesturing like a street hawker. But they all have that inner strength and ability to perform when the going gets tough.

Here are the best batsmen I've seen, in batting order, and a reserve line-up. I never saw Gary Sobers or Graeme Pollock, much to my regret, and I've left out players I didn't see in test matches except for Barry Richards. He was out on his own.

Barry Richards: The best batter I've ever seen. The first year I was in England I watched him knocking up before a game and the ball just zinged off the blade with natural timing. Playing Derek Underwood, a great bowler, he swept him where short fine leg would be so they moved slip there and he played the next one where slip had been. They say that in South Africa he once played an over using the edge of his bat. Watching him bat, I felt I was in the presence of an artist.

Sunil Gavasakar: I didn't see the best of him and never played against him in India but I watched him get 221 against England at the Oval and it was a superb innings. He was obviously a player of great class and his record against the West Indies is amazing. He was a beautiful leaver of the ball and his footwork was fantastic; he never committed himself too early.

Viv Richards: the hardest hitter of a cricket ball I've seen. I watched quite a lot of him in the 1976 series against England and he was absolutely magnificent. A player like Richards against some county attacks is an unfair contest – he just murders them. There were days when you turned up thinking "we'll chase a bit of leather today" but some players, and Richards in particular, make you chase further and more often than others. It was fun in a way watching him in the Sunday slog because you never knew what he'd do next.

Greg Chappell: a clinical, elegant player and a very tough, mean competitor. He had great balance and great presence: he carried himself in that ramrod-straight, aristocratic way that radiated total self-belief to the point of arrogance. His on-side play was amazing and you will never see a photograph of him off balance.

Javed Miandad: No one matches his relaxation out in the middle in a test – he could be sitting on a sofa in his front room. Despite that enviable demeanour, he concentrates very hard and is quite clinical in going about the task. He's also the cheekiest batsman I've come across. He takes the mickey out of bowlers, laughs at them. When a spinner is coming in to bowl he'll be calling "flight, flight, flight" at them or clicking his fingers, giggling away. He'll run the ball down to backward point for a single; there'll be no chance of a second but he'll pretend to be looking for two and call for it just to make the fielder hurry. He's a real streetfighter – anything goes – and opponents have to understand that's the way he's going to play it. He's been that way all his life and it makes him a tremendous competitor. He's not frightened to abuse bowlers if they have a go at him.

He has a tremendous eye and great eye-hand co-ordination and plays the ball very late, adjusting the bat at the last moment to angle the ball away, which makes him very effective in one-day cricket. Although he's so unorthodox in many ways, he does the basics just as all other good players do.

Allan Border: A real sticker, a real fighter – I love his mental toughness. If I had to pick someone to play for my life, I'd pick him. He carried Australia for a long time, particularly against the West Indies. He's another great player of spin because he uses his feet and isn't afraid to go over the top. He can hang in there and accumulate although he has a good range of shots and can take attacks apart in one-day cricket. He doesn't play the pretty shots but he picks the bad ball and puts it away every time. He's a fine cutter and sweeper and has great judgment of line. I think he's been underestimated: he combines resolution with superb technique and ability.

That's the top line-up. The next-best are:

Geoff Boycott: I never found him boring to watch because he was such a tremendous technician. Watching him play the quicks in the first hour of an innings was amazing – the way he could rotate the strike so that if the wicket was doing a bit, he'd face only one or two balls an over. I watched the way his hands and feet went, how he left the ball. Whatever they bowled, he seemed to have an answer to it. You felt he was like a big rock and it was going to take something exceptional to get rid of him.

Gordon Greenidge: An impressive player who's been almost overlooked in the West Indies because he's been in Richards' shadow. He was superb off the back foot and pretty lethal in county cricket. We always used to worry when he limped because that meant he'd get his head down. Sometimes he'd be hobbling so much, you'd think he couldn't hold a bat and he'd proceed to beat hell out of it.

Lawrence Rowe: a brilliant timer, smooth as silk and so relaxed – he used to sing or whistle to himself when he batted. The West Indians rated him very highly and he never really reached his full potential. I'm sure the New Zealand boys in 1972, who had the chance to study him at leisure in his fairly productive debut series, rated him too. His time at Derbyshire was marked by his intense dislike of the cold and it's said that he once wanted to bat in a fur coat. He also had injury problems and once had a fitness test on a green net wicket against Mike Hendrick and Alan Ward. The ball was flying everywhere and the other lads didn't want to know. Lawrence went in and proceeded to smash it around in grand style, then walked out of the net and said "I don't think I'm fit enough to play".

Martin Crowe: I'll discuss Hogan in a later chapter.

Alvin Kallicharran: a superb, compact little left hander who seemed very well-organised, and used his feet and played the hook well. Everything about him seemed so neat and comfortable, I used to think he must be exactly the right height and build for a batsman.

Clive Lloyd: he had a wonderful temperament, very phlegmatic. He used enormously heavy bats with five or six rubbers on the handle and could really punch it – fielding at extra cover to him was like being in a shooting gallery – which made him very effective in limited-overs cricket. He had a tremendous record as a captain and unquestionably had the best position from which to watch test cricket: a very fine first slip to the West Indian attack. A great character and tremendous bloke who became a legend in Lancashire.

Obviously the gap separating these players from one another and from a number of others is very small. One in particular I thought hard about was Zaheer Abbas. I've never seen a wristier player – it was extraordinary the way he could drive the ball that was going away from him: if he wasn't quite there, he'd delay the shot and hit it past point. He used to score bundles in county cricket especially if the tracks were flat. He'd just get in and make a meal of it.

He was very relaxed. Once I was getting psyched up before going into bat and having a pee at the same time when Z walked in. He looked at me and said "forget about it, smile, have a good time". I thought "is that your bloody secret?". He wasn't quite like that playing test cricket.

I saw a lot of Peter Kirsten and rated him very highly: he was one hell of a player, probably the most natural batsman I've ever played with. He was about 5ft 5in and we called him 'The little Don'. We had a lot of big stands together but we had different styles – I played forward to balls he played back to. He played all the shots and loved to cut – the spinners he'd cut really fine. He'd have 30 before you could blink and you'd wonder where they'd come from which is the sign of a very good player. I enjoyed batting with Kirsie more than anyone and we seemed to go well together: in 1982 he got 1941 runs at an average of 64 with eight tons, three of them doubles, and I got 1830 at 55.

He had plenty of coaching as a kid – a lot of English pros spent their winters in South Africa – and had been taught to 'throw' his hands at the ball. He used to grip the bat with the wrist of his top hand on the front of the handle, facing the bowler. Apparently Peter May had the same grip.

He could massacre bowling attacks. Against Glamorgan in 1980 I was run out for 94 in very unusual circumstances. I hit the ball back to the bowler Malcolm Nash who threated to throw the stumps down. I said "go on" so he let fly, winging it wide of the stumps and the wicketkeeper. I thought

Glenn Turner – definitely one of the 'greats'.

it had gone through so I took off but unfortunately slip stuck out his hand, grabbed it, and threw the wickets down with me halfway down the pitch and Kirsie wondering what the hell was going on. Peter went on to 213, getting his last 100 in 67 minutes and he flayed them. He'd get in and move the ball around for a while, then once he was set on a flat one, he'd really smack it. He was an exciting guy to play with and left an indelible impression on me because we played together so much. If he'd played test cricket, he would've been a world-class player.

I didn't see Glenn Turner face the quicks that much but he got heaps of runs as an opening bat so he must've handled them well. He had the stillest head so if he got a short one, he hardly had to move to avoid it. He was a great pacer, mover, and chipper of the ball and so methodical. His knock-up was like a check list: head, hands, feet. He was superb against off spin, chipping it through the on side and flat batting it if they bowled wide of off stump. Glenn, in my view, is definitely in the 'greats' category.

Doug Walters was a brilliant player, a typical product of hard wickets, playing the hook and cut and all the back foot shots. The English wickets simply didn't suit his game and he always struggled there.

David Gower is a beautiful player to watch. If you're fielding in the mid off/cover area to top players, the ball arrives a hell of a lot faster than you expect. Gower seems to caress the ball but it zings at you. He's copped a lot of stick about some aspects of his game with the critics saying he's too loose and flirts outside off stump. When he flirts outside off stump and wands it away for four, they wax lyrical and liken him to Frank Woolley – not that any of them saw Frank bat. If David had changed his game and tightened up, he would've been a different player and maybe not as good. He's performed very well – 7000-odd test runs – and given a lot of people a lot of pleasure and had almost as much criticism for being irresponsible as Boycott got for being over-cautious. You figure it out.

Ken McEwen, another South African in county cricket, was an incredibly effective player. In 1976 I batted with him for the Derrick Robins' XI against Kent. He made 160 and got the best part of them while I scored 50; I thought "Good gracious, I think we're playing different games here".

Then there were guys who maybe won't go down as greats in test cricket but were really rated on the county circuit: Keith Fletcher was a pro, a top player especially of spin. He used to play the ball very late and cut so well; Dennis Amiss was like Fletcher, the very best of the old pros. What a county cricketer! He never seemed to move his feet much but had very strong forearms and could hit the ball square of the wicket on both sides off the front foot. They said he had problems against quick bowling but he got a double hundred against the West Indies in 1976 when Holding was bowling like lightning. He was someone you always liked to see the back of. Graeme Gooch thrashed county bowlers and treated some test attacks pretty roughly without being able to do it consistently.

Lots of marvellous players have emerged from the Indian sub-continent: Asif Iqbal was amazingly quick between wickets and Majid Khan was just a beautiful player. He got a great century against us at Napier in 1979 – everything was so simplified and aristocratic.

Kris Srikkanth goes off like a firecracker, really takes you on, and it doesn't matter where you put the field. In one game Braces came on and we put mid on back straight away – he hit the first one over mid off for six. We put mid off back and he went for it again and cleared him comfortably. Mohammed Azharuddin started like a comet with three centuries in a row; he's another very wristy player like Zaheer. He has his own style which is completely unique, a wonderful player to watch.

You don't need a crystal ball to predict that Graeme Hick is going to be a great player. It's been said so often that he'll be the batsman of the nineties that he's now got an awful lot to live up to when he gets into the test arena. He reminds me of a guy teeing off with a one wood – the cleanest striker of a ball I've ever seen. His ability to hit boundaries off the back foot with what seem like defensive pushes is quite staggering.

The Aussies are very well served with players like Steve Waugh, Dean Jones, Mark Taylor and David Boon, all of whom are just entering their prime and already have impressive test records; Richie Richardson is a very good player in West Indian and Australian conditions and Desmond Haynes is an excellent opener.

The four great all rounders – Ian Botham, Imran Khan, Kapil Dev

Barry Richards – the best I've ever seen.
NZ HERALD

Sunil Gavaskar – sure and serene.
NZ HERALD

Viv Richards – 'Master Blaster'.
N.J. SMITH

Greg Chappell – clinical and elegant.
J.G. BLACKWELL

Javed Miandad – a modern-day genius.
J.G. BLACKWELL

Geoff Boycott – the technician.
NZ HERALD

Allan Border – the ultimate competitor.
D.O. NEELY

Gordon Greenidge – great to watch.
J.G. BLACKWELL

Lawrence Rowe – potentially the best of them all.
NZ HERALD

Alvin Kallicharran – competent and well organised.
NZ HERALD

Martin Crowe – number one Kiwi.
S.D. NEELY

Clive Lloyd – the ball stayed hit.
NZ HERALD

and Richard Hadlee – are all tremendous strikers. In many ways Kapil is the most exciting batsman of the lot: he plays with absolutely gay abandon and on flat wickets, mediocre bowlers had better look out. If you were to rank them as batters, you'd have to put Botham first, on his record, although he's not that great against the quicks. I love the way he plays. He used to come out in county cricket and behave as if it was a benefit match: the first ball was just as likely to go over the fence as back to the bowler. He has a lovely swing of the bat, hits it a mile, and can turn a game in half an hour. As batsmen I'd rank them this way: Botham, Khan, Kapil, Hadlee. Keep an eye on Imran – as his bowling has declined, he seems to have concentrated more on his batting and he's become very consistent. If he keeps going, he might sneak through. The young Botham would be near the top as a bowler but over the long haul Hadlee is out on his own followed by Imran.

Dropping a catch off a great batsman is not something you want to make a habit of. These guys make very few mistakes and if you don't capitalise on those they do make, you're in trouble. Drop someone like Boycott and you could be condemned to an extra day in the field. In Auckland in 1987 I dropped Gordon Greenidge after he'd got a century. He went on and got a double century. Playing Somerset, we missed the stumping chance off Viv Richards early on. A couple of our lads were injured so the Somerset twelfth man, David Gurr, was on the field. Viv, who still hadn't reached 20, went for a big one, miscued slightly, and it went straight to Gurr at long off, who dropped it. We couldn't believe it but the Somerset team out on the balcony were in fits of laughter. We got off lightly because he got a quick 80 then departed.

When you're talking about the great bats, it's fun to think about the not so great. At Derbyshire Devon Malcolm was one of those blokes who'd either hit it for six or miss it. Allan 'Jack' Warner wasn't a bad bat at seven or eight and would cream anything short. He had a quick bouncer – he hit me in the head twice when he was playing for Worcestershire – and if guys bounced him because he'd given them a few, they were likely to have to retrieve the ball from the car park. Nottinghamshire knew all about him and Franklyn Stephenson tried a double bluff: he raced in like a demon and gave Jack his slower ball which was a beauty – he held it back as if it was on a string. Jack had been expecting a bouncer first ball and he ducked what turned out to be a very slow full toss which arched gently over his hunched back and knocked out middle stump.

John Bracewell had a similar experience when he was clean bowled by Simon O'Donnell's slower ball in a one-day international versus Australia at Lancaster Park in 1990. When Braces entered the changing room a couple of lads left the room unable to contain their laughter while those remaining consciously and sensibly stopped themselves from even smiling. Braces sat absolutely still, silent and undisturbed for about 10 minutes. And then remarked to everyone he was looking forward to seeing himself on the television in the Minties advert.

CHAPTER SIXTEEN

Butterfingers

When I think of the countless hours I've spent fielding, I can't help wondering how I could have used that time if I hadn't been a cricketer. I could have made and lost a fortune or learnt everything there is to know about Canterbury rugby off by heart and won *Mastermind*. There are times, especially when you're playing in front of two men and a dog that would rather be out on the street sniffing a lamppost, when it's just a chore. Then you'll do anything – chat to the square leg umpire, have a laugh with your team mates, stir the batters up, have a yarn with the crowd (providing they can talk back), offer the dog some chewing gum.

I can remember the first catch I took in a competitive game of cricket. I'd gone to watch my father play for Kirwee in the Malvern competition and one of his team had to leave early – it was harvest time. I subbed for him and they sent me down to third man. They were playing on a concrete wicket and the inevitable happened: the batsman had a swipe, got a top edge, and the catch came my way. I caught it and one of the Kirwee players told me my father would buy me a raspberry drink on the way home as a reward. Dad said he hadn't dared to look. As the years have advanced and my agility declined, the New Zealand team often feels the same way when I'm getting under a catch.

Recently I've shelled a few that weren't too difficult – I've also clung on to a few blinders so I'm not sure what that proves about the ageing process. The sensation of taking an absolute stunner could be described as orgasmic – metaphorically speaking of course – but the other side of the coin is that there's absolutely nothing worse than muffing a catch. It makes me feel like giving the whole thing away. It's not so bad if it's a really difficult chance – diving, one-handed, trying to drag in something travelling like a shell – but dropping a sitter is a horrible feeling. You have the feeling that everyone – the captain, your team, the crowd, the media, certainly the TV cameramen – are focusing on you and there's nowhere to hide. If you've got a duck, you can sulk in the sanctuary of the dressing room, but when you drop a dolly, you just can't get away from the waves of hostility and derision which come at you from all sides.

Keeping for the First XI.

The poor old captain might've been working on a plan, moving the field around, putting pressure on the batsman trying to force him into a mistake. You've been put in a particular position to complete the trap. Then up goes a regulation catch, the batsman is all but walking off, and you grass it. The crowd goes crazy, yelling comments like "get a bag" and worse and a ripple of something very close to hatred runs through your team mates. Bowlers are seldom sympathetic: I can remember Richard Collinge roaring "get that man out of there" after a slip fielder put down his second of the day. After you've shelled one, you're expecting some attention from the crowd and sensitive souls can find themselves picking up derisive comments they wouldn't normally notice.

In a World Series one-day match at Adelaide, we were defending 190-odd and had the Aussies in a bit of trouble. David Hookes hit an absolute gift to me at mid wicket off Jerry Coney – I just had to run back a few paces and take it. Adelaide is Hooksey's home ground so the whole crowd wanted me to drop it and I didn't disappoint them. They roared their heads off and the team looked at me with pure disgust, as if I was a leper. I felt so stupid, as if I should have been on the beach trying to catch a frisbee rather than playing international cricket. I just wanted to disappear.

Not long afterwards Richard Hadlee dismissed Hookes, I caught Kim Hughes at mid off, and we won the game so it was a let off – it could've been so different. Everyone says "forget about it," "don't let it get you down," "no one tries to drop a catch" – all the old sayings – but you're thinking suicidal thoughts. I once dropped Greg Chappell in a one-day international and he went on to get a century. We still managed to win so afterwards I claimed my fumble added to the day's entertainment value.

Dropped catches – particularly skiers – can have their own entertainment value. There'd be few better examples than Tony Blain's attempt to catch Ian Botham at the Oval in 1986. Botham had an almighty slog and hit the ball virtually straight up in the air. It was up there for so long that we could've held a team meeting and cut cards to decide who'd catch it but the sensible thing in these situations is for the 'keeper to step forward, which Blainy did. He paced up and down underneath it like an expectant father but the ball fell to earth untouched by human hand. When someone holds on to a skier, their relief is palpable: a slight tremble, moist palms, the face drained of blood. Colin Tunnicliffe at Derbyshire would produce an imaginary hypodermic needle and say "let's give him some blood".

In last season's Napier test Danny Morrison bounced Mohammed Azharuddin as soon as he came in and it seemed obvious to us that he gloved it to leg gully. He was their key batsman and we were furious when Steve Woodward gave him not out. Aza was a bit ruffled and on five tried to hit Martin Snedden over mid wicket and sent a very simple chance my way which was declined with regret. It was probably the easiest catch I've dropped in test cricket. I thought it might look harder on TV but the replay only emphasised the very low degree of difficulty. He was 30-odd at stumps and I was completely brassed off with myself and even more so with Woodward. Next morning Aza started off well but then Danny bowled him for 33. As I ran to congratulate Danny I said to Steve: "You and I are the most relieved people on this ground mate." "Yes Wrighty," he said, "but yours was easier than mine." Steve certainly put me in my place.

My problem is that I was never taught to catch correctly. I take the half-cupped approach which isn't too crash-hot technically speaking. It's one thing to get yourself into position for the catch but then you have to get your hands in the right position and I've paid for not being technically sound in that department. I've never been supple so I've had to throw myself around and do a lot of diving, which has been the subject of many taunts along the lines of "who does your washing?" Bill Alley, the umpire, once said that he'd never seen a bloke who spent so much time on his knees, adding: "You're not in church y'know".

There's a seniority factor governing who gets put in which fielding positions: rule number one is that the youngest bloke in the team is the sacrificial lamb at bat/pad. When I arrived at Derbyshire, Eddie Barlow put me there straight away. It wasn't a problem to Mike Hendrick but a different story with the spinners: English batsmen tend to sweep a lot, even from outside off stump, and there were no helmets in those days so I had a torrid time. I got 20 catches that season, certainly my best tally, but at the end of it I had no hesitation in telling them what they could do with the box and shin pads. I've never been back there since. When the left arm spinner Ray East first came into the Essex side, he was made to troop from

Got 'im – to everyone's amazement.

JOHN KNIGHT

third man at one end to fine leg at the other. Finally he got sick of it and borrowed a bicycle to make the journey.

It's not just the batsmen you have to worry about: in England in 1986 Brian 'Basil' Barrett nearly cleaned up Ken Rutherford when he lost control of one of his quicker deliveries and speared it way down legside. Kenny immediately decided that he should be saving the single rather than positioned for a catch. The proximity of a bat/pad fieldsman tells you how confident and aggressive he is – the gung-ho like to get in real close and spit at you and it's obviously a great position to sledge from. It's generally not a position with long-term occupants although Gus Logie has done the job brilliantly for the West Indies. In the West Indies we came across a bloke called Simmons who was about six foot three, didn't wear a helmet, and stopped everything. It was like batting in the nets.

Slip is the most important fielding position in test cricket. Jeff Crowe at first and Jerry Coney at second stand out as our best slippers. Lance Cairns liked to stand at third or fourth chewing a piece of grass. It's a great place to have a chat: out in the covers or mid off can be quite lonely and you can spend whole days without human contact. Square leg is okay because you can chat to the umpire and you'll often notice a fieldsman placed a few yards behind or forward of square ending up right next to the umpire. I'd love to field in the slips, both for the social life and the lack of physical exertion, but my back just can't take the crouching. Now and again I wheedle my way into fourth slip for a bit of social intercourse.

Some slips have a game called Blind Man's Bluff: it involves the slips keeping their eyes closed till they hear the sound of bat on ball. It's a high risk game and not for the hard of hearing. The Derbyshire slips sometimes had funny faces competitions as the bowler was running in, which can't have helped the bowlers' concentration. One Derbyshire slip fielded for an over – at Lord's of all places – with his plonker out in the fresh air; it's not something you'd do if the game was on TV. It certainly gave new meaning to the phrase 'a member of the MCC.' The rest of the team wondered why he'd exposed himself to ridicule.

I quite like gully but I tend to be a bit of a snatcher which is okay when the ball is hit wide of me but not so good when it comes straight to me. I dropped David Boon on 76 in the gully at Perth in 1989. He really nailed it and I got a hand to it and tipped it away for a couple of runs. Boon went on to 200.

Believe it or not, a clear blue sky makes high catches much harder to judge than if there are clouds about. Clouds seem to give you a point of reference and make it easier to get a fix on the ball. At Derbyshire Bob Taylor used to say "blue sky today lads, we'll practise the high ones." The white balls used in limited-overs cricket are harder to pick up than the red balls and seem to arrive a lot quicker. At night, if there's a bit of dew about, they gain pace off the turf. It's difficult to adjust to them if you use them only three or four times a year.

It's easy to tell the standard of cricket you're watching by checking out

We had to dig him out – Andrew Jones at Bangalore.
J.G. BLACKWELL

'The Claw' at practice.

the deployment of the field. The finer fine leg is and the closer to the wicket keeper, the lower the level. Slips are another giveaway: you're not watching anything too serious if they're well-upholstered men of advancing years, particularly if they leave lit cigarettes on the ground behind them and take a drag between balls.

The finest outfielder I've seen is the West Indian Roger Harper. Peter Kirsten was a brilliant cover as was Derek Randall who was cat-like in his agility and anticipation. The Australians put in a lot of work on it and their standard now is very high. In New Zealand teams Ken Rutherford, Martin Crowe and Mark Burgess stand out.

The Indians and Pakistanis are good close-in fielders because of their quick reactions and their suppleness, which enables them to stay down. That's critical: you mustn't anticipate the shot and stand up as the ball is played – you stay down and wait for it. Cliff Dickeson, the Northern Districts left arm spinner, was known as 'Dog' and fielded at short leg a lot. If the ball went past him because he stood up too soon, Lance Cairns would growl "Siddown Dog". It sounded like something from *A Dog's Show.*

CHAPTER SEVENTEEN

Silver Fern

As a New Zealander playing county cricket alongside two South Africans, I always felt that guys on the circuit rated South Africans but reckoned New Zealanders, while they might be able to play a bit, weren't that special. Eddie Barlow said our 1978 side didn't seem to be very organised and thought it must be hard to play good cricket in such a set-up. He was right: we lost three out of three and a couple of years later went to Australia and lost two tests in three days.

The side's attitude has developed. We've realised we can be consistently successful and the players have confidence in their own ability and that of their team mates. There's a lot more discipline in the side and that applies to all facets: touring, fitness, training and so on.

The attitude of touring teams in New Zealand has changed. In 1979 we lost the first test to Pakistan who were without their Packer players. You could see from the way they practised before the second test that they thought they were going to stuff us three nil. The West Indies came the following season, after hammering Australia, expecting a doddle. It's not that way anymore. A test draw a decade or so ago was appreciated as much as a win is now but that's a natural progression. Now we're getting to an even higher level where the players have the confidence to express themselves, back their own ability, and go out to dominate the opposition and guys new to the test scene feed off that and are not overawed.

People recognise us now. It started with the World Series in Australia in 1982. The first time it happened to me was when I was walking down the street in Papatoetoe and an old lady came up and told me how much she'd enjoyed the games in Australia. It gave me a hell of a fright.

Another spin-off of success is the much higher media profile the top players have; in my view this can be a double-edged sword when players criticise team mates in their newspaper columns. I'd hope they could sort it out over a beer or even with a few punches if they felt that strongly rather than publicly sniping at each other. If you're playing for New Zealand, you should be in it as a team, together.

Benefits are an excellent innovation, especially for the bread-and-butter players and the great provincial servants who never quite made it to the top. I hope benefits are handled sensibly to ensure the goose which lays the golden egg isn't killed in its infancy and that players with the greatest need get rewarded. For instance, benefits should be confined to the beneficiary's home province.

Professionalism is not a dirty word. It is not just about money – although there is quite a lot more of that around now – it's about the whole approach. We compete much harder and players coming into the side are expected to have that approach. Guys who go out and let themselves down the night before a big game just don't play.

Against Australia in 1985 and England in 1986 we were the better organised team, we warmed up better, we were more professional. We've had some good sides in the past – the team that drew the series in the West Indies in 1972 was a tremendous side. We're probably not better cricketers than they were but the set-up has improved.

The money comes into it in the sense that if you're being paid, you've made the decision to be a cricketer. You can't just slope off back to the job if things aren't going well; you've got to hang in and perform. Players earning their living out of the game are much more committed. We get more help from the Cricket Council: there are fitness programmes and the tab for training facilities is picked up.

Even the provincial set-ups are becoming much more professional and have full-time executives to run things.

The competitive attitude goes right through the team. It means you don't give your wicket away even if you're a tailender; it means you chase everything in the field. There'll always be some players who are tougher than others but a hard side is one which never stops competing no matter what the state of the game, who they're playing against, what the conditions are, or what the media are saying about them. A good competitor is someone who always keeps coming back.

We don't back off from aggro anymore; we expect it. The media has made a lot of fuss about other teams' behaviour – the Pakistanis for example – but we give as good as we get. John Bracewell seems to be regarded by the public as our hard man and leading sledger but there are a number of guys in the team who are just as hard but perhaps less obvious about it.

The side has been stable, which builds confidence. All selectors make mistakes but generally selection has been good starting with Frank Cameron and carried on by Don Neely and his panel. They've been sound and sensible; mistakes have been made but that solid core has always been there.

But in the end the players have to do the job on the park. Over the time I've played, the focus – particularly overseas – has been on Hadlee and now Crowe but we've had a lot of players whose quality has never really been recognised: Edgar, Reid, Coney, Smith, Bracewell, Boock, Lees, Jones, Cairns, Chatfield, Snedden and Troup plus the young guys coming through like Greatbatch, Watson, Thomson, and Morrison. It's a long list and a talented one. You only have to check out the various performance-based

The Boys from Brazil.

world rankings to see how well these guys have performed compared with their modest international reputations.

That has its advantages: by and large we've avoided the superstar syndrome. Some of the other teams seem to have lots of stars; we've had ours but never a constellation. Often our guys have been as good as the so-called stars. Teams full of stars tend not to knit together because everyone can be more concerned with their own performance than the team's, something that becomes more pronounced when the going gets tough. Our sense of playing for our country is pretty strong and so is the Aussies' but there've been English teams who gave the impression they were playing for their bank balances rather than England.

It's important to have a happy side. That doesn't necessarily mean everyone gets on wonderfully well but the key thing is that they respect each other as players and be positive to one another in a cricketing sense. They put aside personalities and function as a competitive team.

The only time there's ever been strife has been when guys started getting too big for their boots and too big for the team. Although we have personality clashes, we don't have the cultural and class differences you can get in English, Indian and Pakistani teams nor the regional rivalries of some West Indian and Australian teams. We might support different rugby teams but first and foremost, we're Kiwis and Kiwis generally get on pretty well with each other. If they don't, they try to, and if that doesn't work, the stirrer responsible gets ostracised.

Togetherness.

CHAPTER EIGHTEEN

Take me to your leaders

The first time I ran across Geoff Howarth the thing that struck me was that he was a very snappy dresser. He was the first cricketer I saw wearing buckle shoes. It was at the 1970 Brabin tournament – Jeremy Coney probably played in it as well. Geoff was the Auckland captain and was obviously one of the young glamour boys of New Zealand cricket.

Then in 1975/76 I started playing with him for Northern Districts – he, Roddy Fulton and I had all been brought there by John Guy. Geoff made a habit of being tough with young players and I got the treatment too but as soon as he rated you a bit, he was okay. He was a likeable bloke and we got on well. He was a dasher then and I think he was really always a dasher. He was a gifted, elegant player who had style and a hint of mischief – he always had a twinkle in his eye.

He wasn't a big trainer and his temperament wasn't suited to county cricket. Although he loved being in England and in many ways felt more comfortable there, his results show that he wasn't really suited to the grind.

He hadn't been all that successful in test cricket when I came on the scene in 1978. He'd been a bit of a rebel and hadn't had a good tour of India and Pakistan in 1976/77 but probably neither the countries nor the team policy agreed with him. I think he found India and Pakistan pretty intolerable.

He struggled in the first two tests of that 1977/78 series against England and the third test in Auckland was crunch time for him. He got a hundred in each innings. He was pretty determined and Eden Park suited him because he was a good slow-wicket player. During the intervals he didn't say much, just sat and smoked, which was very unlike him. He was certainly more tense than I'd ever seen him playing for ND. After that, his test career took off: he went to England in 1978 as vice-captain under Mark Burgess and played brilliantly, then took over the captaincy in 1979/80. He also became ND captain that year and had an amazing season: ND won the limited-overs competition and the Shell Trophy and we beat the West Indies. Geoff's batting in that series was probably as good as it ever was. From that game at Eden Park in 1978 through to the series against India in 1981 he played magnificently and scored six test centuries. He played very straight and timed the ball rather than forced it and when he was going, he was one of the most attractive batsmen in the game.

When Geoff became New Zealand captain, he took over a pretty young side with one victory under its belt – England in 1978. The West Indies in Dunedin in 1980 was number two. Apart from Geoff and Richard Hadlee most of us were trying to establish ourselves and we were a close-knit team. Geoff was very positive and said with real conviction that we were good enough to win. Paddles cottoned on to the 'win' theme and reinforced it. Geoff had played plenty of cricket, a lot of it as captain, had good cricket knowledge, and was a reasonable communicator in the team context. He wasn't really a 'strong' individual in the sense of being the boss, running a tight ship, and being a bit aloof from the rest of us. He was really just one of the guys.

He did a fine job in Australia in 1980/81 and the Aussies rated him. We lost the series 2-0 but did well in the one-day series where he really established himself. He was an excellent tactical captain in one-day cricket.

Geoff always appeared calm and confident but he was actually quite a nervous person. At the Oval in 1983 he came down the wicket after facing his first over and said "pat me between the shoulders because I feel like throwing up". To his credit he was able to overcome his nerves and perform.

Captaining New Zealand meant more to him than it would to most people because cricket was, and still is, Geoff Howarth's life. He did it for the right reasons – not to further himself but because he felt it was a great honour to captain New Zealand. To beat England at Headingley in 1983, the first time we'd won a test there, we needed 101 in the fourth innings. Bruce Edgar got out at 11 and Geoff came in and smashed a quick 20. I'd run him out in the first innings, really sold him down the river when he was batting beautifully, but typically he didn't make a word of complaint. He got out at 40, I went at 60 and Martin Crowe went straight away which made us 60 for four. By then we were both sitting on the balcony, smoking as fast as we could breathe. He said to me: "Shake, I don't give a shit what else happens as long as we win this one." Because he'd played a lot in England where they'd never really rated us, it meant so much to him and I felt that too. I enjoyed being his vice-captain.

He had a lot of style, panache and genuine leadership qualities and I think New Zealand cricket owes him a lot. On tour all he had as back-up was a manager – there were no cricket managers or physios – so he didn't have the support captains have had in recent years. He enjoyed a few drinks and cigarettes and should've trained harder, but he more than anyone got New Zealand moving up the ladder and he did it because he was a very good judge of the game. He picked the players he wanted and played the way he wanted.

His spell influenced everything that followed. He rated Ian Smith ahead of Warren Lees, and didn't place much emphasis on spin bowlers which

The captain returns.

Geoff Howarth and Viv Richards toss at Antigua.

BROOKS-LA TOUCHE

limited the chances of Steve Boock and John Bracewell. Some players disapproved of his enthusiasm for having a good time – he was a great admirer of the fairer sex – but he had the pro's attitude in that he did what he wanted off the park and knew what he was doing on it. He related well to the media and developed a high profile here and overseas.

Towards the end Geoff didn't work hard enough to be a top-level performer. He was always very much a touch player and he needed to work consistently on his game to retain it. He called a spade a spade and alienated a few players: if he thought a bowler should come off or someone shouldn't play, that was that. A few people in the side felt he was too much the English pro and didn't place enough emphasis on developing team spirit. He wasn't a great communicator on a one-to-one basis.

In some ways he was a victim of his own success. He took a young average side and turned them into winners and suddenly there was a 'we know better than you' syndrome. When he departed, the side was at its peak with a hard core of seven or eight mature players at the height of their individual powers backed up by people who'd learnt the ropes of test cricket and were starting to perform. If he'd kept going for a couple more years, the results would have been just the same and he would've retired as one of the all-time great captains.

Things probably came to a head in the West Indies where he didn't train hard enough. Captaincy wears you out and everybody has a few drinks during a tour but this time it was under the eye of Frank Cameron, the chairman of selectors, who was there ostensibly as assistant manager. The atmosphere in the team had changed and certain players who'd become household names were dissatisfied and were manoeuvreing to get rid of him. I thought Geoff had made a mistake in not going to Pakistan in 1984/85. He returned for the home series against Pakistan, then went to the West Indies where things just sort of snowballed. In hindsight it wasn't a bad tour – we drew two tests but lost the series 2-0 whereas a few sides have gone there and lost everything. Geoff also got an 80 in what turned out to be his last test dig but neither that nor the reasonable result saved him.

People – and I've done it myself – always think they can make a better job of the captaincy than the bloke who's doing it but I never felt that way when Geoff was skipper. I reckoned that making the right tactical decisions was what it was all about and he did that. He was strong enough to play the way he wanted and to pursue his own selection hunches; in the end he made the mistake of not paying enough attention to his own game and his fitness – his booze and cigarette intake meant his V02 level probably never matched that of a healthy asthmatic. Maybe he let his game drift because he felt the captaincy was enough.

His exit was premature and badly handled although you don't expect too much sensitivity in international sport. Before the team for the 1985 Australian tour was announced, Geoff had dinner with two senior members of the cricket council. They knew Geoff had been axed and sat there listening to him talk about how he planned to take on the Aussies.

I found it hard to adjust to being Jerry Coney's vice-captain because I was disappointed at not getting the nod myself, having been vice-captain for four years. I was a pro, away half the year, and I made mistakes as vice-captain. It didn't help our relationship despite the fact Jerry and I were good mates when he first came into the team.

In Pakistan in 1984 he wasn't strong tactically but he was very good off the field, almost the opposite of Geoff. Tactically he needed back-up but off the field he related well to players. He couldn't stand losing, especially to some countries, and his toughness in that respect was good. Sometimes he'd say "I don't like these blokes and I don't see why we should lie down for them." He was extremely fortunate to take over the side when he did because we would've beaten Australia and England in 1985/86 no matter what. He found it difficult in Pakistan – who doesn't – but in the end he was probably the most successful New Zealand captain.

He was a tremendous cricketer, a great fighter, and a great competitor. He and Eddie Barlow would be the best slip fielders I've ever played with – he had a beautiful pair of hands. He underrated himself as a bowler and when he became captain he didn't bowl himself enough. He'd be one of the few cricketers who've bowled a pine cone in a major cricket match – he bowled one to me for a bet in a Wellington versus Northern Districts one dayer at Gisborne.

He was a very resourceful batsman and although he probably didn't work any harder on his game than Geoff, he was probably more talented and better at pulling it out when it mattered. He is a very talented person, good at squash and volleyball and a good musician. He'd learnt the basics of cricket early and was technically sound. He tended to play off the back foot more than most Kiwis, which made him watch the ball very closely, and he played straight.

He could bat two ways – defend for long periods or take the attack to the bowlers, which he did in the 1986 series against Australia where he played really well. There were times when perhaps he should have batted higher in the order although he was tailor-made to be a test number six: if the early life had gone out of the wicket and the bowlers had lost their edge, he could take advantage and if we were in strife, he could defend. He could improvise, adjust his game, and he was a much more natural cricketer than people appreciated.

His five-year banishment to the wilderness is one of the enduring mysteries of New Zealand cricket. Some of the powers at the time gave the impression of being more concerned about the whiteness of his pads and boots: at that stage he wasn't the smartest looking cricketer you ever saw. He probably didn't perform as well as he was capable of for a while after his initial breakthrough, but he'd demonstrated that he had the temperament and he was far too valuable a resource to waste.

The period when he and Glenn Turner ran the team was our most successful. I found it difficult as vice-captain because they were very close which meant I wasn't really involved. We'd have an open wicket practice

Great expectations.

"Jerry, I think they've got us by the . . ."
J.G. BLACKWELL

Automatic pilot.

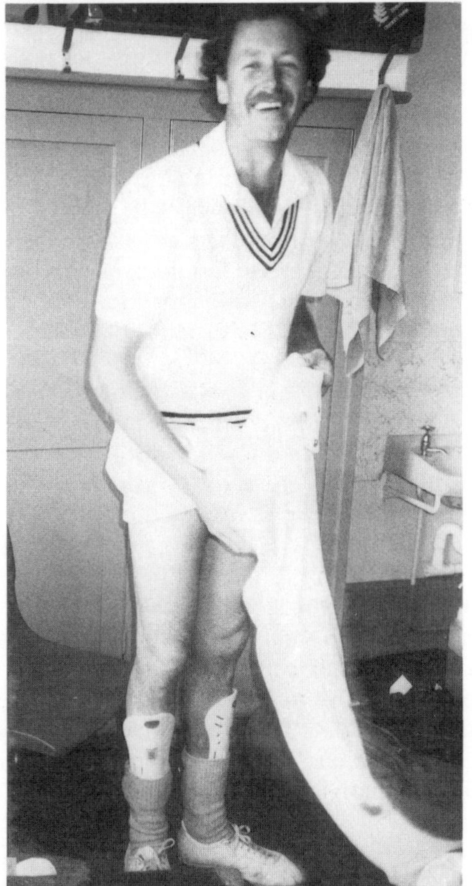

'The Mantis.'

and while Jerry was off doing something else, Glenn would set the fields.

Turner was very good tactically. He did send advice out at drinks breaks and to some extent ran things from the sideline, which Richard Hadlee criticised. But the thing about Jerry and Turns was that their formula worked – they were very successful and that's the bottom line. Jerry would've been a fool not to be guided by Glenn and Glenn wouldn't have been doing his job as a cricket manager if he hadn't got involved. Richard, great bowler that he is, has never captained sides at the top level and until you do, you have no idea of what's involved. I say that as someone who was vice-captain for eight years and knows better than most.

A cricket team really is a team and that includes the physio and the cricket manager. Jerry was not strong on tactics and Turner's input was significant in that area. It doesn't really matter how results are achieved; what's important is that you get them. The captain gets a lot of praise when things go well and cops it when things go badly.

Although the team atmosphere was not always enjoyable and now and again I had to act as an intermediary between one or two of the players and Jerry and Glenn, a lot of the enjoyment in top sport comes from winning. You can score a century but if you've lost, you'll be celebrating on your own.

People talk a lot about motivation but you shouldn't need to motivate people at this level. Any sportsman who has reached international level has shown that he has the ability to motivate himself. If a team lacks the desire to win you have a real problem. Half the time is spent keeping guys from getting each other's backs up because they're so keen to blame someone other than themselves if things go wrong.

Brian McKechnie said he enjoyed the company of rugby players more than cricketers because cricketers had a habit of putting the knife into each other. You have to get them to focus on their own performance. Turner argued that you didn't need to foster team spirit because international players should be professional, self-reliant and should direct their energies into their own performances; if they produce the goods, the rest – success and therefore team spirit – would follow.

Bob Cunis and I believe more in the importance of team spirit. Every leader has his own approach which will suit some more than others. Turner's approach was fine for some players and he put in a lot of time with and related well to our stars – Martin Crowe and Richard. But people who aren't extraordinary players and who feel human things like nervousness and lack of self-confidence can be helped by realising their team mates are going through the same thing. Some guys are strong enough not to give a toss about team spirit, not to need support from their colleagues, but others need the team situation. Kiwis respond to the situation where we're playing for others rather than just for ourselves. People have to look inward but once they lose motivation, they have to be brought out of themselves and made to realise the importance of playing for their country.

At the end of the day cricket is a team game although it depends on a lot of individual performances. Once a player has made a commitment to be part of a side, there are certain standards he has to adhere to, like not letting his team mates down and giving 120 percent. There's nothing worse than playing alongside a guy who's taking the soft option, who doesn't compete, and who'll collapse when the going gets tough. The paradox is that some of the best people in a crisis aren't the best team men.

As Richie Benaud says, captaincy is 90 percent luck. There was a lot of fuss made about how our victory in Brisbane in 1985 was carefully planned but in fact it was pretty simple: we won the toss, stuck them in on a green one under a cloudy sky, and Paddles bowled unbelieveably well. We had the same field most of the time and we caught well and rolled them. We got a reasonable start when we batted, then John Reid got a good hundred and Hogan batted magnificently. Both Jerry and Glenn deserved credit – Glenn for instance spent a lot of time with Richard, working on bowling to lefthanders – but that particular game was a case of us having the best of the conditions and of a few individuals performing heroics.

The strength of the opposition has a big bearing on results. England in 1978 and 1983 were certainly a lot stronger than they were in 1986 and the same could be said of Australia. If you compare the 1985 and 1987 tours of Australia, all three tests in 1985 were played on result wickets. We won the toss in Brisbane and Perth suited us. In 1987 we lost the toss in Brisbane, Adelaide was always going to be a draw, and we were unlucky not to have got a win in Melbourne, which would have put Jeff Crowe's captaincy in a different light.

Jeff was tactically sound and had a good attitude and he was great to work with as a vice-captain. It was just a shame he had the batting blues, especially as he's not as relaxed and laid-back as people think he is. It must've been hard for him on that Australian tour as he'd played a lot of cricket there. I always found that playing for New Zealand in England put me under added pressure to perform.

His batting is a mixture: he tends to get very square and probably found it hard to adjust coming back from Australia – I think he may have got caught a bit betwixt and between the two countries. He's got a good temperament and is a good man to come in at six because he's hard to dislodge and sticking around without scoring many doesn't worry him. He plays the short ball well and got a good century against the West Indies, taking advantage of a follow-on situation – he really took it to them.

The game is very important to Jeff but there's more to life than cricket. He's a very keen golfer and squash player and enjoys himself off the field: when he retires, he'll probably write a book on Australian red wines and the curry houses of England. Being such a level-headed guy enabled him to cope well with his disappointments and bounce back.

CHAPTER NINETEEN

King Dick

My father played cricket for Malvern and on Christchurch show weekend they'd come into town to play a city club. One year the game was at Hagley Park where a cousin of mine was playing in a trial match for the Canterbury third-grade primary school rep team. They were a man short so I played, without whites – I was in standard four and had never played in a competitive game of cricket – and made 28 retired. In the afternoon I went to the circus.

I ended up being picked for that team and we went down to Ashburton on a bus to play Mid Canterbury at the Ashburton Domain. I got run out for two and took a couple of catches in the gully but the thing that made the biggest impression on me that day was a skinny kid playing in the first grade rep match on the next wicket who bowled like the wind. I wondered how anyone could bowl that fast – especially as he was the only bloke on the ground who had skinnier legs than me. It was my first sighting of R.J. Hadlee.

I next ran into him six or seven years later playing for Christ's College against Christchurch Boys' High. I was a fifth former; he was a seventh former with a hell of a reputation. Our openers were Donald McDonald, who was a New Zealand schoolboy rep, and Roddy Fulton and they whacked Richard all over the park. When I went in at number six, he was off a short run but he was still much quicker than anyone else I'd faced. Even then he had an incredibly good action. He was also a very good bat and definitely the star of the side.

The next time I faced him I was 17 playing for the New Zealand Brabin side against Canterbury B. He opened with Ken Ferries and was very quick but I managed to get 90-odd. During that game he was called into the Canterbury team to make his first-class debut. He was one of those guys who always stood out, who had the ability and was going to make the big time.

The thing about him is that he's a natural, born to play cricket. He comes from a great cricketing family: Walter, Barry who was a fine player, and Dayle, who was a gritty performer. It was a great shame Dayle had to come home from the 1978 tour of England with a back problem. I'd have liked to have done a tour with him – in the short time I saw him, he really impressed me. He didn't muck about and at that stage seemed to be meaner and tougher than Richard.

He couldn't have had a more cricket-oriented upbringing and having all those brothers who were good was an advantage. Walter did a great coaching job on the grass wicket in their back yard. Richard and Martin Crowe are similar in that both were obviously taught the sound principles of cricket so that even before they got anywhere near being recognised, they were doing most things right. I envy them that. You can make minor adjustments later on but it's difficult to correct a major fault by the time you reach your twenties, especially if you're playing a lot of cricket. Many habits are formed in the back yard and Richard and Martin were taught the basics well, refining their techniques and mental attitudes along the way.

I faced Richard in my first first-class game and started playing with him in 1978. In my debut test he bowled out England on the Basin Reserve and he'd already done the same to India. In those days he ran in a fair way and his action was a bit different and he was very, very quick. In the second innings he seemed to gather inspiration from Rock Collinge bowling Boycott and he responded well to the crowd, which wasn't huge but really got behind us. Throughout his career he's responded to dramatic situations, particularly at Eden Park.

He was our spearhead and bowled well through that series although Ian Botham gave him a bit of a pounding in Christchurch. He was becoming a world-class player and doing a hell of a lot of bowling for us. At that stage he was expected to get results and if he didn't, the team suffered. Instead of looking at their own performances, some people pointed the finger at him.

After the 1978 tour he was invited to join Essex, which he turned down and ended up with Nottinghamshire. At first he got smacked around in county cricket but he soon came to terms with it and never looked back. He came back from England for the 1978/79 series against Pakistan and bowled beautifully, did Imran like a dinner. England had worked out for him. He loved playing cricket, and had great enthusiasm and appetite for the game so he enjoyed being a professional. It also brought him on as a cricketer – he learnt to run off the wicket and his bowling improved. It was great for him and New Zealand cricket. He had so much ability but he needed two or three years of county cricket to get the best out of himself. He felt at home in England and the impact he made can be judged from Geoff Boycott's remark that if Yorkshire changed its policy on overseas players, the one he'd want was Hadlee.

When Richard became a pro it made life a hell of a lot easier for the other pros – myself, John Parker, Geoff Howarth – to deal with the NZCC, some of whose members were anti-professional. They typecast pros as poor team men who'd been changed through over-exposure to Pommie professionals and were looking after number one.

Then came the short run. When he first used it against Australia at the Basin Reserve in 1982, it caused an almighty stir. There'd been a lot of rain and Australia didn't bat till the fifth day. There were board members mumbling that it was ridiculous and a lot of players were uncomfortable: it just didn't look right – our spearhead bowling off a short run. In the second test he went back off the long run, skittled the Aussies, and we gained a tremendous victory.

The idea must have come from the demands of county cricket. It was a big decision but there was no way he would have survived for long over there bowling off 25 yards – look at the English bowlers. It was a logical and realistic decision and you've got to admire the guy for thinking it through. What he learned to do was utilise every yard of his run to achieve the same momentum and rhythm he got from the long run. There were plenty of people who thought he was taking the easy option, turning himself into a medium pacer when we already had a country full of them; that instead of being a strike bowler, he'd bowl medium pace dobbers. A lot of guys in the team thought that too.

Early on he was a bit woolly round the edges and had no-ball problems at times. He used to get a bit disheartened when things weren't going his way and he wouldn't put as much into his bowling as the team wanted from him. He's never been emotional but he just wasn't as professional as he became and didn't have the goal setting to motivate him. Later he realised that he had to have the ball in his hand to get wickets – and if he could he'd bowl right through the innings.

That tendency to get a bit down re-surfaced briefly before the second test against Australia at Christchurch in 1985/86. He felt like a rest. He'd just taken his 300th test wicket, he felt knackered and he had a niggling injury he wanted to clear up. Frank Cameron and I had to chat to him and convince him that it was vital that he played. I don't think he was ever not going to play; he just needed to be talked into it. But needing to be talked into playing shows that he wasn't in the ideal frame of mind to go into a test match. He went out and bowled 44 overs, took seven for 116, and nine wickets in the match. I wondered how many blokes could take seven wickets in a test innings after having had to be cajoled into playing. Mind you, he did get a duck so maybe it was his batting he wasn't happy with.

He was quite disillusioned for a period in the early 1980s and got involved with Grahame Felton, a Christchurch sports psychologist. One of the things that emerged from that process was the goal setting which has helped him enormously. He's played for a long time and had a lot of success but he's never dropped his standards and he's become a great achiever of targets. He's into competing over a series with his counterpart in the opposition. He's always backing a winner of course and some of his pairings are a bit suspect. He'll say "you take Boycott and I'll take Pringle". He's not one to miss an opportunity either: if he's got three wickets and there's just nine, ten and jack to go, he'll be very keen to get the ball in his hands and he'll probably bowl quicker than at any stage of the innings.

I didn't mind facing him in county cricket and he didn't used to like

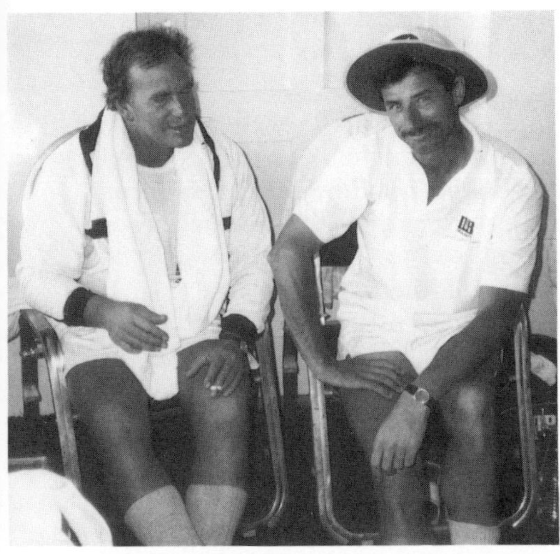

"In my day, Richard, we bowled . . ."

The thoroughbred.

"No, Paddles, it's your shout."
J.G. BLACKWELL

The legs aren't what they used to be!
J.G. BLACKWELL

bowling to left handers. He couldn't get his line right – he used to bowl middle stump swinging in. I obviously couldn't take him lightly but I was able to work him through midwicket. In Australia in 1985 Glenn Turner spent a lot of time with him – Glenn related well to great players; he probably felt he wasn't wasting his time with them.

Paddles and I had the first game off – against Queensland Country – and he spent a lot of time bowling to me in the nets. Turns got him to get in close to the stumps and now he gets in closer than anyone I've ever seen; his balance enables him to do that. If you're bowling wicket to wicket, you'll tend to bowl down a line the batsman has to play but if you bowl from two feet wide of the stumps, the batsman can leave a lot of deliveries because you have to move it so much to get it on line.

Richard became like Dennis Lillee, continually putting the ball in the danger zone and making the batsman play. His accuracy is unbelievable for a fast bowler. Glenn also got him to change his line to left handers, getting in close to the wicket and bowling off stump and just outside. If the ball seams back in, the batsman is vulnerable to lbws; if it moves away, he risks snicking it. In the Brisbane test he got nine wickets for 52 against a batting line-up stacked with left handers: Border, Matthews, Wessels, Phillips. It really was a brilliant exhibition.

His run-up and action are very simple and technically fantastic. His head is very still, his approach is very direct, and he's beautifully balanced. He didn't lose much pace by shortening his run; a lot of bowlers would because they don't have his rhythm. Physically, he's a bit of a freak – for a start he looks exactly the same as when he first played for New Zealand apart from a few grey hairs. He never puts on weight despite a huge appetite, mostly for the wrong kind of food, and he's very supple, which he has in common with the West Indian fast bowlers. He's never been into heavy stamina work but by playing in England he got cricket fit. Any physio will tell you that fast bowling is one of the worst things you can do to your back but Richard's taken the stress out of it because of his balance, rhythm, and suppleness.

As a batter he times the ball better than anyone in the New Zealand team and he's taken amazing catches in the gully which testify to what a superb pair of hands he has. He simply has enormous natural ability with a cricket bat and ball.

He's pretty clinical, single-minded and professional – he has to be to do what he's done. He's a professional sportsman and he realises that, at the end of the day, he's got to make a dollar or two or three out of it so he's directed a lot of energy into his off-the-field revenue-earning opportunities. I've always taken the view that he's New Zealand's world champion and good luck to him. In England in 1986 after we'd drawn at the Oval to win our first series there, Richard left as soon as the game was over and headed back to Nottingham to attend to his benefit. Most of the boys thought it would've been nice if he'd stayed for a few beers.

He's incredibly well-organised. His first-aid kit has about 15 different compartments and I'm sure that if you needed snake bite serum, it would be there somewhere. You know where to go in an emergency and many's the time I've nicked something from him. He thinks and lives in an organised way and bowls that way too. Although we're completely different types of people, I've got great respect for him and we get on well.

He's got to the stage where he's very matter of fact about things – he doesn't get too carried away with success or too down in the dumps over failure. He never displays emotional turmoil. You see guys in the dressing room racked with self-doubt but Richard knows that if he goes out and performs in his usual manner, he'll get people out. He has the comforting knowledge that his technique makes him far less susceptible to vagaries of form than most other bowlers. I've never seen a bowler who sends down as many good deliveries as he does. All bowlers bowl some good nuts and good bowlers bowl a lot but he bowls an amazing amount of them. Sunil Gavaskar told me: "when Richard is bowling well we are all like detectives looking for clues."

I don't think he's quite as effective in limited-overs cricket because he's a better attacking bowler than a defensive one. I also think batsmen who play him off the front foot will do better than those who play back or from the crease. The West Indies played him pretty well, perhaps because they were less intimidated by him. He certainly had the sign on a lot of players in other sides and he knew it and exploited it by being clinical and methodical. He's very good at accepting decisions that don't go his way or dropped catches: he just gets on with the job.

Richard's never been that nasty. The only time I've ever seen him really lose his cool was in Sri Lanka when he left his floppy hat on the stumps and the umpire wouldn't pick it up because he wanted to have it handed to him. There'd been a few lbw shouts that looked pretty adjacent but hadn't gone our way and Madugalle had been caught off the handle – the ball lobbed miles – and given not out which annoyed us because he was their key player. In the end I had to hand the hat to the umpire because Richard wouldn't come in from the end of his run and do it.

There were times when we wanted him to bounce the daylights out of people, particularly tail-enders who were holding us up or blokes who'd bounced Chats, but he seldom did. I'd be at mid on telling him, as he walked back to his mark, "Go on Paddles, bounce the jerk," and he'd just sort of nod. I think he just fancied his chances of getting them out by bowling normally. When he wanted to though, he'd bowl a very quick bouncer and it was the change of pace which made it so effective. I remember one particularly good one he bowled to Zaheer Abbas on a slow Eden Park wicket. Z had to fend it off his nose with his finger pointing towards the scoreboard. Richard is competitive but in a clinical, rather than a hot-blooded, sort of way.

If Paddles hadn't been a bowler, he could've been a hell of a batsman, easily good enough to hold his place in the New Zealand team. He batted very well for Nottinghamshire, averaged 38 in county games and playing a number of fine one-day knocks. He can play two games, particularly against the spinners – he has a better defensive technique against the mediums than the slows – but the main thing about his batting is that lovely swing of the bat and the clean strikes, especially down the ground. He's a superb striker of a cricket ball. All of us clip it well now and again but he smacks it very crisply most of the time. He's great to watch because you never know what'll happen next. Because he really goes for it, he gives it a good nudge or misses it; he's seldom out playing a half and half sort of shot. Sometimes watching him you're thinking "Oh Paddles, why did you flash at that one?" His 99 against England in 1984 was a great innings to watch – it also won the game for us. Batting is harder psychologically so he definitely took the right option.

He's always had this big thing with Ian Botham. In England in 1978 Both bounced him unmercifully and Richard didn't handle it that well; there was a bit of the old tell-tale shuffle of the feet, backing away from the line of the ball. In those days Both was very sharp, tremendously aggressive, and bowled a mean bouncer and he definitely intimidated Richard. The introduction in the '80s of the helmet has done a lot for Paddles' batting and he's certainly given Botham some stick in recent years.

Being the superstar hasn't always been comfortable for him or the rest of the team. Because he's the one and only RJ, he got away with a bit – for instance giving interviews during practice which would earn anyone else a verbal boot up the backside. That's one of the things the New Zealand team has learnt to accept. By the same token no one goes out on the field better prepared than he does.

Some of the team thought he was very mercenary over the car business. My attitude, and I guess it was partly that of a fellow professional, was that he'd already won two cars which had gone into the team pot and put $1800 in each of our pockets, so good luck to him. Besides he probably didn't have an Alfa Romeo in his garage. He'd told me in advance that he was going to keep it and there was a team meeting to discuss it in the transit lounge at Melbourne Airport. The younger guys didn't know what to do when it came to the vote. I voted for him to keep it and so did John Reid but I can't remember who else did. I know Jerry Coney, Bruce Edgar, and John Bracewell were against it and so was Glenn Turner. I thought the vote was confidential but found myself named as a leading light of the 'Let Paddles keep his motor' faction in Richard's newspaper column. The basic problem with that incident was that the ground rules weren't set out beforehand.

I think that the New Zealand team has come to understand him in the last few years, to respect him for his absolutely phenomenal performances for us, and to be more relaxed about his superstardom. For his part, he's enjoyed being a member of the New Zealand side more, and has certainly contributed more off the field. Before that he probably didn't help team mates as much as he could have.

He and Coney had their problems, detailed in Richard's autobiography, culminating in the game in which I had to be a sort of a go-between because

"Not a problem, Paddles."
ALL SPORT

they weren't speaking to one another. I'd be asking Richard if he wanted to bowl another over and telling Coney that Richard wanted another gully – I felt like Henry Kissinger. It was absurd. Both of them came to the conclusion that third-party shuttle diplomacy wasn't a terribly practical way for a captain and his key bowler to communicate during a test match. Richard got a few wickets so I guess Jerry eventually had to congratulate him. At least I can't remember him asking me to "tell Richard the captain says well bowled".

In the early '80s we used to call him 'Super Paddles'. Is it a bird? Is it a plane? No, it's Super Paddles! Lance Cairns was adamant Richard slept at night in phone boxes.

He's got a corny sense of humour and he used to have the most dreadful dress sense although it improved after he started going to England. He and John Parker used to vie for the title of worst dresser in the New Zealand cricket team which Paddles won by virtue of a particularly vile orange shirt which he must've bought during a power black-out. He loves electronics and has a TV set in virtually every room of his house.

He's a good Canterbury man and we go back a long way together – I've even been accused of doing him favours when we've been on opposing teams. I had a really bad day against him once in county cricket and it started early – I was running late and I reversed out of my place into a lamp post. Nottinghamshire batted first and I dropped Richard when he was 20-odd. When he was 99, he pushed one to me in the covers. I rushed in to stop the single and the ball went through my legs and he got his century. I got a lot of stick from the Derbyshire lads about Kiwis looking after one another.

I went in to bat and Richard bounced me first ball. I hooked it in the air to the longest boundary on the ground. This tall guy, standing right on the rope, stretched up his arms and caught it – it would've been six otherwise. The Derbyshire guys were creased up with laughter when I returned to the dressing room. They reckoned I'd been had.

I once bowled him out in club cricket with a fast leg break and ever since I've told him that it was wasted on him.

It's been good to play with him and he's certainly been the main factor in our success. He won't be replaced and the post-Hadlee era won't be easy. He's a captain's dream: you throw him the ball and he gets wickets; it's as simple as that. He gets wickets at the start of the innings, he gets the vital breakthroughs, he cleans up the tail – you can't ask for anything more.

He's always been a great advertisement for New Zealand. He was a guy with great natural ability and enormous promise who was taught the basics well. He represented New Zealand and became a world-class player, then went to England and honed his game. He had a mid-career crisis from which he emerged with good habits and mental skills and clear-cut goals. Then he kicked on and went from strength to strength. He became a champion. If he was a racehorse, his achievements would be the equivalent of winning three classics in a year, the Triple Crown.

CHAPTER TWENTY

Hogan

I guess most people have thought pretty much the same thing when they saw Hogan – Martin Crowe – for the first time: "Here's something special."

My first sighting was at a coaching clinic for promising players run by Martin Horton, who was then national coach. I was 22, back from my first season overseas, and he was 15 and pretty big for his age. There was a game on the last day. The wicket was a bit up and down and I ended up batting with him, chasing a modest target which we knocked off. I couldn't get over how easy he made it look and how technically good he was. He seemed to have modelled himself on Greg Chappell.

In his first-class season in a Northern Districts versus Auckland match in Tauranga he looked pretty impressive. In the return game at Eden Park he was caught behind for five but didn't walk and got away with it. A number of remarks of an uncomplimentary nature were forcefully delivered, some of them by me, which obviously rattled him but he composed himself and went on to get 90-odd. It was good to see a guy his age handle himself that way.

He did a bit of bowling in that match. It was a flat wicket but he was quite nippy, bowling big inswingers which were outswingers to me. He was handy enough but he wanted to bowl at a million miles an hour and sprayed it all over the place. Bowling seemed to bring out a wild streak in Martin: at Lord's in 1986, Jerry Coney was off the field and I was in charge. England had started well but we restricted them and pulled them back. The bowlers were knackered so I gave Martin a trundle. We had a bit of a disagreement over field placings and he told me I had no idea about setting a field because I'd never been a bowler. He dug in a few and got whacked and I told him I'd have to be a genius to set a field for his bowling, then took him off and sent him to fine leg to cool off.

In 1981 he was over in England on the Lord's ground staff and making a big impact. When they played the Derbyshire second XI, the Australian Wayne Phillips went in and thrashed 20 off the first over, then got out. Martin came in and smacked it everywhere, got a big score, and certainly impressed the Derbyshire lads.

He played his first test when he was 19 – against Australia at the Basin. He was the whizz kid, the new sensation. Some players get picked very early because there's no one else. In this case there were alternatives but most of the team felt he was good enough to be there.

Owing to rain he didn't get a bat till late in the game and Jeff Thomson – who bowled pretty quickly in that series when he got it right – worked him over. Martin ended up having a shocking series: at Lancaster Park he played two beautiful boundary shots then ran down the wicket and was stumped for nine; he was obviously pumping with adrenalin. By this time there were one or two murmurs that it was a case of "too far too fast". There's always the danger of putting a player's development back two or three years by chucking him in too early.

Hogan missed the 1982/83 test series against Sri Lanka then came in for the one-day bushfire benefit match in Sydney. He got 66 on a tricky pitch and batted brilliantly, winning the man of the match award. He played in the one-dayer against Sri Lanka at Napier and had a big partnership with Jeff. In England for the World Cup in 1983 he got 97 against England in the first game, then had a moderate test series, but it was starting to fall into place. England came the following year and he got a century in the first test at the Basin in a great partnership with Jerry Coney. He's never really looked back. In the space of two years he'd come of age.

I really admired the way he came back from that horrible start against the Aussies. Getting dropped after that series was probably a good thing. Compare his start with Ken Rutherford's: at 19 Martin was batting five or six against Australia while Ruds was opening against West Indies. Ken was dropped then brought back to play the Windies again. In New Zealand, because of our small player base, you can fail and still come again. The question is, how much psychological damage has been done?

Martin has said that he felt he was left to fend for himself when he came into the New Zealand team and didn't get much help from the senior players. I remember after his test debut against Australia I made a conscious effort to talk to him and help him. From very early on I thought he was a great player and I used to tell him so.

We used to talk about concentrating ball by ball and the mental side of the game which he's worked hard on and feels strongly about. I've always been positive towards him. When you've got stars like him and Richard Hadlee in the team, it's important that they don't turn off and become self-absorbed, that they feel motivated by and comfortable about being a member of the team.

The tall poppy syndrome is never far away: other players can be alienated by the constant focus on the superstars who get much more fuss made about them by the media and sponsors. In Australia in 1981 we were the Howarth/Hadlee team; later we became the Hadlee/Crowe team. Because they're the best players, they do well materially out of the game, which can cause envy. Martin is a sensitive person and at times he's felt he wasn't part of the team. Early on he could be quite moody: one morning he'd say "g'day"; next morning he wouldn't. When a normal player does that, people just think he got out of bed on the wrong side; when a star does it, they think "Oh, he's up himself."

Going to Somerset really helped his game. He became a lot more consistent. In the West Indies he got 188 at Guyana and hardly a run in the rest of the series. He went back to England and thought about why he'd failed after that great start. When he came back to play Australia, he'd really strengthened his game. He'd always been good technically but he'd become very straight, the straightest player I've seen.

Glenn Turner helped him a lot in Australia. Glenn's a hard taskmaster and I don't really go along with his approach of not congratulating a guy who's got a century because he'd been told to get a double hundred. But he did teach Martin to go for the big ones. They're dissimilar characters: Glenn's much more clinical. As a batsman, Glenn mastered the one-day game which Martin has yet to do, mainly because he doesn't like it. It was easier for Glenn being an opener and he maintains Martin should bat three in one-day cricket and I agree: it makes sense to give your best player as much time as possible so you've got to get him in. But I think Martin finds it very frustrating to get out to a shot he normally wouldn't play.

The only question still to be answered was how he'd handle the really quick stuff. No one really likes it and none of us have been that successful against it. His 188 at Guyana was on the flattest wicket of all time and he didn't do so well after that. The West Indies came here straight after the ruckus at Somerset when Viv Richards and Joel Garner had been fired and Martin hired in their place. There was definitely some acrimony. He and Viv had been good mates in the West Indies – Martin looked up to Viv and Viv seemed to relate to him – but out here Richards would've been extremely pleased to see him fail miserably. Somerset's decision would've looked insane if the guy they'd exchanged for Richards and Garner – and in effect Ian Botham because he left the county in protest – had flopped.

Before the series he put in a lot of work with Harold Whitcombe, a stalwart of the Cornwall club in Auckland who's worked with Martin for many years. He failed in the first innings of the first test at Wellington then got a brilliant century under pressure in the second and batted magnificently through the series with another century at Auckland and an 80 at Christchurch. His positional play against really quick bowling was outstanding.

The thing I like about his batting is that he can play two games. He's a good leaver, goes under the bouncer well, uses his height well to play on top of the ball, and works the ball on the leg side, but he also has the strokes of a great player. He can bat defensively without letting the bowler get away with a bad ball – he punishes them whatever the situation. He also works very hard on his fitness.

It would've helped the cause enormously if he'd been in India in 1988. The big hundred he got in his comeback test against Pakistan was a

Where's Jane?

tremendous knock because there was a lot of pressure on him. We'd been through a hard tour of India which made us a pretty tight unit so Martin had to get back into the swing and become part of the team again. It was a technically superb innings.

I enjoy batting with him. He's one of the few blokes I haven't run out and he hasn't run me out, which is surprising given the disparity in our respective speeds between the wickets. He's extremely positive and supportive in a partnership and takes the pressure off you because of his enormous ability.

He and Richard Hadlee are both blessed with tremendous natural ability, both had excellent coaching at home, and both honed their games in England. Hogan certainly had back problems but I don't think he's suited to the drudgery of county cricket. His time there was highly beneficial but he didn't need to stay any longer. Quitting the circuit is no big deal financially with the sponsorship opportunities available to him here. Another thing he and Paddles have in common is that it's easy to see what makes them so good. They're both tremendous technicians in the classic style. Martin is elegant without having the wristiness of the Indians and Pakistanis.

He enjoys a challenge – he loves to take the opposition on and laugh about it and it would be a shame if he lost that attitude. That could easily have happened if he'd carried on playing county cricket. He works hard on the mental side – is maybe too complicated sometimes – but it's a

Bursting to bowl.

Enough said.

Perfection.
J.G. BLACKWELL

A cloud on the horizon?
J.G. BLACKWELL

"On your bike, sunshine!" Danny Morrison gets Dean Jones for 99, Perth, 1989.
GREG PORTEOUS

learning process. He's ambitious – he's pushing himself towards big goals despite having achieved a great deal already.

Middle of the road isn't good enough for him – he's always wanted to be one of the world's top players. That means maintaining a test average of over 40, which is very high by New Zealand standards. There's no doubt that he's going to be our most prolific batsman: he's the most complete player I've ever batted with and I rate him as the best New Zealand player of my time, ahead of Glenn Turner. I don't think he'll match Turner's feat of 100 hundreds which comes back to their differing personalities and temperaments: Turner was very clinical with tremendous discipline and a very level attitude. Whereas Turner and Hadlee are on a pretty even keel, Martin sometimes has his ups and downs.

He's got the potential to be the best batsman in the world. Graeme Hick is a cleaner striker – I've never seen anyone else block boundaries the way he does – but it's hard to compare them because Hick has never played test cricket. At the moment Hick's entire focus can go into county cricket or Shell Trophy or whatever and his results are amazing. Once he's playing test cricket though, it will be difficult for him to avoid focusing on test matches and putting less concentration and effort into first-class games.

In that context, it's worth noting that Martin has also been enormously successful in first-class cricket with a career average of over 50 which puts him in the company of the real greats. I got over 1000 runs in the 1986/87 New Zealand season which normally would've been an oustanding effort. Martin got 1500-odd and was nothing short of awesome – against provincial attacks on good wickets, it's just money for jam for him. The move to Central Districts was a good one. It was almost like leaving home and standing on his own two feet.

He's grown up in a professional age; he's always had a manager and reached a point quite early in his career which took Hadlee some time to get to. Cricket is his livelihood so the bottom line is performance. A lot of benefits come with his star status but without performance people don't want to know you. I wouldn't mind some of the benefits – the money from endorsements for example – but I don't envy him the high public profile. It adds to the pressure.

Despite the move to CD, he remains very much an Aucklander. Aucklanders are different – they comb their hair more and even John Bracewell has sunglasses with a string for hanging around his neck now. Martin is probably the flashest dresser I've ever played with. His clothes, his gear, and his on- and off-the-field demeanour are all part of his search for perfection. In many ways, Richard Hadlee is an ordinary, unremarkable person who happens to be a cricketing superstar. Martin is more aware of it and enjoys it. Like most Aucklanders he projects himself more. He puts a lot of pressure on himself through his quest for perfection and simply living up to his self-image.

It'll be interesting to see how he goes as captain. In some ways it might help his game, especially in one-day cricket, and bring him out of himself. He thinks about it a lot and can get bored just watching it happen – he's played a lot of cricket for a guy his age. He won't have to worry about holding his place in the side, which is a big advantage. His best is ahead of him and I really hope he maintains his enthusiasm and carries on through to his mid-30s. Getting on to the other players' wave-length will be the test. It's going to be quite challenging because he'll be leading a group of players who've come into the team during a successful period and who expect success.

Sometimes at team talks he's been very honest and more open than a lot of players about his shortcomings and how he feels he's let the side down. It's almost over the top. I dare say he'll restrain the emotional, impulsive side of his nature as he gets older but I hope it doesn't disappear altogether.

In 1987 we were opposing skippers when Canterbury played Central Districts at Lancaster Park. The wicket was green but he won the toss and batted. I couldn't believe it. That season he had a theory that the team batting first had more control over how the game developed. We would've been hard pressed to get 150 batting first and CD was two for zilch very quickly. Then Hogan came in and blasted 150.

He was expecting me to declare behind but I like getting five points if they're there for the taking. He thought that we'd effectively killed the game but my plan was to bat on then try to bowl them out and we nearly succeeded, in fact we would have if he'd been given out stumped for nought; we thought he was out but the shadows were getting a bit long for the square leg umpire who probably enjoyed watching him anyway. He was in the dressing room when he heard Peter Sharp on the radio suggesting that CD were to blame for the state of the game. He rushed outside and, in full public view, gave Sharp up in the commentary box the fingers. Perhaps it was slightly impetuous but if he ever does it at Lord's, I'll be the first to congratulate him.

CHAPTER TWENTY-ONE

Comrades in arms

One of the best things about playing for New Zealand is that the other guys in the team are my mates. Sure we've probably all called each other meatheads and wallies at some stage but the odd clash is inevitable in a group of guys trying to perform under pressure and in the glare of the media spotlight.

While the members of the New Zealand team are a collection of strong and distinct individuals, they all have a hard competitive streak, an inner drive to succeed for themselves and the team; you couldn't ask for better men to enter the fray with. And because they're all good blokes, they've been great companions on and off the park, at home and abroad, in success and failure, in victory and in defeat.

Ewen Chatfield has been a great foil for Richard Hadlee and you can count on the fingers on one hand the number of times he's bowled badly for New Zealand. You know he's going to put the ball round about the right place and make the batsman work for his runs. Writing in his benefit brochure, Stephen Boock listed the ten terms most frequently used to describe Chats as: reliable, consistent, durable, dependable, accurate, evergreen, solid, not out, older than Stephen Boock, and number 11. The last two, said Boocky, were used almost exclusively by himself and members of the Stephen Boock Fan Club.

Javed Miandad paid him a great compliment when he said he'd like to take Chats back to Pakistan and use him as a bowling machine. Chats, it should be said, was not thrilled by the thought of spending the twilight of his career in the Karachi nets.

The wicket might look flat but he'll hit the seam and if there's something there, he'll find it. He'll find a little spot and work away at it. His nickname was 'Farmer' which got shortened to 'Mer' and if he gets a ball to go, there'll be a chorus of "Mer, Mer, Mer," starting in the slips and going round the side. When Boocky kissed the Eden Park pitch during the 1989 Pakistan test, in the course of setting a record for the highest number of runs conceded by a New Zealand bowler in a test innings, he reckoned he was trying to create a damp spot on the wicket for the Mer.

Normally one Chats over takes as long as any other, almost to the second. Because he just bowls then gets straight back to his mark. But when a delivery does a bit, he gets a glint in his eye and a little spring in his step, and walks back to the end of his run a little quicker. There were times when the metronomic briskness with which he bowled his overs made me cross, such as when the opposition were nine down with half an hour's play left and I wasn't keen on batting that night. I'd be suggesting to Chats that he take his time but he'd carry on at exactly the same pace. Danny Morrison and Willie Watson could take a leaf out of his book when it comes to getting through their overs.

Chats sometimes found it hard to adjust his line and length to bowl blockholers in one-day cricket but he's just what you needed at the start of an innings. You can't hit a guy like that to all parts of the ground, and in the end he usually got those who tried to slog him. One of the few times he was really collared was in the World Cup in India when Sunil Gavaskar and Kris Srikkanth threw caution to the wind and belted him over midwicket or went inside out over the covers. They were good enough on the day to do it and Chats went for 39 off four overs which I'm sure he'll enjoy being reminded of. But he has a great temperament and was very philosophical when he did get hammered.

He's definitely been one of New Zealand's most entertaining batsmen. He has a wonderful ability to play and miss — we call it the withdraw shot.

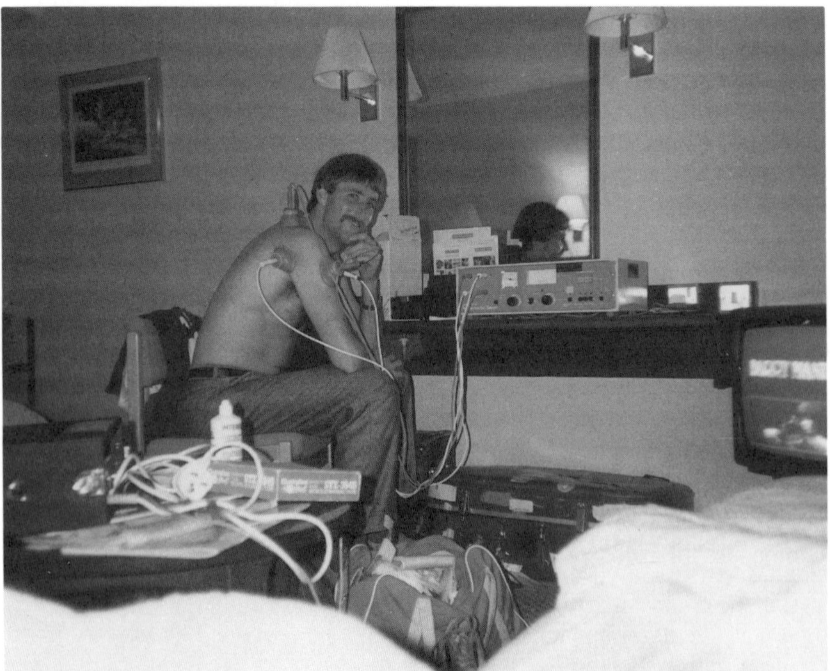

A minor malfunction to the bowling machine.

His partnership with Jerry Coney at Carisbrook to beat Pakistan was marvellous. It was a lively wicket, he had a lot of the strike and had to face a few bouncers. He obviously got over that horrible early-career injury but was still understandably nervous before he went out to bat. A lot of guys would've flagged batting away after that experience. Chats stepped right up again even though he knew very well that the quicks were going to bounce him.

Early on he wasn't a great fielder but when we took part in the World Series for the first time in 1980-81, he spent an awful lot of time on his fielding and made himself very proficient.

Chats enjoys a beer and, as you'd expect, he goes about the task methodically and with good rhythm. He's also a fitness fanatic and can run for miles. On tour in England I got out early in a county game and went for a run with him. I'd heard he was a bit of a gun and sure enough, he took off at a brisk pace. I thought "he's just trying to burn me off, he can't keep this pace up for long". As the run proceeded, the gap between us got wider and wider till he was just a dot in the distance. If he hadn't played cricket for New Zealand, he would've been a useful marathon runner. He's also a very good squash player and he and Jeff Crowe have had some epic battles. Predictably it was Chopper who played the shots while Chats just kept hitting it back down the walls.

He should've played for New Zealand earlier but he made up for it and playing for as long as he did was a tremendous achievement. He liked touring and was a good tourist although no more immune to the ravages of Delhi belly than the rest of us. In that infamous test at Bangalore he asked me part way through an over if he could go off to answer a scream of nature. I told him to finish the over. He had his hands full as he scuttled through the official section of the stand and in the dressing room Bob Cunis, ever helpful, suggested he add cornflour to thicken it.

Chats loved playing for New Zealand and would have liked to've gone on till he was 50. If he'd been an All Black, he'd have been one of the guys in the back of the bus who set the standards and made sure they're kept. On tour the social committee fines people for minor misdemeanours like being late, wearing the wrong clothes, or being loud in the pub. It would have been easier to pin an offence on Mother Teresa than Chats and in the end we had to resort to making things up, like claiming he'd been seen exchanging deep and meaningful glances with Maggie Thatcher.

I've known Johnny Bracewell's family for years: I was good mates with his older brother Doug, who wasn't that far behind John as an off spinner, and got to know Brendon on the 1978 tour when he showed tremendous composure for an 18-year-old. They're one of New Zealand's great sporting families – four of the Bracewell boys have played first-class cricket and four have played first-class rugby. Three have done both.

As kids they used to bury tennis balls for three weeks to make them nice and hard then shave them and play one another in timeless test matches in which no quarter was asked and none given. John once batted for three weeks for 180 then dismissed Brendon straight away and enforced the follow on. You couldn't design an environment more likely to produce fierce competitors.

He came into the team in Australia in 1980/81 with Martin Snedden and they were a brash young pair. I had quite a few throw downs from him on that tour and he's never let me forget it. He warns new guys in the team not to get sucked in to giving me throw downs or they'll be doing it forever. For a while we never really hit it off. He probably classified me as a professional and I was vice-captain in a regime that wasn't giving him a lot of opportunities.

In those days he felt under pressure for his place in the team whenever he bowled but it was obvious he had it because he was such a big turner of the ball, the biggest I've seen. When he bowls well, he bowls sides out because he's an attacking bowler. He's more comfortable attacking, more mentally relaxed, because he's not really a containment bowler. Despite that, he hates to have runs hit off him, especially in the first couple of overs.

He has been the matchwinner in several tests, which is a great achievement: not too many spinners apart from Indians in India have turned sides out in tests recently. His all-round effort in Bombay in 1988 was tremendous and his century at Trent Bridge in 1986 was a key contribution to winning the test, which he followed up by dismissing David Gower, probably their key player, with a ball which turned miles. His wrapping up of the Australian second innings at the Basin in 1990 was a big factor in New Zealand's victory.

He doesn't really have a slow bowler's temperament and I hate to think what he'd have been like if he'd been quick. He's got a good nasty streak. The opposition don't like him because he's intimidating. He can be as hard on himself and his team mates as he is on the opposition. Early on, as he'd be the first to admit, he could be too tough on his team mates. You'd be sprawled on the turf having hurled yourself full length in a vain attempt to stop a screaming drive and he'd ask you if your feet were stuck in concrete. Some players, especially those who weren't used to it, got a bit upset.

He's a world-class sledger: in a one-dayer in India he was given out caught behind by their new wicketkeeper Pandit. He was absolutely convinced he'd been sharked out. Pandit came out to bat with India needing only 20 with five wickets in hand and copped a ferocious barrage of abuse from Braces who was out in the covers. Whenever the ball was hit to Braces, he returned it to Ian Smith like a rocket, which meant Pandit had to keep his wits about him. Pandit got completely flustered and soon spooned a catch to mid off.

In the test against Australia at Wellington this year, Allan Border was dropped at short cover at a vital stage of the game. Braces rushed in from mid on and yelled at the top of his voice "Shit the cricketing gods – they're against us." When he dismissed Ian Healy later in the same innings, he barked at him "you're out, Four Bats Healy. Some people – notably Aussie journalists with short and selective memories – criticise Braces for going

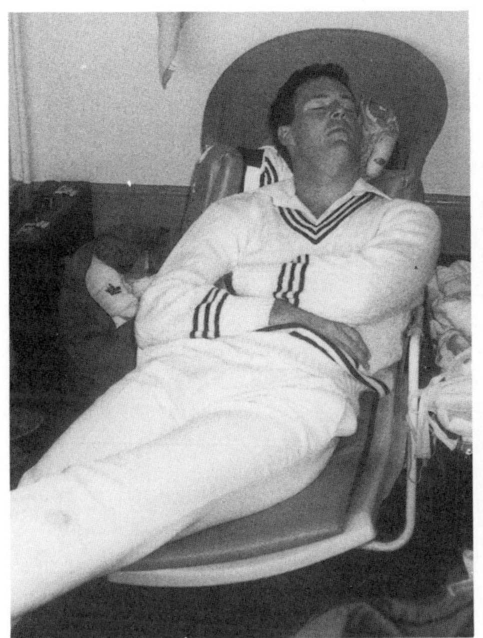

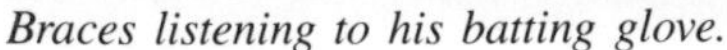

Braces listening to his batting glove.

"Gee, it's great to be alive"
ALL SPORT

too far but I like having him on the park because of his boots-and-all approach.

He's suffered a lot from back problems and sometimes played in considerable pain but never complained. He's taken some good catches at slip. His batting is like the rest of his game – attacking; he makes things happen. He's playing the spinners better and never flinches from the quicks. He sets high standards for himself in all departments and expects high standards from his team mates.

Australians bring out the best in him; he usually plays well against them and they really rate him. It's a great compliment to him the way Australian crowds appeal after his first ball and I think he enjoys it. He's certainly always happy to bandy words with them. In Adelaide a cabbie said to him: "You're Bracewell, didn't you used to dig graves?" Braces replied: "Don't you still drive a cab?"

Braces' sense of humour keeps people on their toes. He said of Franklyn Stephenson, the West Indian all-rounder who took part in the Hadlee benefit matches, that he had a smile "like the grille on a Cadillac". At a reception in Jamaica we were having a drink round the pool when Radio New Zealand's Bryan Waddle strolled past, all dressed up and obviously with somewhere to go. It was quite dark but it may have been Braces who sent him head first into the pool with a delicate and precisely timed nudge of the shoulder. Wads isn't the best of swimmers and had the added handicap of being weighed down by a fair amount of gold jewellery. He still talks about the incident in hushed tones.

Ian Smith is one of the most gifted players of my era, a natural sportsman with great hand/eye co-ordination. He first played for Central Districts as a specialist batsman and looked like a Kiwi version of Doug Walters. People talk about Jeff Dujon but I think Smithy's been the best gloveman of those who've consistently played test cricket in recent years. It's actually hard to remember him dropping catches. He forced his way in at the expense of a good player in Wally Lees and has become the yardstick for the up-and-coming 'keepers around today. Perhaps he hasn't had as much experience standing up as the English 'keepers but he gloves the ball as well as anyone. He has that unobtrusive quality which is the hallmark of the good ones. He has developed as a player and grown in stature with New Zealand cricket: as we've become more successful, his confidence has grown and the more confident he is, the more dangerous he is. He's also a big help to his captains because he's good tactically and sorts out very quickly where the bowlers are bowling and where they should be bowling.

Stockley (that's what the S in I.D.S. stands for) loves to be on top of his game and is a big touch player. When he's batting well, he plays square of the wicket a lot, cutting and hooking. One of the Indians apparently asked at a team meeting: "How do you bowl to this guy, he cuts and sweeps everything." Because he murders anything short, we tell him to get forward although the quicks can worry him when he's on the front foot. He's a fantastic player of spin bowling, playing it from the pitch and late. Anything can happen when he's batting and he can turn one-day games very quickly because he's so aggressive.

His 173 against India at Eden Park was a staggering innings – I've never seen anything like it in test cricket – and demonstrated just how devastating he can be. In the second innings, the Indians were scuffing up the pitch for Hirwani. More, the wicketkeeper, pointed to the footmarks and started telling me how hard it would be for lefthanders – "you've got lots of lefthanders: you, Greatbatch, Hadlee, Snedden . . ." "And Ian Smith," piped up Singh out in the covers. They were so shellshocked by Smithy's innings, they weren't sure which side of the bat he stood on.

Surprisingly for someone who plays with such freedom, he gets nervous before he goes in. He concentrates very hard on the first delivery because he feels a golden duck is far worse than the ordinary kind. He's not a man for half measures and that shows in his results – he doesn't get many "in between" scores. His 'keeping though is remarkably consistent.

He's niggly on the field and gets right into the opposition. At Sharjah, Mohinder Armanath, who was having his benefit at the tournament, was caught behind but given not out. Stockley suggested he was taking his benefit a bit too far and the pair of them had to be separated; they were at it like a couple of fox terriers.

He enjoys being part of a team set-up, loves having a bet on the horses – always trifectas rather than win and place which says a lot about him

"Where are we going tonight, lads?"

"Chats, we need a bigger tray." Wally Lees has the pork pies.

A hard day in the field.

The Barbados beach looks good – what about the bodies?

Shoot-out.

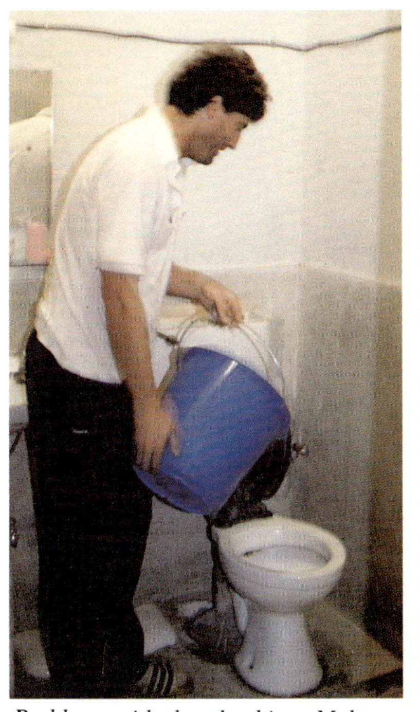

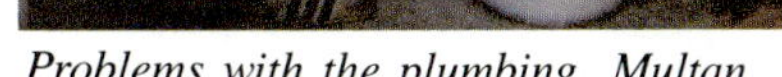

Problems with the plumbing, Multan.

"C'mon, Braces, it's Friday!"

Boocky (centre) looking for his relations in Peshawar.

A day at the races with Boocky, Ruds, Brian Waddle and Iain Gallaway.

A snake-charmer in Hyderabad – up the nose and out the mouth.

The Peshawar Handicap Trot.

Dentist's rooms in Pakistan.

– and has a good, cutting sense of humour. He finds touring quite tough going and looks forward to getting home more than most.

In the West Indies he played very well at Guyana, getting 53 in a big partnership with Martin Crowe, but he didn't enjoy Malcolm Marshall telling him he'd be dead meat on the much quicker pitch at Barbados. The Windies did their best to keep their promise and Stockley got smashed on the hand by a ball from Winston Davis. He was surprised to be met at the hospital by a little boy wanting his autograph. The kid reckoned the hospital was the best place to get visiting players' autographs.

John Reid played 31 innings in 19 tests; he passed 50 eight times and converted six of those fifties into centuries. His test average is 46 and only two New Zealanders – Martin Donnelly, who played seven tests and Stewie Dempster, who played ten – have a better one. He reached 1000 runs in test cricket in 20 innings, a New Zealand record.

Reido was a superb technician and our soundest player of spin bowling. He worked out the angles of playing spin bowling. He played straight on to the ball, not across his pad, seldom got done on length and very rarely hit in the air. He coped better with spin than pace because he'd grown up on Auckland tracks which don't bounce but his century at the Gabba in 1985, when the ball was bouncing, demonstrated how he'd developed.

His unflappability made him an ideal number three. He'd just key in and do it over and over again. When he got his rhythm going against the slows, he'd milk them here, milk them there, and hit the bad balls for four. He didn't seem to take a lot out of himself when he batted. In Sri Lanka the rest of us had only to walk outside to be pouring sweat but Reido would come in after batting through a session looking as if he'd been sitting in the shade, sucking an ice block. He wasn't the fittest guy in the team either.

The century he made against Northern Districts in 1988 in his one-off comeback showed how technically good he was. His technique made him less susceptible to fluctuations in form than other players. He very rarely had extended bad trots and could come straight back after a poor game and succeed spectacularly. In Pakistan he got two and six in the first test then made 106, 26, and 97. In Sri Lanka he was close to being dropped after getting seven and nought in the second test; in the third he batted 11 and a half hours for 180.

He didn't enjoy fielding as much as batting although he was very good in the gully. Like Zaheer Abbas, he saved himself for batting. Quite often after he'd got runs, he wouldn't appear on the field for a while, which was very sensible of him.

He was a good team man, very quiet and considerate to his team mates, and in those days enjoyed being a geography teacher. His analyses of land formations during bus trips in Pakistan were much appreciated by those team members with a burning interest in geology.

I guess he gave up because he wasn't enjoying it – he certainly didn't enjoy touring, being very much a family man. It was a big loss to the New Zealand team but a good thing for the game because he's doing a tremendous

John Reid – the NZCC could do with a few more like him.

Ian Stockley Smith looking forward to another day in the field.

job as chief executive of the Auckland Cricket Association. He's professional, attentive to detail, and a sound thinker who sees the game in terms of a business. He'd make an excellent cricket manager – he took the Auckland squad pre-season training in 1989/90 and was very good and has a great deal to offer New Zealand cricket in a number of areas.

Bruce Edgar was a stalwart, one of the nuts and bolts men. There were times when his contribution was overlooked but he was out there doing the nitty gritty stuff. He set up our test win over Australia at Eden Park in 1981/82 with 161, and his 74 at Perth in 1985 put us on the way to victory. If he had his time over again he'd probably be more aggressive; he's certainly batted brilliantly for Wellington since he retired from test cricket. I believe that if he'd continued for another two or three years he would've reached the stage of playing more freely in test cricket – I've certainly evolved that way. He gets asked every year if he'll play test cricket again but he made his decision and stuck to it.

In England in 1986 he told me he might give it away. In the end he weighed up the family situation, his career outlook, and the amount of enjoyment he was getting from test cricket, and decided to get out. He'd played 39 tests and was a better player than his record suggests and we've missed him, that's for sure. When you looked around at the guys in the side, seeing Brucie gave you confidence – he was a class player, by far the best New Zealander I've opened with.

There may have been an element of disillusionment in his decision to leave the test scene. It must have been galling for him to be dropped on the tour of Sri Lanka and against Pakistan here for players who were inferior, either as openers or simply as batsmen.

Bruce was very determined. He prepared well and put a lot into training – his throwing arm developed enormously when he started doing weights. He was probably the first of us to get seriously into physical preparation and was very fit. He was compact and technically sound, a nice driver and a good accumulator, working it well behind square. Like all left handers he had a slight weakness against the widish ball outside off stump – he used to get squared up. I always felt he was more likely to get out to that ball than the one on off stump moving away, which he judged very well.

We had a good one-day series together in Australia in 1981 but were never really allowed to develop as a one-day combination. He played a lot fewer limited-overs games than I did but in many ways was better suited to it because he deflected the ball so well. One or two players used to give him a hard time for being slow in one-dayers but once he got going, he worked it round well. We're now learning from the Aussies that batting in one-day cricket is more about singles than boundaries. They stop the opposition getting singles by bowling a very tight line and length and fielding aggressively and they make the singles when they bat.

Bruce and I had a lot in common: when we were batting together, we had an intuitive sense of how the other was feeling. If one of us was going through an uncertain patch, the other would know when to give

With Bob Taylor and Bruce Edgar, two great mates.

encouragement although we were never great talkers. After he'd got a pair at Perth in 1981, he was so hosed off he went and sat in one of the big dressing room cupboards and only emerged when the team was on the bus. I knew how he felt – he just didn't want to talk to anyone. We ran between the wickets quite well. There was a run out in Pakistan but he couldn't blame me because he was a yard past the stumps when the bails were removed.

His nickname was Bootsie – he bought a pair of leather boots in Canberra in 1981, someone called him Bootsie, and it stuck. He was a good room mate – a nice, solid, quiet guy with a sense of humour. I was probably sadder than anyone when he gave up. We were still developing as an opening pair and could've achieved a lot more.

I've given a lot of people throw downs but no one was as frightening to give throw downs to as Lance Cairns because he just pummelled them and I was constantly in fear of one being blasted straight back at me. I used to throw them wider and wider on his off side so he couldn't hit them straight.

Lance was a great card player and his bowling reminded me of a shrewd gambler: he had a selection of deliveries and he served them up like a card player going through his hand, fishing out the appropriate card. He was one of the few New Zealand bowlers in recent times who could swing the ball and he had a good slower one and a useful bouncer. He could look quite innocuous and just as the batsman was taking him for granted, he'd come up with a wicket delivery. He wasn't afraid to experiment and, being as strong as an ox, he could bowl all day.

As a batsman he was great for cricket because of his entertainment value – everyone loves a bit hitter and they don't come much bigger than Lance. He used an absolutely huge bat and had two grips: defensive and offensive. Defensively, usually against the quicks, he'd drop his hands down the handle and turn his top hand around.

Like everyone else I used to love watching him bat, particularly against sides who thought they could sucker him out using spinners. Against the Windies at Carisbrook in 1980 we really had to battle – Edgar batted 300 minutes for 65 – and we'd ground our way to 168 for seven when Clive Lloyd gave off-spinner Derek Parry a trundle. Cairnsy hit him for three sixes in two overs and got 35 in next to no time, which proved decisive in a very tight game.

In a Northern Districts-Canterbury game at Dudley Park, Rangiora, played in a howling north-westerly, he was dropped five times scoring a half century, hitting huge skiers which swirled around in the gale. Technically speaking, it was a chanceless innings because no one actually laid a hand on any of them. Sometimes he preferred hitting against the spin rather than with it on the theory that the ball spun into the arc of the bat. Against New South Wales in 1980/81, he absolutely murdered the Aussie leg spinner Bob Holland, making 68 with seven sixes.

Some teams didn't bowl to him all that cleverly. If you bowled into his chest, you cut his options down but if you put it in the slot, you'd be trying to catch sight of the ball in the sun. He was never quite the same, certainly not against the quicks, after being hit on the head by Wasim Akram and who could blame him?

Lance was a pretty direct individual and didn't muck around at team talks. He had fixed ideas on how the game should be played and who should play it. He felt I was too professional in my approach to test cricket and thought I should be more attacking; I felt he sometimes overlooked the difference between test matches and first-class games. He was pleased with the way I batted last season; so was I – maybe I should have taken his advice.

His nicknames were Lancer the Dancer, Spring Creek or Springers (he hailed from Spring Creek in Marlborough), and Monsoon Bog, owing to his ability to shatter the tranquility of a bus trip. He was not a person to get stuck with in a lift. He had a wonderful smile and infectious enthusiasm and his delight at taking a wicket or pasting the ball over the fence was there for all to see. He was a great tourist and enjoyed the comradeship of touring, the rivalry on the field and the socialising off it. He often complained of feeling 'poorly' in the morning after a few beers with the opposition or a night out.

He and Chats are the folk heroes of New Zealand cricket; the game's followers took them to their hearts because of their distinctive and completely individual styles and methods. Both of them played in a way the enthusiast, who turns out for his club every Saturday afternoon, could identify with. Lance is the first of my generation to get to work on a cricketing dynasty and he takes great pleasure in the progress of his son Chris. I think Chris will score more runs than his old man because he's better technically. His 28 in the second innings at Perth in 1989 was an admirable innings under the circumstances.

Stephen Boock – nickname Boocky or Backa after a big backgammon performance in the West Indies – has been one of the great characters in the changing room. He was always very committed to the team cause, straightforward in his views, and not afraid to disagree with anyone: he's had the odd brush with administrators and has been tagged a rebel. One manager's response to a perfectly logical but typically pointed query was "Stupid, Boock"; it became one of our catchcries on the tour.

Like John Bracewell, he often suffered the frustration of not knowing if he would be in the playing eleven. Spinners have this difficulty at the top level: to develop they need consistent play – it's not a craft that's learnt overnight – and the confidence that comes from being able to put the ball where they want it and get good players out. If they get picked only when the selectors think the wicket's going to turn, they're always under great pressure to perform.

I firmly believe that if he and John had been allowed to play together more, they would've developed into a formidable pair, New Zealand's 'spin twins'. Operating as a pair would have lifted both of them a notch and given us the option of preparing turning wickets, especially for sides like the West Indies who play the quicker stuff pretty well.

We made our test debuts together and have gone right through. I regard him as one of the best left armers I've faced and I've never been able to dominate him. He's tight, a very good defensive bowler who can tie good players down, rather than a huge turner, and a top competitor. It would be fair to say he's been the best bowler in domestic cricket in my time.

Boocky's a great sledger – I remember him having a real go with Border when we played Queensland in 1981. It must've been nightmarish for young players going down to Carisbrook when he and Braces played together for Otago and with Wally Lees behind the stumps. He loves playing for a good team and enjoyed playing for Otago when they were doing well. Otago in turn owe him a hell of a lot.

He never had a decent bat,but he had pretensions to batsmanship and it could be said that he always played within his limitations. Most importantly though, he was a gutsy batsman and took part in some important partnerships, notably in Sydney in 1985 when he and Braces put on 124 and in Barbados where he hung around and gave as good as he got, albeit with his mouth rather than his bat. His most ignominious batting failure was at Guyana. Martin Crowe was batting well but gradually running out of partners. At each break Boocky would tell him: "Don't worry if these other idiots can't hang in there with you – just take your time, you can rely on me to keep an end up till you get your century." He even sent out messages in note form with the drinks. When the eighth wicket fell, Hogan was 170-odd and Boocky strode out to bat exuding confidence and giving Hogan a reassuring wink. After a build-up worthy of the second coming, he was comprehensively skittled first ball by Holding, leaving Martin helpless with laughter. He was replaced with Chats who, needless to say, was not out at the end of the innings.

He enjoyed touring, took a lot of photos and liked to get into the local culture, even to the extent of putting henna in his hair during the World Cup in India. In Pakistan we had a three-hour road trip to Hyderabad for the second test, some of us in a bus and the rest in a mini-van equipped with a loudspeaker system, the sort you see during election campaigns. As we tore down the freeway at excessive speed, flouting the road code and defying common sense as Pakistani drivers are prone to do, Boocky was bellowing out over the loudspeaker, at a volume which must have startled camels halfway up the Khyber Pass: "Pakistan – this is God coming – repent, repent." He's a great shopper: in Karachi he visited a rug shop which boasted of having 1000 rugs. Boocky insisted on seeing every single one.

He, Bruce Edgar, and Evan Gray did a lot of scoring during the one-day internationals in Pakistan in 1985 in a way that the Statisticians Association wouldn't have admired. They figured that seeing the opposition had the umpires, it would even things up if we had the scorers on our side.

Boocky is not a man to trifle with in the practical joke department. He has a long memory and a flair for exacting retribution. He takes it as well as he dishes it out: as a fine he once had to crawl down the aisle of an aeroplane to the rear toilet and he did it with a lot of class, as if it was the most natural thing in the world. On the same tour of Australia he and

Boocky feeling a little light-headed.

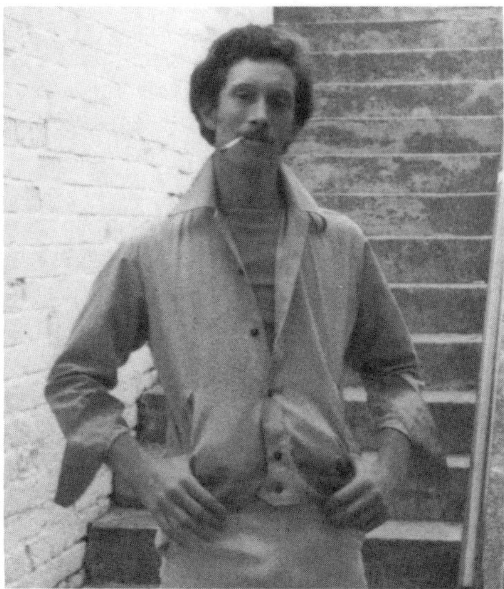

Punk Boock.

"I'll miss you, darling." Stephen Boock kissing the Eden Park wicket in his last test. His one for 229 off 70 overs was a record.

J.G. BLACKWELL

I bought a rubber snake, a fierce looking item which turned up now and again in cricket bags or showers. Someone stuck it in my bed but I didn't notice it and it was discovered by a Greek cleaning lady who got such a shock, she had to be sedated. The management then confiscated it till we left the hotel.

Andrew Jones has always had a hell of a lot of talent. He didn't get picked till he was 28, maybe because he didn't have as many scores behind him as a few others, but no one sat down and thought about how good he was. He comes from Nelson, where they've produced some tremendous cricketers over the years – Wadsworth, Congdon, Edwards, the Hamptons, Blain – and he's another in the line.

He came into the side for the tour of Sri Lanka in 1987 then went to Australia at the end of the year. He batted for a long time for not many in the first innings at Brisbane and got 45 in the second when we were in a lot of strife. They bounced him and he got tangled up trying to hook but played some great attacking shots. It wasn't the usual New Zealand approach. The Aussie media reckoned he wasn't up to test cricket and were thoroughly dismissive of him; I think the guy had guts to go for it when we were on the back foot. He played beautifully for 150 at Adelaide in the second test, confounding his critics and establishing himself as a top test player after just three matches.

People say he's unorthodox but when bat meets ball, he has good body position, great head position – perhaps his greatest asset– and good balance. He makes it simple. He goes into the ball, shuffling down the wicket even against the quicks, which is one of the reasons he's a very good fast-wicket player. He doesn't get tied up with technicalities. He picks the bat up in an individual way but brings it down straight and his point of contact is excellent. He's an extraordinary talent and I'd love to bat like him. Sometimes he doesn't play what the purist would regard as the correct shot to a particular ball but the result is what counts: if he can get away with hitting a leg spinner over midwicket off the front foot, why not do it? In many ways, day in and day out, he's the equal of Martin Crowe: he doesn't miss out very often.

His immediate success and subsequent consistency testify to how mentally strong and well-organised he is; he comes from the school of hard knocks and sorted out that side of the game – the need to be a tough competitor – very early. He's perhaps the toughest competitor in the side: a streetfighter and a sledger who likes to get up the opposition – we call him 'The Doberman'. He has great focus out in the middle and is a big match player who can get the best out of himself when it counts. He'll probably hit a rough patch at some stage but he's a tremendous fighter. Jonesy and I are both pretty self-absorbed in the morning when we're batting. Bob Cunis will walk past and say "Morning Wrighty" or "Morning Jonesy" and get no reply so he'll say "Morning Bob" to himself.

During the Bangalore test I walked past his hotel room. The door was open and Jonesy had his bat out, practising his shots. He asked me: "how am I going to play these buggers? It's turning square and I've never played that before." I told him to do it his way. He went out and got runs because of his ability to adapt.

We'd have been in the mire if he hadn't succeeded as soon as he came into the team because we'd lost Howarth, Edgar, Reid and Coney one after another. He's an example of the natural ability we have in New Zealand and of someone who really wanted to make it. He played first-class cricket very young but didn't get the opportunities some others got and it made him hungry.

He has strong views and speaks his mind. He's good to captain because you can have a real disagreement then go and have a beer. We relate well to one another – old Otago Varsity boy as is Martin Snedden – and he's been a great source of support to me, a great mate. In Australia in 1989 I was feeling a bit negative about the whole enterprise and Jonesy gave me a bit of a talking to and got me into a more positive frame of mind.

Sometimes he wanders in the field and he gets really irritated when I tell him to get back to the right position. He gets his own back on the odd occasion he has a bowl, moving me a foot this way and a foot that way. He has his own particular way of encouraging Danny Morrison from mid on: "Come on D.K. Chapter one, verse one – line and length."

Jonesey's a non-comformist, always the one in the different coloured shirt, and a bit of a rebel who sometimes finds the restraints of the team set-up difficult. I've always tried to back him when someone's objected because I feel the same way myself half the time – besides does it really matter as long as he's performing on the park? He gives great interviews. The team particularly enjoys watching him being interviewed by Peter Williams. The questions are longer than the answers.

Mark Greatbatch decided he wanted to play for New Zealand and worked very hard to achieve it. He worked with Martin Crowe, went to England, and when he couldn't get a place in the Auckland team, he went elsewhere. He's gone to England every winter for eight years and has built up an affection for the people of Yorkshire.

He came into the side in 1988 like a cyclone. He was 12th man against England at Lancaster Park and normally it takes newcomers a couple of tests to get used to things. But when Paddles got injured, Batch (after Paddy Batch, the Australian rugby player; the Aussies call him 'Scones' as in great batch of) came on, took a couple of catches, and generally kept the boys going. Then he got a century in his first test, the next game, and helped save the match.

When you're fielding in test cricket, you've got to keep geeing the team up, keep the chat going. Batch's call is "keep fizzing boys" so we call him 'Fizzing Boy'. He's the team leader on the field; the captain needs someone like that because he can't concentrate on the tactical things and do the constant geeing up as well. Batch was a tower of strength straight from the start and it's uplifting to have a young guy come in with so much confidence and zest. The introverted guys won't say much on the field, maybe out of shyness, maybe out of laziness. When we've got two wickets, he'll be saying "come one, let's concentrate on the third". In the field he sometimes looks like a flying walrus – he's the sort who'll chase the ball all the way then crash into the advertising hoardings – and he's always got some part of his body taped up as a result.

He's very correct for a left hander but he can go over the top as well so he has two options. He struggled at first in India but gradually worked his game out and ended up having a successful tour. He had expectations of himself and he lived up to them. In the third test he and Smithy were batting together and got through to the last over before stumps; a situation most guys would rather not be facing – I haven't seen many players turn down a single which would get them down to the non-striker's end. Batch glanced their first ball of the over to fine leg but didn't take the run and played out the rest of the over instead. It was really impressive: he was in control of the sitution and prepared to take responsibility.

His innings at Perth was an extraordinary display of sustained concentration and refusal to give in in the face of overwhelming odds – perhaps the greatest innings by a New Zealander I've seen. He confessed that he had negative thoughts during the innings and the fact that he overcame them as well as the Australian bowlers underlines his achievement.

Batch doesn't let his disappointments affect him too much. If he fails, he'll be angry and his bat may suffer some maltreatment but he doesn't sulk and he'll still be supportive of those who've done well. He'll get better and obviously has a big future. There's a long way to go but I believe he's got leadership qualities.

Martin Snedden has one of the best cricket brains in the side and did a great job as vice-captain in India. He's a good thinker, a good tactician, and could've ended up leading the side if he'd played test cricket more regularly. I made sure he was on the selection panel for this year's England tour, along with myself, Martin Crowe and Bob Cunis, although I generally favour a three-man panel.

On occasions over the years the odd person has asked "how come Snedden's in the team?" but he has a lot more ability than he's given credit for. He works hard and keeps coming back and performing when it counts. He contributes a lot more to the team set-up than people realise and in many ways has been one of New Zealand cricket's unsung heroes.

Sneds had his good days and bad but in recent series he's put it together and taken wickets regularly. He's probably lost a yard or two of pace but his bowling is very grooved these days. He's likely to swing it a bit more than Chats without being quite so consistent and, like Chats, if there's anything in the wicket, he'll find it; he's a very effective bowler on a seaming wicket. He bowled very well in the 1989/90 season, so well that we didn't miss the Mer, which is a great compliment to Sneds.

He's had to bowl at the death in limited-overs games a fair bit and does it well. He was once dubbed 'the Auckland trolley bus', which he hates, and wasn't amused when, after going for 105 off 12 overs against England

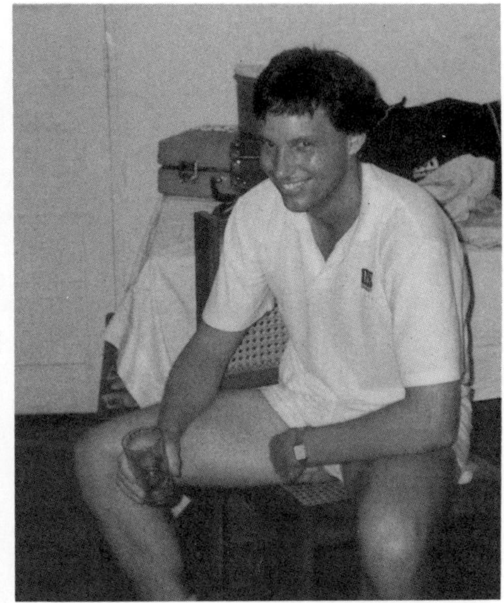

Martin Snedden – a great team man.

'Paddy' Greatbatch – fizzing boy!

in the 1983 World Cup, someone said "the Auckland trolley bus wasn't running too smoothly today".

His other world record was being on nought for 106 minutes after being sent in as nightwatchman in the Wellington test last season. Straight after that game, the Auckland team flew to Napier for a Shell Cup match and the flight seemed to take forever. When someone complained, Sneds pointed out that he'd batted without scoring longer than we'd been airborne.

He and Boocky have been the most regular church goers and perhaps it's just coincidence that they both like to take the mickey. At a team talk before a West Indies test, when most of the discussion had revolved around how to cope with their fast bowlers, Sneds piped up: "This fellow Marshall – he's a bit quick is he?" When we inspected the Eden Park wicket with Allan Border under heavy skies before a one-dayer last season, AB asked Sneds where the rain usually came from at Eden Park, hoping to get the benefit of his local knowledge. What he got was: "From above, I suppose." These little one-liners are known in the team as "Sneddisms".

I hope Martin stays in the game because he'd make a hell of a good administrator.

Danny Morrison didn't play cricket till he was 12 and started out as a wicketkeeper. He can remember keeping for a North Harbour age group rep team to Willie Watson who was pretty quick and the big star. When he was 13 he saw Richard Hadlee bowl on TV and was hooked. He talked his coach into letting him have a bowl and took five wickets for 13.

Danny's a great kid. He's got the heart of a lion, tremendous stamina, and is very professional for a young guy: every night after play he goes back to his hotel room and does 20 minutes' stretching. Early on he used to smile at batsmen which I thought was unhealthy in a young tearaway fast bowler. It was just his way of relaxing and he doesn't do it much now. Not too many batsmen smile at the prospect of going out to face him – he really is very quick and he has the great asset of being able to move the ball away from right-handed batsmen. I really hope Danny develops into a great opening bowler because if he does, New Zealand cricket should do very well over the next few years.

He wasn't very well during the Napier test last season – although he still got five wickets on a flat track – so Bob Cunis decided to take an interest in his health. After checking out Danny's diet, he decided he was eating too much bean sprouts and fennel and not enough red meat. "You don't want to eat fennel," Bob told him, "that's the stuff cats and dogs pee on." Phase two of the recovery programme was sitting next to Bob in the dressing room when he had his first cigarette of the day. "Breathe that smoke boy," said Bob. "It'll put hairs on your chest."

Danny's on the short side for a fast bowler – so is Malcolm Marshall – and in the test match at the Melbourne Cricket Ground in 1987/88 he had to field down in front of the notorious section 13 quite a bit. One bloke kept bellowing: "Morrison, you garden gnome, where'd your mother find you – down the bottom of the garden?"

CHAPTER TWENTY-TWO

The dirt trackers

A dressing room is like a cave – there's no code of conduct, no false politeness. Anything goes and it's all very honest, sometimes painfully so. Facades are down – people don't care if they stand on each other's toes, literally or figuratively, and at times the language would make your hair curl. You can lie on the concrete floor in your jock strap if you want to, and if someone's in your way the correct form of address is "butt off" rather than "excuse me". If I block someone's view of the television, he'll ask "am I in your way, Wrighty?"

Guys let it all hang out in the dressing room. Some players throw bats and rant and rave. One batsman came in from making a match-saving 150 but the skipper didn't utter a word of congratulation. He was so browned off that when the skipper left, he stood in the middle of the dressing room and hurled half a dozen glasses against the wall, calling his captain every filthy name in the book while he did so. A long silence followed this performance, then the dressing room toilet flushed, the door opened, and out stepped the skipper.

Dressing room humour doesn't take prisoners: there was a guy – let's call him Peter – whose team mates call him Derek. He told so many lies, they were not sure they believed his name really was Peter.

After I'd put Australia in at Perth in 1989 and we were sitting in the dressing room at the end of the first day's play contemplating the outcome of that tactical masterstroke – Australia 290 for two – Martin Snedden said "look on the bright side, Wrighty – they could be 290 for one".

The best nicknames are dreamt up in the changing room. Bruce Taylor, now a selector, was known as a lucky cricketer. He was called 'Haystacks' because the team reckoned that if he fell out of a plane, he'd land in one. Another player, who suffered from the short arms/deep pockets syndrome, was known as 'Budgie' because he wanted everything on the cheap.

Old yarns get recirculated: whenever we're playing a team with a nasty fasty, some will recall how Phil Horne's grandmother rang to congratulate him when he was picked to make his test debut against the West Indies in 1986. Remarking how fiery their bowlers were, she told Phil not to forget his chest protector. When he said he didn't have one, she said "well then, don't forget to wear a vest."

The bonds that hold 11 individuals together and make them a team are forged in the changing room. If you've got a good spirit there, the side will tick and work as a team. You take your dressing room spirit onto the field and if the guys are unhappy there, it will show on the park. Any team has its stars, then its bread and butter players, and finally the guys who perhaps aren't quite good enough to hold down a regular place. Often it's the third category – the blokes sometimes called the dirt trackers – who can make people laugh, at themselves and others, and who mould everyone together. Every team has to have these sort of characters. They do the same job in club, first-class and international cricket. Often their role isn't recognised but they're worth their weight in gold, especially to managers and captains.

Dirt trackers can laugh at themselves: Gary Robertson has played one test – against Australia in 1985 – and taken one wicket for 91. After Dipak Patel got his first test wicket in Perth last year, Robbo sidled up to him and said "congratulations, you've finally caught up with me".

Dirt trackers come into their own when you're in strife. They have a philosophical approach to life which enables them to put things in perspective. Robin Penharrow, a leg spinner who played for Northern Districts, personified this attitude: the first time he got picked for Poverty Bay, he turned up with his girlfriend and fishing rod but forgot his boots.

The other thing about these guys is that they make playing the game enjoyable. All the statistics and achievements that the public and the media fuss about pale into insignificance in the end; what I remember – and it's the same for everyone who relates to people – are the guys I've played with. It's the same whether you're an international or a club cricketer – there's something about guys who get off their butts and away from the TV and go and play on a Saturday afternoon. You've still got to get the selectors' nod of course: my mate Harry reckons the only reason he gets picked for an Auckland musicians' social team is that his wife makes a great bacon and egg pie.

I remember the characters more than the centuries and the great grounds. You might've met a guy only once or twice then he retires or gets dropped or whatever but you've had a bloody good discussion over a beer. When you get to international level, friendships are much harder to make because it's so intense and competitive. Even within a team, people are competing. Having a good mate in an international set up is different from having a good mate outside cricket. I'm great mates with the guys in the New Zealand team but I don't see a lot of them at home.

But when you're up against it in Pakistan or you pick up a newspaper at home and read a headline like 'One day wimps', then there's a great comradeship which is special and inspiring. Guys support each other – I remember Evan Gray and Chris Kuggeleijn during the Bangalore test; they were rooming together and one was as crook as the other but they really helped each other out.

It may be a slightly rose-tinged view but I've always felt club cricket

Dad (with the pads on) and my uncles, Ness and Alan.

is full of dirt trackers and therefore a lot of fun to play. My father was a pretty good player who played first-class cricket and used to score centuries in North Canterbury club cricket. School holidays coincided with the harvest and when I was 13 and 14 I used to open with Dad and we put on a few century partnerships which was a wonderful experience. Ever since then I've had a good feeling about club cricket although I haven't played very much of it and have scarcely set the world on fire when I have played. Once I got into county cricket and the New Zealand team, I didn't have much opportunity to play club cricket and when the chance did arise, my inclination was usually to take a rest.

Holmesdale, the club in Kent I played for in my first season in England, was almost the definitive English cricket club. There was a lovely pavilion and a superb wicket in a picturesque little ground. I opened with a bloke called Keith Wooding who was easily good enough to play county cricket but he hadn't seen eye to eye with the person who was running Kent cricket – besides he made more money in the real world. The women were very involved, more so than I was used to, and it was very social. We had a fixture with the Thames Valley Gentlemen, a team associated with the hell-raising actor Oliver Reed. It was a pretty social affair. Whichever captain could de-cork a bottle of champagne first won the toss. The side batting first would start their innings at dusk and at the end of the innings, we'd break for some serious celebrations and resume the next day. The Gentlemen had a guy who'd eat plates and glasses as his party trick and it was rumoured that once they played for a prize of a crate of champagne and a lady of the night.

The other club I have fond memories of is Metro in Pukekohe, which

I joined when I moved from Gisborne in 1979. Don Ingle, known as 'the Monk', was the president. In my first game for Metro we had to get 117 to beat Ardmore and I was expected to get 100 of them in double quick time. The Monk turned up in time to see me dismissed for 14 and greeted me by telling me I was "bloody useless".

I opened with 'Cutter' Curtayne who played the quicks very well – he stood right in front of the wicket and what he missed, hit him. His legs were constantly bruised so he started wearing towels as thigh pads. He was very competitive and whenever he got a bowl, he ran in with great vigour off 15 yards. Unfortunately the velocity of the delivery didn't match that of the run up but he made up for it with the odd bit of sledging, generally out of frustration.

Jack Snell, our slow left armer, was knocking on for 50. He fielded exclusively at silly mid on and crossed the pitch between overs with a stately stride and then bowled his 15 overs for not many. Once the opposition batsmen got in an almighty mix-up – the pair of them must have sprinted the length of the pitch three or four times without actually completing a run while we made a botch of running them out at both ends. Jack stood bemused at silly mid on while frantic batsmen and fielders pounded back and forth past him. When order had been restored, Jack pronounced his verdict: it was, he said, "the biggest balls up since Dunkirk".

I used to bat at five and bowl off spin, my best figures being three for 20 against Tuakau. They were a man short and when wickets started tumbling, they persuaded one of our supporters, who'd spent the afternoon emptying a well-stocked chilly bin, to don the pads. I have to admit he was one of my victims but they all count. We'd have lunch at the Tuakau pub and send the first three batters back to get the innings underway while we finished lunch.

Bill Massey was a pretty laid-back customer. I was 40 not out and we were chasing a hundred-odd when he came in down the order. I was a test player by then while he played only occasionally. As he walked past he said he'd just take singles to give me the strike. His first four scoring shots were 6, 6, 4, 6 which made it pretty obvious what he thought of my batting.

The Counties selector was Richard Halliwell, known as 'the Head'. He played for our arch-rivals Pukekohe and once dropped me from the Counties team for not turning up to practice regularly enough. He did me a favour because there was a race meeting on that day.

Alan Stimpson was a great source of amusement for the Northern Districts team. If he was told to play a long innings, he'd take five minutes to get out to the middle, two or three minutes to take guard and survey the field, then he'd continually stop the bowlers in their run ups, pretending he had something in his eye or someone was moving behind the bowler's arm. One day he was reading a book before he went out to bat and he arrived at the wicket with it tucked in the flap of his pad. It fell out when he played a forward defensive and Bert Vance at silly point asked him if it was a good read.

Raising the fire alarm.

The blaze is extinguished.

Suspected arson.

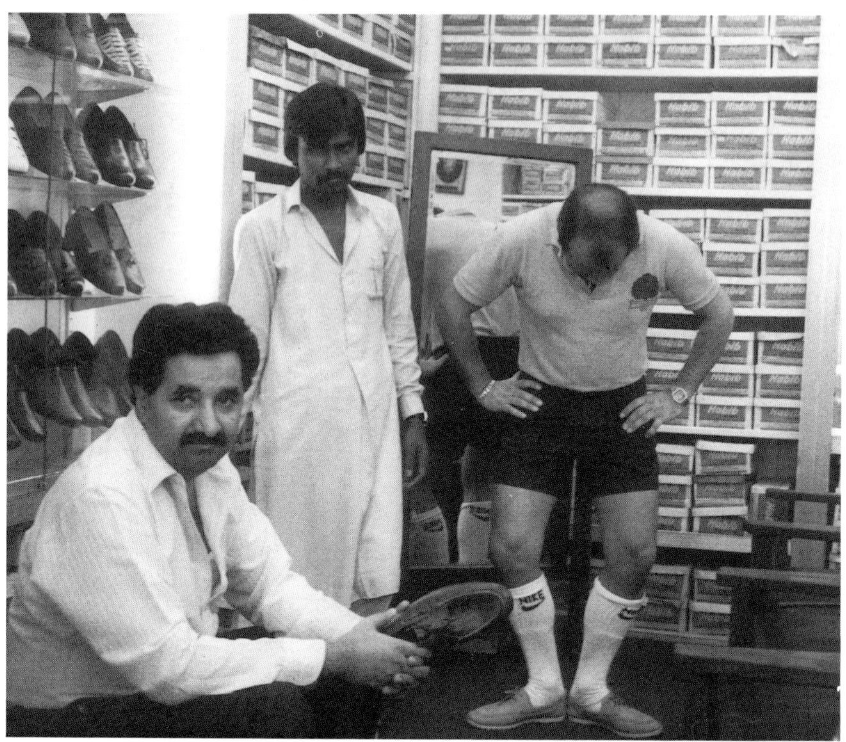

Brian Waddle, Radio NZ's commentator, sizing himself up in a Karachi shoe shop.

"Well, Mer, will you share it with your team-mates or put it in your garage?"

Brendon 'The Bro' Bracewell and his trusty blade 'Centurion' preparing for the big one.

Accompanied by delighted schoolboys, Gary Troup leaves Carisbrook after he and Stephen Boock saw New Zealand to victory by one wicket over the West Indies, 1980.

The Wild Bunch – Metro Cricket Club, Pukekohe.

True grit – Evan Gray personifies Kiwi pride.

'Victor Trumper' Stirling.

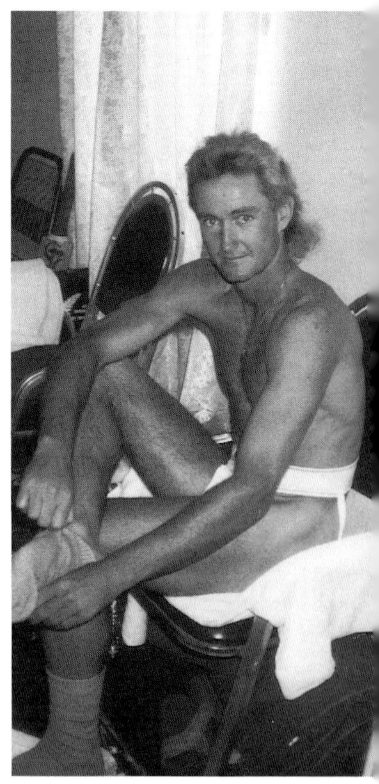
Tony 'The Hunk' Blain.

At Seddon Park in Hamilton there are air ducts between the dressing rooms so you can hear what the opposition are saying. In the middle of Mystery Morrison's team talk, Stimpo got on a stool and boomed down the air duct: "Wellington, this is God speaking; give up, you haven't got a chance".

In my time the New Zealand team has had some tremendous dirt trackers. John 'Tube' McIntyre had a long and distinguished career with Canterbury and Auckland before he was chosen for the 1978 tour of England. He was probably picked too late but he was a very good tourist and the whole experience was an almighty thrill for him. He and I and Warwick Larkins the scorer used to make up tapes for the team which were a review of events and a bit of a mickey take – for the benefit of the Hadlees and Dick Brittenden we imitated Jack Sullivan announcing an All Black team consisting of 15 Cantabrians.

Tube was knocked out by Lord's and when we arrived there for the first time, he immediately disappeared on a mission of exploration. He came back half an hour later to tell us what a fantastic place it was and how it even had a sauna. That turned out to be the room where players put their sweat-stained gear to dry.

I first played with Chris Kuggeleijn in a Northern Districts South Island trip when he was 19. I think it was when he came down to breakfast in Dunedin smoking a cigar that I twigged that he was a bit different from your average cricketer. I'd come across him earlier, at a Rothmans tournament in Christchurch in 1973 when he was 17. The first day was washed out and Kuggs, being a great gambler, got into a card school with Trevor Luke, Dave Dempsey and Paul McEwan from the Canterbury side. He had only about $15 to see him through the whole week but that didn't last long so when he drew three trumps in three card lieu, he borrowed $10 from Murray Childs and went for it. Unfortunately Dave had three higher trumps and Kuggs was left without a cent.

He borrowed a few more bucks and drowned his sorrows at the pub, making his way back to his billet late that night. He had to scale the fence and his feet had just touched the ground when there was a wolfish growl from across the lawn and he realised that he'd forgotten the name of his billet's alsatian, an ill-tempered beast which was quite impervious to Kuggs' charm. He's come a long way as a card player since then and is definitely a man to play with rather than against. We used to team up against a couple of the press guys on the the train trips in India and cleaned them out. I hope the journos' employers didn't check their expenses claims too closely.

Kuggs loves a punt; when I pointed out to him in India that the number six spot was up for grabs, he replied that he'd love a go in a Group one race. In his debut test match he got off to a good start when he held a slip catch to give Richard Hadlee the world record. Then he got sick and it turned into a nightmare: he got a pair without actually hitting the ball, given out lbw and caught off a bat/pad which was 100 per cent pad. No one said a word when he came into the dressing room after the second zero. He sat down, lit a cigarette, took his pads off, then said "I think I'll go up to the scorer's box and check out my run charts." Throughout the tour he called me 'Johnny Hapuka' because every time he tossed out a line, I'd rise to the bait.

Because of that ability to keep his chin up, I was surprised to see him looking really glum down on the boundary during a one-dayer against Pakistan in 1989. He hadn't got runs, they'd taken 50 off his ten overs, and he'd dropped a catch but normally it took more than that to dampen his spirits. I discovered later that he'd just heard from a spectator that Blackie O'Neill, a horse on which he'd placed a large each-way bet, had run fourth.

Jock Edwards would be the most talented New Zealander I've seen when it comes to striking a cricket ball. He was such a natural that it was a shame he never really fulfilled his potential; he got caught halfway between batting and wicketkeeping. Unfortunately he never played in an era which emphasised fitness and was always carrying a little bit of excess.

Jock went to England in 1978 as the only 'keeper, which was pretty tough on him, got quite homesick, and was the subject of plenty of barbs from the likes of Trevor Bailey. He once let four byes through at five minutes to one and a spectator told him to stop thinking about lunch. He had a pretty complicated card trick called Black Sambo; he and I and Rock Collinge went to a pub without too much cash between us but Jock did his card trick and we didn't buy a drink all night.

Tony Blain has been unlucky to play in Ian Smith's shadow, competing against the best in the world, although I think he's batted better day in, day out than Smithy. Blainy's a great team man, a guy who'll never let you down. He's not the most punctual of people and his sartorial inclinations are often at odds with those of the management, not to mention whoever designed the New Zealand team uniform. He turned up to one function wearing a punk rock studded belt and bracelet, which didn't impress Bob Cunis too much, and has an amazing selection of shirts including a turquoise suede one.

Blainy couldn't get to sleep during the Sharjah tournament so he took a few sleeping tablets when one would've been ample. The next morning the rest of us were in the bus and someone had to go and wake him up. We had only 10 fit players so he had to play; we just hoped to field first but we lost the toss and got inserted. He lasted three balls from Qadir, then went back to sleep again. He missed out on the England trip this year but I am sure he'll come back; he's a very good one-day cricketer.

Trevor Franklin's comeback to play first-class, let alone test cricket, after his dreadful injury is a wonderful achievement. He was in an English hospital for five weeks and the get well card from the NZCC arrived the day he left. He loves his food and the Auckland and New Zealand teams have given him the job of marking lunches out of ten, a task he goes about with due seriousness. When we had Australia 90 for eight wickets in their first innings at Wellington this year, someone remarked that it was turning into a clinical operation. "Without an anaesthetic," added Franko.

I've always admired Evan Gray's commitment. He's been in and out of the New Zealand team, his best stint probably being the 1986 England tour when he batted well at number six and won the most valuable member of the team award. There have been times when he probably didn't make enough runs and wasn't a sufficiently penetrative bowler to secure a place but he took his disappointments philosophically.

India was a bit of an ordeal for Ev because of his aversion to curry – the rest of us would be tucking into an arse-rattling good brew and he'd sit down to a bowl of breadsticks and a can of coke. He taken the precaution of bringing $250 worth of chocolate with him which made him the most popular man in the team.

Last season Ev went up to Auckland before the rest of the Wellington team and as social organiser of the side he made a restaurant booking for 14. The others were delayed at Wellington airport and didn't get to Auckland till after 9 p.m. When they got to the motel at 10, there were frantic messages to ring Ev at Chez Daniel where he was sitting in splendid isolation at a table set for 14, surrounded by eight opened bottles of red wine.

Gary Troup was a solid guy, a great team man held in a lot of respect by the players. At the end of the West Indies tour Frank Cameron asked Gary to write a summary of each player's performance on tour and mark them out of 10, which indicates how much weight Gary's opinions carried. Another in that mould is Chopper Crowe, a good guy to have around because he's so solid and even tempered. The various pressures he was under as captain did get to him but he never let it show.

My first international opening partner was Jumbo Anderson who experienced severe culture shock in Pakistan. He found life there rather trying as did any Pakistani who encountered him. He once summoned room service and told the waiter he wanted a boiled egg cooked for exactly four and a half minutes, threatening death and destruction if it wasn't delivered in three minutes.

Perhaps the best team man of them all Brendon "the Bro" Bracewell was only 18 when he went to England in 1978 and on the way down to play Glamorgan at Swansea, we told him he'd need his passport to cross into Wales. We stopped for morning tea at a motorway cafe and Brendon was out in the carkpark pulling suitcases out of the bus's luggage compartment, hunting for his passport. Bevan Congdon had just bought a fancy new suitcase and was outraged to see it being unceremoniously dumped on the concrete as Brendon's search continued.

Ken Rutherford is just starting to feel part of the side now after being in and out for a few years. Not surprisingly, his premature selection to the West Indies blew his confidence away – I didn't help by running him out for a duck in the first test in the West Indies by taking on Roger Harper which isn't a smart thing to do. As he walked off some barrackers screamed out "hard luck Noughtaford". But despite things going wrong, he was the most mature 19-year-old I've ever met.

He enjoys a beer and whenever we couldn't find him, the bar was the first place we'd look. When we batted together on the way to beating Australia at Eden Park in 1986, I couldn't get over how relaxed he was. Although I normally don't say much in the middle, he had me chatting away about horses. We even got a congratulatory telegram from the NZ Racing Conference which we both enjoyed.

Bob Cunis has always been a great contributor in the dressing room and that still applies. He's always been a very hard competitor. I remember him batting for ND with Mike Wright in a tense situation. There was a big appeal against Mike for a bat/pad, Bob rounded on the umpire and told him: "You can't give that out – you've given nothing all day." Mike was quite upset about it afterwards, saying that he'd never cheated in his life. "You didn't cheat son," said Cuni. "The umpire made a mistake."

Brendon Bracewell's efforts to find his passport to enter Wales attract the attention of Bevan Congdon.

There's a story about Cuni captaining Papatoetoe against University in Auckland club cricket. The first day was rained off and the captains agreed that both sides would declare their first innings after scoring one run so they could play for outright points. Varsity completed their side of the bargain but Papatoetoe battled on then rolled Varsity in the second innings to win outright. In the clubrooms afterwards Bob remarked that it was funny that none of the Varsity boys had stuck around for a beer.

As cricket manager Bob's instilled that hard-nosed attitude in the team but he's still one of the boys, someone you can have fun with and very much part of the changing room. With his bandy legs and shorts he's a distinctive figure at the nets. At Adelaide he left his white floppy hat, along with his cigarettes and lighter, on the ground where we'd been having a selection meeting and went back to the nets. While he was away I started a fire under his hat, using a cardboard box that cricket balls come in. Soon puffs of smoke, like a Red Indian's smoke signal, were emerging but Bob pretended not to notice. When he finally retrieved it, there was a big hole in it but he kept wearing it anyway, prompting the comment that he'd always been a bit of a hothead.

Billy Stirling is the funniest guy I've ever toured with. He's a wonderful impersonator, his repertoire ranging from a Maori All Black centre warming up, shorts down around his knees practising sidesteps, to his grandmother's swimming freestyle action to every fast bowler in the business. He never had a bad word to say about anyone and there were plenty of laughs when he was around.

The selectors treated him badly. We went to Pakistan without Hadlee and Billy bowled really well, making Zaheer and Miandad hop about on good batting wickets. We thought we'd found a partner for Paddles. Back home he played a couple of games for CD on flat wickets and didn't do too well and they dumped him. He should have been part of the squad so he could train with us, get coaching and stay part of the international scene. But they left him to wallow and he never reached the heights again although he performed usefully in England in 1986.

He almost caused a diplomatic incident in Barbados. Struck a painful blow on the thigh bone while batting, Billy had to lower his trousers to apply the pain-killing spray. He had only a jock strap underneath and treated the crowd to a view of his white bum, not a familiar sight in that part of the world. It happened to be pointing at the main grandstand where the official party, including the Governor General, was sitting. There was quite a fuss as the locals seemed to think that a white boy giving the Governor General a downtrou, however unintentionally, was a severe breach of protocol and apologies had to be made.

CHAPTER TWENTY-THREE

Planes, trains and automobiles

My first tour was to England in 1978. Since then I've been pretty lucky and there's never been a tour when I've thought "I might miss this one". However, you never know you've made the trip till your name's read out and being a W meant my name was usually last.

For players on the fringe missing out must be terribly disappointing. I'm in favour of taking as many players as possible. Some of them might not get many games but for the younger guys, tours are a great learning experience. They get a feel of what it's like to be in the test arena. I wish I'd gone on a tour and had a chance to bat myself into the test team before I became a front-line player. That's the best introduction.

Touring means you're there to do nothing but play cricket. People say it must be great but normally you get to the ground an hour and a half before play starts. That's 11 o'clock in England, 9.30 in Pakistan and in India the one-dayers start at 9 a.m. Travelling to the ground normally takes 15 to 30 minutes but in India and Pakistan it can take a lot longer. In Pakistan we played a one-dayer at Sialkot which is 75 minutes from Lahore and another in Faisalabad, 90 minutes away. The hotels in Lahore were far superior so we preferred to travel down which meant getting up at five o'clock to get to the ground at seven.

Say play finishes at six: you wind down in the dressing room for 30 minutes or an hour although the trend these days is for players to skip the socialising with the opposition and get back to their hotels as quickly as possible. That's a pity because it's a great learning experience for the likes of Willie Watson to yarn to Terry Alderman. We tend to do it more with the Australians although it didn't happen much when Greg Chappell was captain. In Pakistan you can't drink anyway and the changing rooms on the sub-continent aren't, for the most part, places you want to hang around in any longer than is absolutely necessary.

The days are long and you don't get too much of an opportunity to sightsee. It's a heavy work commitment, especially if you're a front-line player. When you're not playing you're either travelling or practising. It's not uncommon on a seven or eight-week tour to have only two or three days when you're actually free to do as you please.

If you're confident of being picked, you've generally got a fair idea of the itinerary. You look to see where the tests are and batters and bowlers see things differently. If you're a quick bowler, you're happy if there's a test at Perth; a spinner going to India can expect to play on turning wickets.

Then you look at the build-up games before the first test, which are a crucial part of the tour. I always check to see what hotels we're in. When you're not playing, you're in the pub so the standard of them is important and, in India and Pakistan, absolutely crucial. If you strike a bad hotel at the wrong time – and there are varying standards of hygiene – you can find yourself with three or four players crook on the eve of the test.

In 1985 we arrived in Karachi and stayed at the Inter-Continental which probably doesn't feature prominently in Inter-Continental's glossy sales brochures. Down the road was a Sheraton which we checked out the next morning – it was miles better. It doesn't do much for the team's spirit when there's a better hotel down the road so Ian Taylor, Jerry Coney and I negotiated a deal that involved us playing a benefit game at the end of the tour and staying at the Sheraton when we came back to Karachi. It's really important for morale that you get good accommodation.

Generally the Cricket Council relies on information from other teams which have toured the particular country recently. From what I've heard from Graham Dowling, the former New Zealand captain, now Chief Executive of the Cricket Council, and Bob Cunis the standard has improved out of sight since their day. In India in 1988 the standard was generally excellent. Sometimes we drove past the places they'd stayed in in 1969 and we were pretty pleased with the change. Dowls' 1969 team actually stayed at the ground in Hyderabad in a room above the players' changing area.

In 1986 we stayed at the Waldorf when we were in London. It's next to Covent Garden in the West End and it was wonderful to come back from the game and be able to get away from cricket by going to the theatre or to all sorts of different restaurants. It was a tremendous standard of accommodation considering what top London hotels cost.

There's always a great feeling of optimism at the start of a tour. You're setting out on an adventure together and everyone wants to do well. People have high expectations of themselves and the team and the general atmosphere is postive. The good feeling is tempered, for the married guys, by the fact that they're going to be away from their wives for quite a while. Because the destinations were generally en route to England or after the English season, Sue usually travelled with us for part of the tour which helped me enormously. I had a good mate with me and saved a lot on phone calls. It wasn't easy for her: the novelty soon wears off, she had to watch a lot of cricket, and the players are uptight a lot of the time.

Certain administrators – perhaps those who fancy a couple of months away from their wives – have opposed wives being on tour. I've always felt that as long as the relationship doesn't infringe on the team aspect – and there's only one occasion on which a wife has upset the applecart – it's a good thing because it takes some of the pressure off. The team room is off limits to wives and media. Some captains have had a more liberal attitude but I feel it should be a place where the players can go to relax by themselves, particularly for a few beers or a chat after the day's play.

Being away from home is no problem for the young single guys – it's bloody good for them in fact – but for the others it can cause strain. You get the situation where the phone call home hasn't gone well and the player's down. Variations on homesickness can affect performance. Some cope better than others; some enjoy the travel and adjust to touring and others never do; some players don't handle India and Pakistan at all. They can't wait to get home so they just drift through the tour and if you've got that attitude, there's no way you're going to perform. You have to establish in your mind that you're there to play cricket.

The manager and cricket manager are important. A good manager is an asset – he makes the whole thing run smoothly – and the reverse applies. We've had a manager who had never been out of the country before: at the team meeting before we left his biggest worry was how we were going to get sticking plaster – in Australia! Mystery Morrison suggested we float some over in a bottle. Another manager was too lazy to walk up four flights of stairs to check on a sick player's health when the hotel lift broke down.

It's a result of the 'jobs for the boys' syndrome. They're queuing up for the good trips but no one wants to go to Pakistan. Generally it's best to have someone who's been on a few tours and knows the ropes. They also have to be there for the right reasons: their job is to look after the team and represent the NZCC. Some take their wives with them and you hardly ever see them. The players know if they've got a good manager or a dud very quickly.

In England managers have to spend a lot of time waving the flag in county committee rooms and need the constitution of an ox. But the main job is to get players from A and B, make sure accommodation is up to scratch, keep people punctual and generally keep the show on the road. Only the very knowlegeable ones get involved on the cricket side – there's nothing worse than a manager who's had a snort or two getting into a discussion on the shortcomings of the team or an individual. That gets on players' goats more than anything. That sort of manager has to be taken aside by the coach or captain and told to concentrate on looking after the side.

The logistics can be daunting. In India planes are delayed so often that you can spend half a day going backwards and forwards to the airport. Fortunately the trips to India and Pakistan have been well managed and we've had tremendous liaison officers who've done plenty of tours. They are paid by NZCC: they can speak the language, they know the hotels and know the ropes.

"What's the dress for tonight's function?"; "what time does the bus leave?" Unless someone is addressing these questions, you can get half the team turning up in ties and blazers and half in smart casual. Basil McBurney related best to individuals, Dave Elders was a father figure and Ken Deas who was the manager in India in 1988 was the best we've had from the NZCC. Leif Dearsley was excellent – he had exceptional organisational and administrative talents.

In the last few years we've developed a system where guys in the team do specific jobs:

Assistant manager – Ewen Chatfield has done this on the last few tours and does a tremendous job and will make a great manager in future. There's almost a case for appointing someone to do the job on an ongoing basis. Chats makes sure the manager is doing his job and that a notice goes up before 11 p.m. outlining what's happening the next day.

Accountant – these days you're given a meal allowance and a laundry allowance and how you spend it is up to you. The accountant is in charge of everyone's money on the tour. His book reveals that some guys eat very well and enjoy themselves and others scrimp and save and eat Big Macs and do their own washing so they can spend up at the duty free or get souvenirs or whatever. Jeff Crowe lives pretty well; Stephen Boock is a great shopper as is Richard Hadlee, especially on electrical goods, but management takes the palm in this department: Ken Deas and Ian Taylor are the all-time champion shoppers. I'm known to be pretty frugal. I get my washing done as cheaply as possible because it costs plenty. If Sue's with me the allowances have to cover both of us.

In Peshawar in Pakistan the handicrafts, carpets and onyx were superb and they were pretty good in India too. Singapore on the way back is the place for buying the family presents. On one of my trips to Australia I bought a motor mower and Lance Cairns bought a gas barbecue which made us the butts of several jokes. You have to watch your spending. In Australia in 1981 Paul McEwan, Lance Cairns, Ian Smith, Ian Taylor and I went to the Cox Plate in Melbourne and had a few bets. We didn't eat very well for the rest of the week.

Bruce Edgar was a great accountant and Martin Snedden is pretty good too. One manager in Australia took care with money to extremes, trying to deduct prescriptions from the players' allowances. When our physio Mark Plummer bought a $7 inner sole for a fast bowler, he wanted to know who it was for so he could dock him. We knew the NZCC was a bit strapped for cash but that seemed ridiculous. However, the senior players sorted it out and nothing was charged.

When we beat India in a crucial World Series one-dayer Taylor threw a party at which $300 worth of toasted sandwhiches were consumed. Some managers would've checked who was there and how many toasties they ate. Ian was a good manager and one of the reasons the 1985 Pakistan trip went so well.

The social committee – I've had a fair bit to do with this and Jerry Coney did early on. In places like England and Australia it's not that big a deal: there are plenty of things to do and the players tend to go their own

"Guilty as charged." A court session in Pakistan.

way. There are a few court sessions where the new guys have to give a speech on a subject like the manager's wife, nominated by the social committee. You have fines and that sort of thing but it's not an integral part of the tour.

In Pakistan, India and Sri Lanka it's important to have a fairly active social committee. In Sri Lanka Boocky, Jerry and I organised a treasure hunt in this huge hotel we were staying in up in the highlands; tourists and the hotel staff watched in amazement as hordes of young men went racing through the place identifying objects. We also had a tennis doubles tournament won by Martin Crowe and Ron Brierley. Fancy-dress parties, cards and quiz nights bring guys out of themselves and help them relax, forget about cricket and let their hair down. Things like that break down the barriers that sometimes grow up between players. In India and Pakistan it relieves the tedium of the hotel.

In India we got a daily telex from the New Zealand Press Association. It was eagerly awaited for such things as share prices, political news, club cricket scores, and race results. In Rajkot we got the Melbourne Cup field and the night before the race we had a calcutta. A lot of excess meal money was involved. You drew a horse, then they went into an auction. The seller kept half and half went into a pool. Guys were forming little syndicates and buying several horses. The top horse went for 1500 rupees and the first prize was 3000.

The next day we eagerly awaited the results which came through during play and only David Leggatt, the NZPA man, knew. He gave the finishing order to Chris Kuggeleijn who harboured a desire to be a race caller and that night he called the race to a group of very expectant cricketers. The two-mile race lasted seven and a half minutes but he got the finishing order exactly right. I had mixed feelings about it. My syndicate had the winner but Might, a horse I'd bred, finished last.

Timekeeper – you have fines for lateness because there's nothing worse than one bloke keeping everyone waiting on the morning of a test match when the guys are pretty toey. It's $1 a minute but the bus goes after five minutes and the late one has to get a cab.

On one tour we played a game way out in the middle of nowhere. After the match there was a function at which the two women present were mobbed. A member of the touring party struck up a friendship with one of the ladies and there was no sign of him the next day when we boarded the bus at 6 a.m. for our nine and a half hour bus trip to our next destination. The manager left a message for the missing bloke saying he had to show up by a certain time or else!

Needless to say his whereabouts was the subject of much discussion and speculation on the bus trip and when he passed us eight hours later in a rental car, it provoked much animation and a variety of earthy gestures.

Lateness causes all sorts of aggro, especially if it's the same guy all the time. Cairns and Chats did the job and generally had the upper hand. Since the system of having a timekeeper came in, punctuality has improved out of sight although Tony Blain has problems with it. You can't have rules for some and not for others – it has to be no exceptions and that includes the captain and the manager. Geoff Howarth, for instance, wasn't renowned for his punctuality.

In charge of dress – John Bracewell has done this recently and he's a tough taskmaster: in 40 degree heat in India he issued orders for jerseys or tracksuit tops. You can get the order for number ones and someone will turn up in red shoes or a punk rock belt. Andrew Jones is particularly fond of his red shoes but they don't really go with a uniform of grey slacks, light blue shirt, and black blazer. Martin Crowe is the flashest dresser and has the biggest laundry bill. I was always a little bit rebellious on dress but the more senior you get, the more you see it from the other point of view. It's a discipline thing. Bob Vance made Blain wear blazer and tie for three days on the England tour for breaking dress regulations. You've got to look like a team, be smart and together. It's important that the senior guys set an example and have a word to the youngsters when they're out of line. The All Blacks have had tour discipline and traditions associated with touring for years but we're only just getting into it.

There are a lot of advantages to being in a touring team: your luggage is usually looked after, people make a fuss over you, you don't have to queue at airports much; you're privileged compared to the average tourist. On the other hand there are standards of behaviour to live up to – you can't forget that you're ambassadors for your country and that discipline off the field generally reflects discipline on the field.

Autographs – the hardest job is to get 15 guys to sign an autograph sheet. In India there's always someone who wants a sheet for each of his 16 brothers and sisters so you have to go back to the team for another 300 autographs. They only want originals – no photocopies. This task always gets assigned to one of the new boys.

Balls – it's not unknown for New Zealand teams to turn up for a one-day international and want to do some bowling and fielding only to find that the person who should have brought the balls has forgotten them. Willie Watson is very good; Danny Morrison not so good. It's amazing how many balls are lost to or acquired from the opposition depending on whether your thieves are better than theirs. Balls are a potential sore point, so to speak. Some bowlers like to use new balls in the nets and they save them and look after them lovingly but a moment's inattention and someone's using their pristine cherry to knock up with on a wet outfield much to the bowler's annoyance.

Beer – always well handled by Jeff Crowe and Ken Rutherford. It's their job to make sure the team room is stocked with cold beer to be shared equally after the game and for team meetings. It's a precious commodity in India and Pakistan and when a bloke has had a bad day on the first day of a test, he might knock off his quota that night.

The flag – Hadlee has been a bit hampered with his media commitments and so on and he's made a very poor job of looking after the flag which we take with us to fly at the grounds. Quite often it's followed us around in the post.

Tickets – They used to be Ian Smith's speciality before he took over rooms and was replaced by Bracewell. You get so many tickets per test to share out. On tour you usually give them to people who help you, like hotel staff, seeing not many of us have relations in Lahore. They're a great bargaining chip and can ensure your room is well-cleaned. At home they go to family and friends. We don't sell them.

Allocating rooms – the captain, vice-captain and senior pro, if numbers permit, get single rooms. You have to pay for your wife and in the West Indies, where accommodation costs are astronomical, Hadlee saved Sue and I a lot of money by giving up his single room for us. The great advantage – perhaps the only one – of being a vice-captain is getting a single room. It means you can go to bed when you want to.

Sharing can be tricky because you get on with some guys better than others and some people have definite preferences, for and against. Andrew Jones and Tony Blain have known one another for years so they like to room together as do Martin Crowe and Mark Greatbatch. You don't put a light sleeper and a snorer together. One player used to smoke during the night, his nickname was 'Glow worm', and another was an exceptionally loud snorer and farter; others talk in their sleep. During big games it's important that guys are sharing with people they're comfortable with but you can't let cliques develop either. Some people are introverted so every now and again they're put with someone who'll pull them into the team. If a player's having a bad trot, you put him with someone who can help him out.

I hate rowdy hotel rooms and have a reputation for changing rooms. Traffic noise gets on my wick – I'd rather have a quiet dingy room on the wrong side of the hotel than a flash one with a view close to the street. Often no one can find me because I'm not in my allocated room. I remember the good rooms – 2020 in the Melbourne Hilton is away from everyone and there's one on the 18th floor of the Boulevard in Sydney which doesn't get traffic noise. Some guys could sleep next to a motorway. Indian drivers are compulsive horn honkers and there's nothing you can do about it.

In India and Pakistan health is always an issue. We have a list of doctor's dos and don'ts and you must follow them, or you're letting the team down: you could get crook and not be able to play. There have been times when guys have made a point of eating salad or seafood out of bravado. Even if they don't get sick, they're over there to play cricket, and must make sure to do everything possible to keep fit. Anyone doing that sort of thing gets hauled over the coals pretty smartly.

We played at Swansea before the third test on the 1986 England tour. The cricket ground is the St Helens rugby ground so we decided to have a few kicks and a run around on the famous turf. Turner and the physio Graeme Hayhow told us to stop and they were probably right. You don't go roller skating in the middle of a tour: you've got a responsibility to look after yourself. If you get injured, you make sure you turn up for regular treatment. In India our physiotherapist Mark Plummer's day started at 6 a.m. with sessions on Hadlee's ankle and my back and he had to repeat the treatment after play. If someone was crook during the night, he got up and sorted it out. The physio's really important on tour and in places like India and Pakistan can work 16- to 20-hour days.

Everything on tour stems from the management. If the manager is good everything happens on time, the practices are well organised, and if you

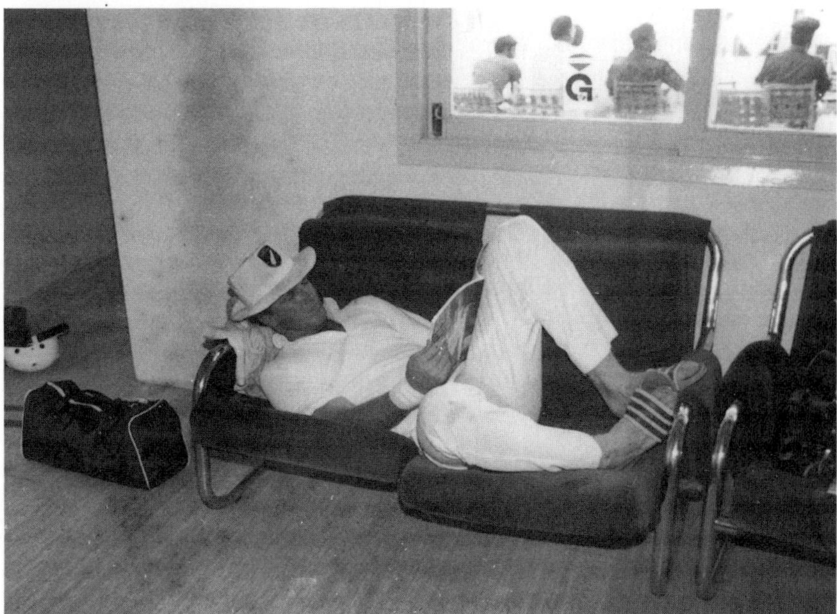

Back to the coaching manual.

need something done about your wife's room or flight reservations, you know it's taken care of. One manager was asked to organise air travel for a group of wives and didn't do it. The wives ended up travelling separately and it caused a lot of anger. A bad manager will do things more efficiently for the captain or senior players than for the troops. Some guys get incredibly upset by managers but if you're well organised yourself, you can go the whole tour having very little to do with them.

The cricket manager is important. He's got to make sure the net sessions go well, that people are involved, that he's sensitive to each team member so everyone feels part of the team even if they're sitting on their bums for five days. Not playing on tour is tedious. These days guys who have a game off are sometimes allowed to have a day or two away from it.

Living and travelling together wears people down. Some get homesick, some aren't doing well, and by the end of the tour the tolerance level is lower. All these things are influenced by how the team is performing. Things run smoothly when the team and individuals are doing well. In India and Pakistan you have the tiresome dietary restrictions – you have to chlorinate all the water you drink or use to brush your teeth. You can't have salad or a drink of milk or a tomato sandwich and the so-called western cooking isn't like New Zealand food. A couple of blokes with a sense of humour are worth their weight in gold – people like Stirling, Blain, Kuggeleijn, the late Andy Roberts, Mystery Morrison – as are the steady eddies – Chats, Gary Troup. In Australia in 1989 Robbo and Bro – Gary Robertson and Brendon Bracewell – made an invaluable contribution despite not making the test side.

The media generally fit in well and are part of the group. Problems can arise when someone sends a clipping from home and players find they've been rubbished. There have been confrontations but they're generally sorted out over a few beers. At least you're away from the pressure of the home media. The press guys have come a long way to cover the tour and have the same frustrations as the team. In India, Pakistan and Sri Lanka we've had good relationships and friendships have formed; everyone's stuck to the rules and been professional. There have been occasions when a player who feels he's been unfairly rubbished has found himself next to the rubbisher on the bus resulting in stony silences all the way to the hotel. Generally a camaraderie, a sense of being together through thick and thin, develops. One of Bob Cunis's strengths is his ability to deal with the media in a no-nonsense way. In Australia in 1989 we got, for the first time, a tremendous press from the Aussies.

Occasionally we get a laugh at their expense. Security was so tight in the Sikh city of Chandigarh during the World Cup that we stayed in the best hotel in town while the press were consigned to an establishment called the Sunbeam.

A very bedraggled mob of pressmen used to turn up in the mornings to be regaled with stories about how great the food in our pub was. Apparently Iain Gallaway's boiled egg arrived with a knife and fork – and he needed them! The air conditioning in their rooms was so noisy it was like sleeping with a helicopter.

India and Pakistan are more than a tour – they are a mind-expanding experience. In Peshawar, near the Afghan border, there are three million refugees from the war. Horses and carts ruled and we drove to the ground through people tending flocks of sheep. It was a biblical scene. We took our own food, a microwave, a television and video player. Breakfast was muesli and canned fruit and milk; lunch, cheese and biscuits or sardines; tea canned beef or tuna casserole and dehydrated vegetables.

For Sue, being in Bahawalpur was like being in captivity – there were no other women around; she couldn't wear shorts or short sleeves, and when she was watching the cricket, there'd be a crowd staring at her. We travelled to the games in vans and the drivers would race each other – it was mayhem. The priests chanted verses from the Koran over loudspeakers at dawn and dusk. The wickets were good, the umpires bad, and we didn't get the results but we were well managed by Ian Taylor, and Masood was a very good liaison officer.

On the rest day in Hyderabad we were taken for a bus tour and were followed by a busful of cops. We saw the most incredible poverty and when we went to a shopping mall, there were crowds everywhere wanting to touch us and the shopkeepers gave us little gifts. The cops had to keep the crowds away. We saw a snakecharmer whose pièce de résistance was to put a snake, half a metre long, up his nose and out his mouth so the snake's head and tail were protuding from the two orifices. We watched the Pakistan golf open on TV; the greens were very bumpy and one of my enduring memories of Pakistan is that the tournament leader was wearing Wrangler jeans.

The hospitality was superb; they couldn't have done more to make the tour go well. It was just a pity about the umpiring hassles which soured relations. A lot of Pakistanis watch on TV and can see what's happening and there were articles in the papers saying enough is enough. It's a bit like rugby here – a disaster if Pakistan lose. There's a lot of competition for places in Indian and Pakistan teams.

Before the tour, the itinerary is just a lot of names; you have no conceptions of the distances and in Australia and India they are vast. There is a tendency for itineraries to get more and more punishing. In India in 1988 we finished the final test match in Hyderabad a day early and had a day off before the one-day series, which went like this:

Day one – left Hyderabad at 10 a.m. on a two-hour flight to Vishkapatanam. One-hour drive to the hotel. Practised in the afternoon.

Day two – Practised.

Day three – Played 9 a.m. to 4.15 p.m. Back to the hotel for a mayoral reception then caught train at 10 p.m. Not too bad but not the best night's sleep I've ever had as we were woken at 5 a.m.

Day four – Arrived in Cuttack at 6 a.m. Went to hotel for a few hours' sleep. Practice in the afternoon, a light training run at a local school, a game of rounders – married vs singles. Reception in the evening attended by the president of the local cricket association, the secretary, their wives, relatives, friends, and probably pets – a cast of thousands.

Day five – Up at 6 a.m., an hour's bus ride to the ground. Played. Back to the hotel at seven.

Day six – Got to the airport at nine. Flight delayed. Hung around at airport with gear till midday. Back to the hotel. Flight to New Delhi finally left at 9 p.m. and we got to the hotel at midnight. Something to eat then bed.

Day seven – Arrived at airport for 10 a.m. flight which left at midday. Two stops and arrived in Indore at 3 p.m., hotel by 3.30. Too late for practice because it's dark well before six.

Day eight – Arrived at ground at 7.30 a.m. Played. Caught train to Baroda at 9 p.m.

Day nine – Arrived in Baroda 5 a.m. Hotel by 5.30. Morning in bed. Practised in the afternoon.

Day ten – Up at 6.30 a.m. Caught in traffic jam after the game and not back in hotel till 6.15 p.m. Flight delayed so didn't leave for airport till 8.30 p.m. Arrived in New Delhi at 11 p.m.

Day eleven – Up at 5 a.m. for 6 a.m. flight to Jammu. Two stops en route but couldn't get off planes because it's Sikh country and security is tight. Arrived 9 a.m. Hotel by 10. Day off.

Day twelve – We awoke to the sweetest sound we've heard in months – rain on the roof. Game rained off. Cunis told the press we're disappointed not to play. Left Jammu 6 p.m., flew to New Delhi, arrived 9 p.m. To a hotel for a couple of hours then back to the airport for a midnight flight to Bombay. Arrived 2 a.m.

Day thirteen – Sleep most of day. Leave for home at midnight.

When I read this itinerary before the tour it looked tough but I had no idea of the distances involved. The Indian cricket authorities wanted to spread games around the regions, and fixtures tend to be awarded to the highest bidder there. Dilip Vengsarkar, the Indian captain, said he'd never played in half these places before. But they weren't bad places to play – Cuttack for instance, in the middle of nowhere, had a great stadium and superb changing rooms.

Umpiring in India and Pakistan is just a fact of life with which you've got to come to terms. In the second test in Pakistan in 1985 I was sawn off in both innings. It was incredibly frustrating because it's absolutely beyond your control. On the last day of the test I went up to the umpire who'd done it and said "Allah knows, he'll get you, you cheating bastard." He just laughed at me. I had no idea if he was a cheat or incompetent but I didn't feel like giving him the benefit of the doubt.

Despite what people here may have thought of him in 1989, Imran

"Danny boy, this could take us a while!"

Late for the team bus.

Smithy smiles for the fans on an Indian overnight sleeper.

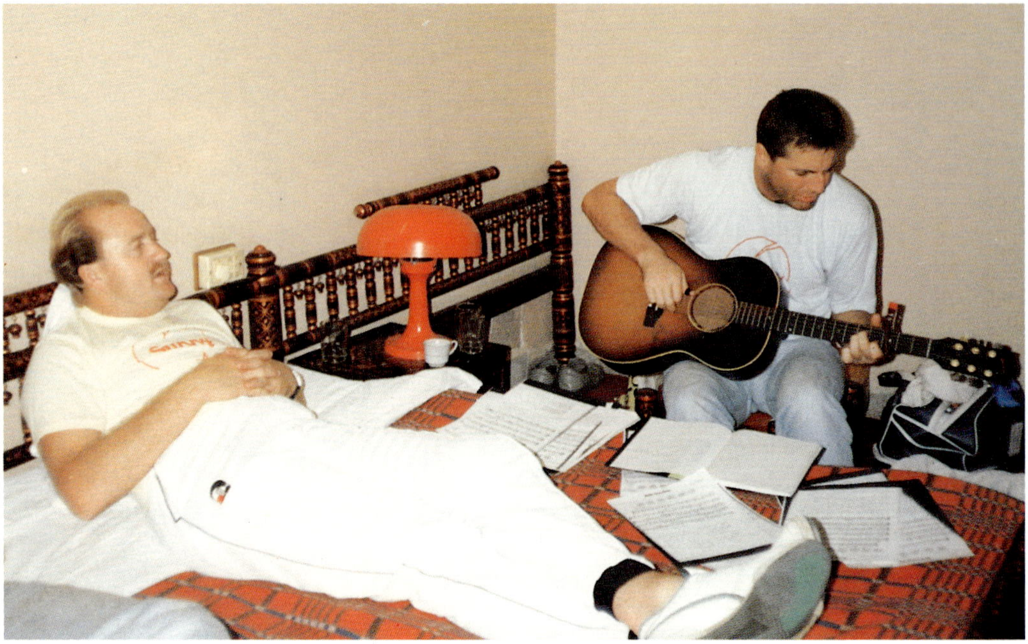

"Twinkle, twinkle, little star . . ."

A communal soak after a day's play at Hove, 1978.

The Members' Stand, Hyderabad.

"This is not a screw-top!"

"Your deal Cairnsy."

Exchanging fishing stories.

The Whisky Club convenes in Rajkot.

was quite a reasonable, positive influence. In 1985 Zaheer was in charge; he really wanted to win and the umpiring was diabolical. Miandad was given not out off Bracewell and it was all on. Coney was going to take the side off the field and had a shouting match with Shakoor Rana, the umpire, who was saying "I swear by Allah, he didn't touch it" – you could've heard the snick in the pavilion. Meanwhile Miandad and Bracewell were setting up a meeting behind the grandstand after the game to resolve their differences. I ended up getting involved in the argument with Coney and the umpire, telling Jerry that we should at least finish the over, then walk off, by which stage of course there was no point.

Coney reached the point where he took every decision personally. That was understandable – Miandad isn't the sort of guy you want to get two bats every innings. Exactly the same thing has happened with Allan Border and Mike Gatting there but you've got to become philosophical when you're the captain – once they put the hand up, they're not going to take it down. At least I've never seen it happen. The Pakistanis now are campaigning for neutral umpires – presumably they're also getting tired of every tour turning into an international incident – and part of that campaign involved belittling our umpires.

It's very political there. For some reason they wanted Mohsin Khan out of the team, even though he was one of their best players. The word was out and he got a shocking lbw. The Pakistani players are under a lot of pressure at home and not many of them scored that heavily.

We weren't angels. The umpires got a lot of abuse from us. The wicketkeeper Dalpat sharked me out in the second test and before the third I told him if he did it again, I'd wrap the bat round his head. He kept his mouth shut. At the end of the day though, they were the better team and deserved to win the series. The umpiring in India wasn't as bad but I still felt the odds were stacked against us. It was very subtle: we'd work our way into a position of strength, then suddenly a couple of key wickets would go.

The West Indies tour was really hard and followed an intense period of cricket. We went to Pakistan, Pakistan came here, then we went to Australia for the World Series, then to West Indies in March. We had two warm-up games, then the first one-dayer, then the first test. There were no easy games: if you weren't playing Holding, Marshall, Garner and Davis you were playing Merrick, Walsh, Gray and Co., guys who were just as quick. I also played every game whereas some of the other guys had a lot of time off. That meant three or four days off in ten weeks except when we got cleaned up in the tests and finished early.

The little islands – St Kitts, St Lucia, Antigua – were lovely places to play but Kingston is a tough town and we were advised not to leave the hotel after dark. We had two weeks in Trinidad in the Holiday Inn down by the wharves. The Windies were in the Hilton which wasn't by the wharves. Everything was incredibly expensive and there was a perceptible colour thing – we were advised to only go out in groups and we often heard the line: "You white honkies, you're going to get your licks."

I didn't enjoy the tour but the cricket was good. The wickets were generally flat and I was psyched up for it although I didn't get the results I wanted. In my first three test digs I got a roughie, a run out, and an lbw to a Holding bouncer which went along the ground. Guyana was the flattest wicket I've ever played test cricket on. It was also a tricky place, very restrictive. Going there was in doubt because the All Blacks were meant to be going to South Africa. There was a lot of poverty – it had apparently been very wealthy but had gone down hill under the government of Forbes Burnham. Our hotel was one of the few places because of flour shortages that had white bread. Sue and I went out with Michael Holding and a couple of his friends who were teachers. They couldn't get enough books for the kids. There were rows of buses standing on drums because there were no replacement tyres, beautiful big houses that hadn't had a coat of paint in years, and a thriving black market. The West Indies players said the place had really gone downhill since they first played there.

Some players make themselves unpopular on tour. When the world's right with them, everything's fine but when it's not, look out because they don't show any sensitivity to their team mates. If things aren't going well, good tourists don't take it out on the rest of the team. There's only so much whinging you can do if flights are delayed or the food's not too good before everyone gets heartily sick of the sound of your voice; it's also inane to go to a foreign country expecting to find everything to your taste. You've got to try to be cheerful and have a laugh and there are plenty on tour.

In Kandy in Sri Lanka Boocky fell asleep after a few drinks and I covered his face with talcum powder. He got a hell of a fright when he woke up and looked in the mirror. At the next hotel, I had a huge ceiling fan in my room. I had all my suitcases open and gear spread out when I turned the fan on and powder went everywhere. He'd put a whole tin of the stuff on the blades of the fan. It took me an hour and a half to shake the bloody stuff out of my clothes.

In India Bob Cunis bought some gems which he kept in his wallet. He didn't trust the hotels to look after his wallet so he took it everywhere. On the rest day of the third test, the Kiwi media had a game against the local media and Bob played. Kuggs and I ran into him coming out of the lift on our floor after the game and he was extremely vexed. It turned out he'd lost his wallet and was sure it'd been stolen. The hotel management was rung. He thought he'd left it in his room so a detective was summoned. This went on for about an hour with Bob getting more and more grumpy before the wallet turned up. Someone had found it on a seat in the lobby, where Bob had been sitting, and handed it in to reception. He was happy as a sand boy, though he got some ribbing.

The next morning, to while away the time on the physio table, I rang him in his room and said I was Inspector Patel of the Hyderabad police and would he come down and make a statement. I'd just done it on the spur of the moment but Bob fell for it. "It's all right officer," he said. "It's been found." "We understood it was taken from your room," I said, "and we've held five suspects overnight for interrogation. If you can't come down and make a statement, I'll send Senior Sergeant Ranji to the ground to collect one."

When he came down to breakfast, Bob got stuck into the liaison officer for bringing the local constabulary into it and the guys were giving him a hard time. At the ground we got one of the multitude of cops to pose as Sergeant Ranji but before he could open his mouth, Bob had him baled up against a wall, warning him not to touch those innocent men. When we went out for warm-ups we told him and he took it very well. He didn't have much choice with 15 guys hysterical with laughter.

The new boys are always good for a laugh. On being introduced to the former British Prime Minister Ted Heath at a reception in London, Brendon Bracewell opened his side of the conversation with "Do you work here, Ted?"

In Pakistan a young female Karachi cricket fan showed some interest in a young and single Billy Stirling. Cairns gave him a bollocking, saying Pakistan was not the place to even look sideways at the local women and that he could end up in jail. That night I rang him up, putting on an accent, and introduced myself as Mr Butt from the firm Butt, Butt & Pervez. I said I was Hani's father's lawyer, that this was a serious matter, and I was coming over to talk to him.

Then I got the hotel porter to ring Billy and say there was a Mr Butt in reception to see him. Billy wouldn't go down so I got the porter to ring and say Mr Butt was on the way up. Billy barricaded himself in his room for five days. The guys were telling him he'd have to stay in Pakistan for the court case and Bryan Waddle of Radio New Zealand said he didn't know how he was going to explain to New Zealand why one of the team wouldn't be coming home. Others were saying we'd have to try and smuggle him through the airport. Martin Crowe was counselling him that the New Zealand Embassy would be able to help him. By this stage Billy was petrified he might have to stay in Pakistan. Martin Snedden wrote a letter purporting to come from Mr Butt saying he would be taking legal proceedings, that Billy would have to stay behind for the court case, and that the maximum penalty was a 50,000 rupee fine and 50 lashes.

We got a policeman to deliver the letter. Billy read it and went white. There was a reference in the letter to 'wrongdoing' and Billy kept shouting "it's a lie, nothing happened". When he finally found out what was going on, he was too relieved to be angry.

CHAPTER TWENTY-FOUR

Christmas in Rarotonga

The wickets for the 1987 World Cup in India had been excellent and I was looking forward to cashing in when we returned for the three-test tour in late 1988. The warm-up games were played on fantastic batting strips but their spinners were so good they could get assistance from them. In the West Zone game at Rajkot the off spinner Radia was able to get turn off a very flat wicket – he might've chucked it mind you. In the nets there'd be kids of 13 and 14 who could probably play first-class cricket in New Zealand.

The first test was at Bangalore, which is a magnificent stadium. The seating is very close to the ground and very high, which creates atmosphere. We went to the ground two days before the game and one look at the wicket was enough to see that it would turn square: the wicket was absolutely bare and the ground staff were simply rolling grass clippings into it. But the Indians had obviously decided that our spinners were nothing to worry about or at least no match for whichever three or four they picked from the 50-odd they had to choose from.

The press asked me when I thought it would turn. I felt like saying "in the eighth over, when the spinners come on" but you've got to be optimistic before a test so I said probably at the end of the third day. I was thinking that if the test pitches were all like this we could easily lose the series 3-0.

I lost the toss, Hadlee got a couple of early wickets and broke Botham's record, Chats and Evan Gray bowled well, Bracewell not very well at all. Sidhu got 116, Vengsarkar 75 and they ended up with 384. We batted a long time for 189 and got hammered by the press for it. The point was, it was a square turner and it went quickly because their spinners have that great ability to create quick turn. Then most of us got ill.

On the evening before the rest day we had a function that none of us wanted to miss: it meant the chance to meet a thousand or so local cricket administrators in a room the size of a lift. We left at about ten and I went straight to bed when we got back to the hotel. Within ten minutes I was shaking violently. It was a bit like the plague as someone went round putting crosses on the doors of guys who were crook. There were nine doors with crosses on them.

Paddles' dose struck the next day when he was downtown doing some shopping. The Indians had treated him like a superstar from the word go and about a dozen people rushed him back to the hotel. His room was like a scene from Emergency Ward 10 with four doctors arguing about what they should do with him. One of them wanted to inject him with paracetamol and I thought "Well that's Paddles knackered one way or another".

India batted for just 28 overs for their 141 in the second dig with Srikkanth playing incredible shots, hitting Gray's left arm spinners over extra cover for 6. We went in again late on the fourth day. I felt really crook but very detached and Franko played well and we batted through to stumps. At the start of the fifth day we thought we could save it but then I got fired with what I thought was a bad lbw, Jonesy got a bad decision and all of a sudden we were three down after an hour. Kuggs also got a roughie to complete his pair in his debut test but it was the timing of them which really hurt us. I was ropable because I thought we could hang in there. I'd also spent a lot of time talking to the umpires, P.D. Reporter and S.K. Gosh. That morning I'd said to them, "You understand these guys are going to put you under a lot of pressure today". The Indians play it hard and appeal a lot but they aren't like the Pakistanis.

After the game I did a TV interview with Ken Nicholson and I thought "I could be doing this after the next two tests as well". We felt we'd tried like hell but been on a hiding to nothing. But regardless of the result, I felt that we'd played with a lot of courage and I was really proud of the team.

Then it was on to Bombay for the second test. From the dressing room the pitch looked quite green and historically the wicket there has given some assistance to seamers but up close it was the same thing: grass clippings rolled into a shaven wicket but it didn't look as bad as Bangalore. I thought it would turn by the third day and would be really going by the fifth.

We made a couple of changes. Tony Blain is a very talented cricketer and a great team man, one of the best I've been away with, and worth his weight in gold for that. If you had 15 Blains in the side, you'd never have any problems but when the pundits are assessing team selections, they never take that factor into account. I don't think Chill's that far behind Ian Smith as a 'keeper although his keeping hasn't come on because of the lack of opportunities. He and Kuggs had scored centuries at Goa so it was tough on Kuggs to be dropped. It was also tough on Evan Gray because he'd bowled better than Braces at Bangalore but we decided to gamble and go back to the old New Zealand formula of three seamers. We figured it didn't matter what Paddles had to bowl on, that Chats could hold up one end, and we'd let Danny Morrison have a crack at them.

I don't think anyone in India and very few in New Zealand gave us a bolter's chance and it was pretty clear from what they'd done with the pitch at Bangalore that we were looking down the barrel of three-zip.

Bombay is another great stadium with lots of atmosphere. Someone told me that I needed 26 runs to overtake Bevan Congdon and become the greatest New Zealand run scorer in test cricket. Congo had taken 61 tests and this was my 60th. I've always been a little disappointed with my record in tests: I should have got there in 50.

I won the toss. One of the marvellous things about being a captain in India is that you never have to worry about what to do when you win the toss. You don't spend two days worrying about whether you'll look like a pillock if you insert them and it doesn't work. If you win the toss there, you bat. That's it.

When you win the toss, especially when you're playing on turning wickets and it really counts, everyone thinks you're God. I can remember Paddy Greatbatch booming out "great stuff captain". He was so positive, it was like having someone underline your decisions in red ink.

It's humid in Bombay and the wicket was damp. Franko played well. Ayub came on the over before drinks and he made it turn a foot. I thought "Oh God, here we go again". Franko came down the wicket, almost walked past it, and got stumped down the leg side. Jonesy came in and shouldered arms to Dev – not a bright thing to do in India – and was lbw.

Twenty minutes before lunch I played forward to Hirwani and got a fine edge. My angle was all wrong, I was playing towards cover instead of straight back to the bowler. It wasn't a huge mistake but it was enough and it's a bugger to get out defending. At lunch we were 72 for three – not good. At lunch Don Cameron of the *New Zealand Herald* asked me how it felt to have broken Congo's record. Under the circumstances, it didn't mean a hell of a lot.

Greatbatch, who hadn't had a good first test, was in and playing well.

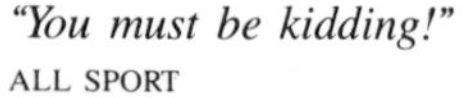

"You must be kidding!"
ALL SPORT

I felt sorry for Ken Rutherford batting at five. He'd opened against the West Indies when it was flying about and now he always seemed to be going in when it was turning. He got out not long after lunch which made us 83 for four. The storm clouds were gathering. Blainy played really well but Shastri, who was their least effective spinner, came on and bowled an absolutely unplayable ball: it turned quickly and bounced off a length, got the shoulder of the bat, and lobbed to slip; 110 for five.

Richard Hadlee went in and tried to smack it around. Paddy was still going well and I thought he was unlucky to be given lbw for 46 – 121 for six. Paddles got out at 141 and Ian Smith at 158 for eight. In the dressing room Cuni and I discussed where we might spend Christmas.

Danny Morrison went in about an hour before tea, joining Braces who hadn't been playing the spinners that well. He'd been defending when he's better off attacking. Danny's six previous test innings had yielded a total of 16 runs. At that stage I thought we'd get 170 as Chats is better at batting for time than runs.

They got through to tea when everyone had a chat to Danny, telling him to play for Braces. He defended brilliantly and played Ayub as well as anyone. It was one of those partnerships where you're not expecting much so every run is a bonus. Braces was talking to Danny a lot and he got more confident and hit a couple of fours over the top. At stumps we were 231 for eight and the partnership had lifted the side. We knew we hadn't done well but felt we were back in the game when at 158 for eight, we'd been out of it. Braces had batted well, swept well. The umpires hadn't got involved because they hadn't been given a chance to. They passed the previous ninth-wicket record against India and in a way it was a continuation of the resolve the team had shown at Bangalore.

Afterwards someone asked Danny what he and Braces talked about in their long, intense between-overs chats. He said they were discussing whether they'd have lamb or goat curry for dinner.

Martin Snedden, the vice-captain, had been injured early in the tour, missed the first test, and hadn't been able to fight his way in for the second which was a great disappointment to him. He's a good thinker about the game and an excellent selector. Sometimes captains and vice-captains don't get on that well because the vice-captain is the one who'll take over if a change is made. Martin gave me great back up. He took the drinks out to Danny and Braces. It was a little thing but he relates well to both of them.

Mark Plummer the physio fits in really well with the side. He's a real solid, consistent guy. At Bangalore he'd been working 20 hours a day. He was the one people rang when they felt crook at 2 a.m., he took round the pills and drinks, and in the morning he'd be working on Hadlee's ankle and my back. He was a great source of information to me because guys relate to him and tell him things when they're on the physio table because he's neutral, a bit detached. Without breaching confidences, he'd pass things on to me: "Paddles is okay but needs careful handling; Kuggs isn't right no matter what he tells you." He took the drinks out with Sneds and you couldn't have had two better guys. I'd probably have said the wrong thing if I'd gone out.

We went back to the hotel knowing we weren't out of the game. Danny particularly had shown that you could block forward to Ayub and Hirwani. We were thinking that we might get 275 to 300 but it didn't work out that way. The innings only lasted a few more overs – all out for 236. In retrospect one of the most remarkable of the many remarkable things that happened in this test match occurred that morning and was hardly noticed at the time: Chats was clean bowled by Kapil. Normally he misses the ones off the stumps and blocks the ones on them.

We were in the field after half an hour. There was a big crowd – 20-30,000. Danny was straight into it and in his first over Arun Lal snicked one to Greatbatch at first slip, who dropped it. Paddy would feel it more than most. It was a blow because we were keen to get Sidhu, the danger man, in while the ball was new. He hadn't faced Hadlee much at Bangalore and when he did, he just wanted to get down to the other end.

Then Paddles got Lal and Sidhu lbw – 34 for two. The umpire who gave them, Gupta, is one of the best in world cricket. Vengsarkar joined Srikkanth who really went for it and suddenly the game was starting to slip: they put on 100 in 118 minutes and we were looking at a score of 400.

Throughout the series the sight of Vengsarkar was like a red rag to a bull to Braces. For some reason Braces didn't like him much. Vengsarkar had a bit of luck and Braces sledged him continually. In the end it got to him and he played a horrible shot. At tea they were 141 for three.

I've taken a long time to get to know Braces even though his elder brother Doug has been a mate from way back. He's one of the guys I'd want with me going over the top. You need him out on the park because he makes life uncomfortable for the opposition.

One of the nice things about playing in India and Pakistan is that you play only five and a half hours with a 90-minute session after tea. You have to bowl 82 overs in the day and at tea we still had a lot of overs to bowl. Cuni and I talked about it and decided we were going to do it at our own pace.

The crowd had built up even more for the final session and they got their money's worth: in the first five overs India scored 31 and lost three wickets. Generally Richard likes to bowl a few overs before tea but he had a dicky ankle and I had to be careful with him so I'd held him back. First Braces got Azharuddin caught by Greatbatch. Franko was in the gully and I wasn't sure if he was the right guy to be there. He wasn't our best gully and if you have the wrong man in the wrong place at the wrong time, it can cost you the match. As captain you can think about something like that but decide to do nothing. Then the exact scenario you were running through in your mind happens and no one knows you screwed up except yourself. Hadlee caught Srikkanth halfway, the ball went not that quickly to gully, and Franko hung on to it – 150 for five and we were back in the game.

Shastri came in. The crowd seemed to dislike him in most parts of India and particularly in Bombay and they gave him the funeral chant as

"No, Braces, he's staying just where he is."
ALL SPORT

he walked to the wicket. I've never heard a cricketer get more stick from his home crowd. I think it's because he's been a controversial figure in their domestic competition. He's a good player and handled Paddles better than anyone in the Indian team. He'd climbed into Braces in the first test and Braces wanted a long-on straightaway. The conversation went like this:

JB: I want mid on back.

JW: No. He's just come in. Let's gamble.

JB: Wrighty, I want my bloody mid on back!

JW: He's staying where bloody he is.

The big thing with Braces is to get him into his rhythm and he loves to get through a couple of overs without being whacked. Going for runs early on upsets him. I don't want to upset him but it wouldn't have mattered if mid on had been 20 foot tall and standing on the rope because Shastri hit the first one he got way over the fence. I gave Braces a long on and thanked God it hadn't dropped ten yards in from the rope. A couple of balls later Shastri smacked one over mid wicket for another six. He took 14 off the over and I took Braces off which isn't an easy thing to do. He wasn't pleased.

Kapil thrashed the first ball of the next over for four and they'd got 18 off seven balls. Then Paddles bowled a really slow one outside off stump; Kapil tried to hit it out of sight and dragged it on to his stumps – 172 for six. We'd had a couple of drinks breaks and gone over time and it was starting to get darker. The Indians didn't like it but we had only four bowlers and had to take our time.

Shastri was playing well, which was frustrating because I wanted Paddles to bowl at the guys who didn't play him well. I gave Chats a trundle and he bowled Shastri with a dead straight ball which he just misjudged; 209 for seven. I brought Paddles back for a few overs before stumps and he bowled very fast. Patel took a fearsome blow on the arm – it hit him so hard I thought he'd never bowl again – then was caught at bat/pad fending another one off. Ayub snicked one to second slip where Braces took a brilliant catch – 232 for nine.

The little leg spinner Hirwani came in at number 11 looking nervous. I wanted Paddles to hit him on the fingers rather than get him out but as usual Paddles was more interested in wickets although he did make him fend one off his nut. The final session, scheduled for 90 minutes, had taken nearly two and a half hours. Richard had taken five wickets for 49 off 20 overs. We'd pulled back from the dead a second time.

Next morning Paddles bowled Kiran More for 28 and we had a two-run lead on the first innings. It was quite cloudy when we went in to bat and Kapil, getting the ball to swing, had Franko caught behind in his first over. The wicket had turned on the first day because of the dampness but not a lot since and we knew that if we got runs on the board, we could put the Indians under pressure. Jonesy, who hadn't had a great tour, came in. Neither of us says a lot in the middle so between overs we meet halfway down the pitch and grunt at each other. We went to lunch at 46 for one.

After lunch I felt good. I'd even gone down the wicket to Hirwani and whacked him over the top. Then he bowled one well outside the off stump. I went forward and got a big edge and squeezed the ball between bat and pad. They appealed like hell for lbw and Raswami, who had a shocking test, gave me out. I've been fired before and have to expect it because I don't walk – it happened twice in the same test in Pakistan – but I'd never been angrier about a dismissal. Something almost snapped and I gave the umpire a load of abuse on my way off the field. Of all the bad decisions I've ever had this was one of the worst and I couldn't accept it. It took me ages to calm down.

At tea we were 133 for two and Jonesy and Batch were playing well. We had them. At 149 Paddy played a bad shot and was bowled by Hirwani. Then Jonesy was lbw. Ruds came in and the ball started to turn. Blainy got a bad lbw. We ended up losing six wickets after tea for 49 runs. Ruds never looked at home, Hadlee got out having a whack again, and I sent Danny in as night watchman which didn't impress Braces or some of the others at all. I wanted Smithy to bat in the morning. Realistically he represented our last chance: he's not a good defender and if we were going to win, I wanted him to have a chance to play his natural game. He was in good form and can take spinners apart. Danny got out at 182 for eight so Stockley had to go in. It was the wrong decision in that it didn't work but it did mean Stockley didn't have to bat for too long.

I was so depressed that night at the hotel because of the decision and because it looked like we'd blown the chance of winning. Sue suggested we go and buy a leather jacket to get my mind off it. I didn't want a leather jacket – they're far too trendy – but I was that browned off I went out and bought one. It turned out to be a good decision because I wore it all winter.

Tomorrow was another day and we had to be positive. I don't think three guys have ever had as many throw downs as Braces, Stockley and Chats got that morning. The big fear was that one of them would get fired. They played brilliantly and we went from 182 to 250. In the end Stockley was fired, given out caught at silly point off Ayub. Chats survived for an hour, another legendary innings, and 29 more runs were added. Braces' batting in this game was brilliant. He was part of three amazing partnerships and it was typical Bracewell: never lie down.

India started batting after lunch needing 282 to win. That morning the wicket didn't turn much and it looked like the venom had gone out of it but it was probably just the batting which made it look that way. Throughout the game, the further on in the day, the more the ball turned. It was a Sunday and there was another big crowd.

Srikkanth shouldered arms to the first ball and was so plumb he almost had to walk. Then Sidhu and Arun Lal played pretty well. Sidhu had played Braces well and can hit the ball a huge distance but I gave Braces a bowl and straightaway he got massive turn. He was also bowling well. Sidhu was always looking to hit the ball over the top so we had to make the same decision about mid on. It was academic. Sid charged down the wicket looking to hit it into the stand, missed, and was bowled. That was 48 for two with ten minutes to go till tea. Just before the break, Braces bowled Vengsarkar with a great nut – 54 for three.

At tea we could smell victory. Straight afterwards Paddles got Arun Lal who'd always seemed the guy who could get a big hundred because he was prepared to be patient, unlike the other Indian batsmen. What's more that day I'd had the feeling he was going to get a score. I was also worried because I'd been bowling Chats with a slip and a gully and thinking it might be better to have two slips and a backward point. While I was mulling it over, Lal had gone for a cut and top-edged the ball to where second slip would have been. At the time I thought that could be a decision – or non-decision – I'd regret forever. But then he snicked Paddles to Paddy Greatbatch at first slip; there aren't many people who are happier than Paddy when he takes a catch but there was one that day. Three balls later Azharuddin was caught close in by Ruds; 89 for five.

Shastri walked in to the chant and immediately started playing well. Braces had a couple of good appeals, an lbw and a bat/pad, turned down by Raswami. The batsman was Kapil and he was the one guy I thought could turn it. I was wild but Braces went off his head and got stuck in to the umpire. Raswami came over to me and told me to tell Braces to stop abusing him. The crowd could see what was going on. I told the umpire that Bracewell was very competitive, that we'd thought it was out, that we were playing for our country and so on. Then I called Braces over and waved my finger at him for the crowd's benefit. They thought I was giving him a dressing down but anyone watching on television would've been less

impressed because neither of us could stop laughing.

Shastri and Kapil took it through to 134, scoring 36 off 37 deliveries. I brought Danny on, who bounced Kapil and got whacked. Paddles came on and, typical Paddles, made the breakthrough. Shastri snicked one and Stockley picked it up in front of first slip. Some of the lads didn't think it had carried but Shastri had no complaints. The session had been so intense, it seemed to have lasted only five minutes.

Meantime Kapil had been smacking into Braces, stepping away to give himself room and blasting it inside out over wide extra cover. Chats was at deep mid off and I was at extra. One went through Chats' legs for four which had Braces raging. I was wondering where the hell to put Chats because he wasn't the guy to have at deep mid off. With Kapil you get only one chance and you've got to take it so it was frightening the hell out of me. I moved mid on straighter and kept pushing Chats and myself squarer. Kapil went for it again and drilled one just wide of me to the left. I dived and it stuck and I never took a catch that gave me more satisfaction. The guys converged from everywhere – Jonesy ran from deep square leg. He and a few of the others had never been involved in a test victory. Later we heard that when Kapil was out, Srikkanth got up and went into the dressing room and said "that's it".

At stumps they were 137 for seven and everyone was ecstatic. In the lift at the hotel Arun Lal said to me, "well done, we admire the way you committed yourselves today". Azharuddin and Kapil, even More who is very competitive, said the same sort of thing. They were very open and sporting about it. I don't think they'd ever really thought we could threaten them.

The two teams got on pretty well. Paddles and Kapil went out together on the rest day the next day. There were one or two personality clashes – Bracewell and half the Indian team on the field for instance – but otherwise we got along. Azharuddin asked Smithy: "Is Braces always like this?" "Not on rest days," said Smithy.

We had the rest day to recover so we had a big night. Ruds filled up the fridge with Kiwi Lager and we threw the team room open to the media and our supporters. I went to bed at a reasonable hour but at 3 a.m. some of the lads conducted an experiment to test the velocity generated by full Kiwi Lager cans dropped from the 20th floor. I don't think they extended the frontiers of scientific knowledge.

We didn't expect rain at Bombay and people were telling us we had it in the bag. I kept thinking of a Benson and Hedges game at Derby in 1981 when the last Yorkshire batsman Mark Johnson came to the wicket at 123 for nine with them needing 81 in nine overs. Bluey Bairstow, who was 27 when Johnson came in, got 103 and they won from a situation you'd have said was impossible. Besides I'm a bit of a pessimist.

Paddles' ankle wasn't that good but the next morning he bowled very rapidly. Braces bowled More, the wicket we wanted, off his body with one

"Braces, you beauty!"
ALL SPORT

that spun a yard and poor old Patel came in to face the music. He was caught behind to give Paddles his tenth wicket in the match then Hirwani swept Braces to Chats at deep square and that was the ball game.

A lot of guys had contributed: Danny took part in that vital stand and bowled well, loosening up Kapil with the short stuff on the fourth afternoon; Jones, Greatbatch and Smith had batted well; there'd been some great catches and help off the field from Sneds and Evan Gray. Then there was Paddles with his ten wickets. But in the end it was Bracewell's match: eight wickets for 131 and innings of 52 and 32. If the side had been picked purely on performance on tour, Gray would've played ahead of him but we knew what Braces could do.

There were 2000 people there to see us win on the last day and I think that while they believed India were the better side, they respected what we'd done. They also respected us because we didn't whinge as touring teams usually do in India and Pakistan. You know what the score is when you go there, that there will be times when the umpiring goes against you; teams that come here think the same thing. The Indian people love their cricket and they could see for themselves what happened. There's one drawback with not whinging: when people look back on the tour, they tend to judge people purely on performance whereas if there'd been a hell of a row over the umpiring, they would take that factor into account. Blainy, Kuggs and Ruds all got sawn off and they were at the mercy of people picking teams later on who weren't there and might just go on the figures.

We'd been stuffed in Bangalore but it was almost like a victory just to get the game into the fifth day. People made a big deal of the illness but I thought we played with great skill in that game, which we've never been given the credit for. It was such a learning experience – most of our batsmen had never played on a real bunsen before – and I think that what we learnt and went through there was the reason for our win at Bombay.

And in the end, that is what it was: a win. I think of it as the greatest game I've played in but if we'd lost, it wouldn't be getting a chapter in my book.

That night we went back to the hotel and finished what was left of the beer. We even had some champagne, which costs a fortune there, and a team photo. Sometime during the evening Bob Cunis murmured to me "maybe we'll give Rarotonga a miss this year". "Yeah," I said. "I guess we can put it off for a little while longer."

CHAPTER TWENTY-FIVE

Teamwork

I spent the winter of 1989 studying economics, playing and watching the odd rugby match, poring over old Wisdens and New Zealand Cricket Annuals to remind myself of what had happened during the last 12 years, and occasionally seriously considering giving cricket away. When spring arrived I decided to play, although any enthusiasm I felt was stifled by my annoyance over the short tour of Australia.

I thought the tour was absolute madness from a playing point of view. The New Zealand team sent on a suicide mission to earn a few bucks because the NZCC's finances were in a bad state. Most of the senior players felt the same way – we were being sold down the river. My preparation 'in the middle' consisted of two innings on artificial wickets for my new club Papatoetoe – a glorious two against Eden Roskill and a scratchy 40 against Cornwall. The rest was in the indoor nets and the gym.

We got over there and Western Australia cleaned us up in a one-dayer then rolled us in the first innings of the first-class game. We had to bat a day plus a session to save the game, which we did. Ian Smith and I got centuries but I never thought during that innings – in fact throughout the entire tour – that I was in any sort of batting nick. But we worked bloody hard – we had to because we were going up against a team that was much better prepared than we were. As we went through the lead-up games everyone chipped in with a performance at some stage – the Crowes got centuries in the draw against South Australia – and we reached the test match with our record more or less intact even if the team seemed to be coming apart at the seams. Richard Hadlee had withdrawn before we left New Zealand and injuries put Andrew Jones and John Bracewell out of the test.

I won the toss and made the – in retrospect – horrendous decision to insert the Aussies. It seemed the attacking thing to do: we had a young pace attack and the WACA wicket had seamed all over the place on the first day of the Western Australia game. It looked a good batting wicket so it was always a gamble; one we lost because the wicket turned out to have very little in it. 'Wright gets it all wrong' was one of the headlines the next day. I don't think I've ever felt worse than on the first two nights of that game.

We battled away, keeping up our optimism, our team work, our team spirit and our sense of humour. They'd dug the hole and were lowering in the coffin when Paddy Greatbatch, with a little help from his friends, saved us with a magnificent, inspirational innings. He and Martin Crowe had played well in the first innings and in the second Chris Cairns made a quality 28 and Martin Snedden batted for a very long time. What had begun as a no-win situation turned out to be a fantastic way to start the season. Instead of skulking home with our tails between our legs, we walked away from the WACA with our heads up and pride intact. Under the circumstances a draw was almost as good as a win, even though it was largely due to one player. It was great to be back with the lads again and we were still hanging in there. The Aussies were very confident going into the game – understandably so, following their tremendous performance in England – but we weren't prepared to lie down.

During the tour I spent a lot of time in the nets. In 1988/89 I hadn't felt comfortable in the upright stance, standing up straight with the bat held almost at the top of the backlift. I'd adopted that stance because of my back problems and it had served me well but I felt things were going wrong technically which I'd been able to correct in previous years. In the nets I reverted to the orthodox stance with the bat resting on the ground and I found I could do it without discomfort, perhaps because I'd had a winter off after playing more or less 12 months a year for over a decade. The work I'd put in in the gym must've helped as well.

I had a chat with Bob Simpson who said he didn't know how I could bat in the upright stance. He told his players they had to have the bat on the ground to get rhythm into their batting. A couple of remarks I made after the test in Wellington later in the season were written up as if I'd changed my stance purely on Bobby's advice. (I'm not quibbling with the stories – it was a good angle.) I've got a lot of time for Bob but in fact he just reinforced my growing conviction that I should change; I also talked it over with Bob Cunis who felt the same way. During the last two days of the test, when I was no longer playing an active part, I spent a lot of time in the nets in the orthodox stance and it felt good: I hit the ball really well. Ken Nicholson of TVNZ bowled to me a bit and I broke his thumb with a nice, crisp straight drive.

I reckoned that I didn't have long in the game and it would be nice to finish up playing more naturally. Holding the bat up had worked and felt comfortable if not entirely natural. Back home I played in a benefit game for Martin Snedden and got a 70 using the orthodox stance then I agonised over whether to use it or go back to the tried and tested upright stance for the first Shell Trophy game against Central Districts. I had to clear a psychological hurdle: I'd used the upright stance for a long time and achieved reasonable success and I worried that if I changed, I wouldn't be the same player. My wife Sue, who's always been a source of good advice,

PETER BUSH

New Zealand defeats Australia at the Basin Reserve by nine wickets, 1990.

MARGOT BUTCHER

FOTOPACIFIC

FOTOPACIFIC

Mark I.

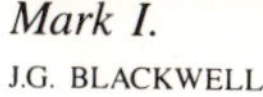

J.G. BLACKWELL

Mark II.

J.G. BLACKWELL

told me I had to be myself. CD batted first and we rolled them but I didn't make up my mind until just before I went in. Then I thought "Bugger it, I'll go for it" and I got 70. I got 90 in a match in Gisborne then played in an Evan Gray benefit in Wellington just before Christmas; I got 150 and punched it everywhere.

I found I was getting into position much more quickly, my feet were moving better, and my head was stiller. Everything was simplified: I didn't have to worry about how far back my bat was. Whereas I'd been static in the upright stance, the pick-up and movement into the ball gave me more rhythm – I guess a comparison would be with trying to generate a nice, rhythmical golf swing starting with the club near the top of the backswing. Most important of all, my back was standing up to it.

The Shell Trophy series went reasonably well although I didn't score a century, and I was feeling pretty good when we arrived in Christchurch for the first test against India. As usual we gathered two days before the game and practised. Richard Hadlee, who hadn't played all season after an operation on his achilles tendon, turned up at the nets and had a trundle. The selectors had decided that they weren't going to risk him in a test until he had a first-class game under his belt and he was down to play for Canterbury against Otago. He didn't bowl at full pace but he was there. It was like turning on a machine after it hadn't been used for a while: it took a while to warm up but nothing much had changed – it still did the business. He felt fine and said how great it was to be able to bowl without pain.

Willie Watson had scored a century in club cricket the previous weekend then taken a knock on the thumb fielding in the slips. At practice he couldn't grip the ball properly so we sent him off for an x-ray. When we got back to the hotel, his arm was in plaster. We knew Paddles was worth three or four wickets against the Indians because he had a psychological edge on them so we rang him and asked if he could manage 15 overs a day. "I'll do 20," he said. Willie looked on the bright side: he reckoned there weren't many guys who'd been replaced by Richard Hadlee when they pulled out of a game.

I'd had a good look at the wicket and knew I'd bat if I won the toss so the pressure was off in that respect. The ball swung and seamed in the first hour and I played and missed a bit and squirted one between third slip and gully to reach 50 but then it settled down and I got 185, my highest test score. Danny Morrison got among them, Paddles picked up his 400th test wicket, and we played really well: good, attractive, winning cricket. Some people felt it wasn't good for the game that we won with so much time to spare; Sir Donald Bradman said the aim of test cricket was to win by the biggest possible margin in the shortest possible time, but what would he know?

Then it was on to Napier which was a real disappointment. We thought the wicket was going to have grass and replaced Dipak Patel in the squad with Shane Thomson. The pitch turned out to be bare. The Indians had been criticised for indisciplined batting in the first test – that's the way they play; if it had come off, they'd have got 400 in a big hurry. At Napier they tried to tighten up and played with a lot of inhibitions and took a long time for their runs. It rained a fair bit and we didn't get a bat till just before lunch on the fourth day. There was nothing on the game so I went for my shots and got another century. I've averaged around the 30s or 40s in most test series and always wanted to have a big one, to "dip my bread in the gravy". Now it was happening and I couldn't really believe it.

The test fizzled out and we got unjustifiably slated for not wanting to play on the fifth day. What really annoyed me was that not a single journalist asked us what the story was, yet here they were, ex-players included, making snide remarks about how the New Zealand team should be paid by the hour. For the record, what actually happened was that there was a mishap with the covers and a lot of water got dumped on the bowlers' run-up at one end; the Indians were unhappy about it and didn't want to play till the area had dried out which wasn't till after tea so the game was called off. We were quite happy to play. Think about it: we were one wicket down and I was 113 not out on the flattest wicket in the country with the opportunity for some batting practice; why the hell wouldn't we want to play?

In the third test at Eden Park we were right out of it at 60 for five. Paddles played brilliantly, going for it as only he can, and Ian Smith gave the most incredible display: I've never seen anyone strike the ball so cleanly for so long in a test match. I was in the physio's room with Bob Cunis and by the time we got to 150 for five, we were too scared to move in case the spell was broken so we stayed there. It was a great day's cricket with the wicket doing plenty early on, us losing wickets, then coming back to score 390 in a day.

Azharuddin played superbly and we ended up trailing by 90 on the first innings; I dropped the number 11 when they were 20 ahead and he got 50. Despite the number of runs that had been scored, there was still a lot of the test to go. I batted pretty well again in the second innings and probably blew it when I had another century there for the taking. Martin Crowe and Andrew Jones got centuries and then it hit the fan: I didn't set them a realistic target and got dumped on from a great height.

I don't have any qualms about my decision. My first responsibility was to my players, to ensure that we won the series as we deserved to do. In 20 years' time I may feel that I should've declared and had a fun game but I had no doubts at the time. I got a lot of critical letters but people don't understand that if the boot had been on the other foot, in most other countries, the opposition would simply have batted out the day. Their attitude would be "Get stuffed; if you aren't good enough to force your way into a winning position, don't expect us to open the door for you."

And it would have been an irresponsible act of charity to set them a gettable target because the likelihood of their getting it was a damn sight greater than the likelihood of us bowling them out. We didn't play a spinner, which really annoyed me, and Paddles was knackered so I was down to three bowlers, including Shane Thomson in his first test. India had scored at 4.7 an over in their first innings; I set them about 6.1. The wicket was so flat that they could've got to seven down and put the shutters up and we couldn't have bowled them out. India wouldn't have gone to the bitter end – a miss may be as good as a mile but they didn't want to go home as two-zip losers, especially after the controversy over the team's selection. The bottom line in test cricket is that you declare to win games; if you declare and lose, you've got it horribly wrong. I didn't feel, given the pitch, the depth of their batting, and our lack of bowling firepower, that we had a realistic chance of winning so it wasn't a difficult decision to make.

The triangular one-day series came next. We beat India in Dunedin and I missed the next two games with tonsillitis: the Aussies creamed us in Christchurch and we lost a knife-edge game to India in Wellington. We were on course to beat the Aussies in the second preliminary game in Auckland when the rain came and they beat us out of sight in the final after I won the toss and batted and the ball moved all over the show. The same wicket had seemed very flat the day before.

After that no one gave us a chance in the test. The Aussies were saying that on the day there wasn't a team in the world that could beat them. Our pundits couldn't have agreed more, especially when Martin Crowe pulled out. With our non-appearance at Napier, killing the game at Eden Park, and general hopelessness in the one-day series, the old New Zealand knocking machine was having a field day with the notable exception of TVNZ, whose people were being positive. None of it really worried me because I have great faith in the team's ability to keep competing.

It was pouring when we arrived in Wellington on Monday and it poured all day Tuesday and Wednesday morning. Then they looked under the covers and they'd leaked – there were damp patches all over the pitch. Terry Brindle of *The Australian* newspaper heard groundsman Wes Armstrong ask one of his staff what he found when he lifted up the covers: "it's piss wet right through," was the reply. Wes told me that if the weather didn't clear quickly there'd be no play before Saturday. That afternoon the sun came out and the wind blew.

We'd had a couple of indoor nets, but when you don't know when – or even if – the game will start, it's hard to maintain concentration and keep building up: the momentum drops and players start to relax instead of being keyed up. The authorities had a meeting on Wednesday night to decide if Thursday's play would be abandoned; they were going to ring us at our team meeting if that was the decision. The call never came. At the meeting it was stressed that we had to expect to play next day and we had to be ready.

Thursday was fine and there was a helicopter in, doing some drying. I've never worried so much about a toss. The wicket had no grass and looked bare and flat. It wasn't going to break up – Basin wickets never do. I asked John Morrison the Wellington coach what he reckoned – he said "bat". I spoke to Wes Armstrong; he said I should bat, but if I wanted to gamble, bowl. That really clarified things. It was a freaky replay of Perth. After that disaster, I'd sworn I'd never insert again yet here I was, four months later, considering inserting the same side. In the end I'd decided I'd bowl if I won; I was such a nervous wreck, I wouldn't have been much use as a batter anyway.

Allan Border won the toss and batted; I knew he would because that's the way they play these days. It was a great toss to lose; it was certainly the slowest wicket I've ever played test cricket on and they didn't cope with it. They'd been in the indoor nets where the wickets are quickish, which wouldn't have helped but they just weren't really there. But our seam attack bowled brilliantly: Danny Morrison was right into it and swung the ball, Sneds chipped in with a couple, and Paddles got his 100th five-wicket bag. I took a hot catch at mid off; when I caught it, I heard the whole stand go up behind me.

We bowled them out for 110 in just under three hours and suddenly we were back in fashion and everyone was saying they know we'd come right when it mattered. I guess it's human nature.

We never set out to bat slowly but we knew the wicket was terribly slow, we'd seen the Aussies get out trying to force it, and we told the guys not to let the pitch frustrate them out. If you're not getting runs, we said, focus on the partnership and be patient. It simply wasn't a pitch that you could just decide "I'm going to play some shots" and do it. In many ways they bowled better than we did but we were more patient. Trevor Franklin and I put on 48, then Jonesy and I went through to 90. I got out just before stumps when I'd set myself to bat for a day or a day and a half because I felt that any lead on that wicket would be crucial.

Sneds batted for 94 minutes without scoring and ended up with 23 – he slowed things down but he did a job for us. We were criticised for being negative but we had to have a lead. It was psychologically important: the Aussies had to get 90 in their second dig before they were on the board. We ended up chasing 171, which everyone thought would be a tough target; 260 would've been a lot more intimidating. People are too quick to make judgments and tend to look at passages of play in isolation rather than in the context of a five-day game. It's significant that none of the three players who tried to attack in that innings – Ken Rutherford, Ian Smith and Paddles – got runs.

We got Mark Taylor and David Boon out before stumps when they were 50 for two. Bob Cunis emphasised that although Australia were a good side, they hadn't been under pressure for quite a while. We bowled badly at the start of the second innings; the wind was on the wrong angle for Hadlee and he's so finely tuned that it was enough to throw him off and have him bowling on leg stump rather than off and Geoff Marsh worked him through the on side. We got Marshy, then Border and Peter Taylor batted very well. Danny made the breakthrough, getting Taylor caught behind and Dean Jones with a lucky lbw, and Paddles got rid of Steve Waugh.

I'd always fancied Braces on that wicket. He bowled most of the day without luck but when he gets it right, he's unstoppable. He was into them like a fox in a henhouse and there were blood and feathers everywhere. It was a magnificent exhibition of attacking spin bowling. I was thrilled for him: I'd backed him all summer against the doubters, some of them in the highest echelons. He'd dislocated his spinning finger in Australia and that took a while to come right but people have amazingly short memories: a few moderate Shell Trophy games and his achievements, the match-winning performances, were forgotten about.

Franko and I had to survive four overs, which seemed to last for ages after the intensity of the day in the field. I thought 171 would be a tough target but batting conditions had got better as the game went on. The wicket was turning but Braces turns it more than most and Peter Taylor hasn't had a lot of experience as an attacking bowler in test cricket – he's mostly been a one-day specialist, bowling to contain.

Day five was a big, big day: a chance for us to perform and win in front of New Zealanders, to show we could hack the pressure. I just wanted to contribute to the performance, get a solid 30 or 40. In the dressing room I normally focus on the team – how we've got to stick together and work for each other. That morning I talked about there being an opportunity to excel as an individual, that if two people could do that the team would win and everyone should be wanting to do it. It's nice to be right now and again.

Franko and I made another solid start, which was important. If the Aussies had got a couple of early wickets, it would've lifted them and really put the pressure on us. Jonesy came in and we grafted through to lunch.

After lunch the game started to go our way and we grabbed the initiative. I took 10 off an over from Taylor, reaching 50 with a shot over extra cover, which surprised me so it can't have done him much good. As the season had gone on I'd found it much easier to go over the top from the natural stance than I had standing up. When I was in the 80s Jonesy, maybe sensing that I was loosening up, said I had to get a century. In Evan Gray's benefit game early in the season I'd hit him over extra cover for six and I thought it would be nice to do the same to Border. Next ball I galloped down the wicket and did exactly that to reach 99. Then we were home and hosed. Campbell came back on and I slogged him here and there and it was all over. Once the momentum had started to go our way, it just went with a rush.

It was a great way to round off a season in which I'd played the way I'd wanted to play for years. It was the result of hanging in there, working at it, believing in myself – I've always believed that if you want something enough, you'll get it in the end. I'd played with freedom in first-class cricket and now and again in tests but not consistently and it was enormously satisfying to do it throughout a season in New Zealand.

We were thrilled to bits but we tried to be humble when we went into the Australian dressing room. It's important not to go overboard when you win. Then we got back in our dressing room and Braces said "Well, we gave them a real dicking, didn't we." Smithy said it was almost as good as Bombay, Paddy Greatbatch poured a bottle of champagne over Bob Cunis in his underpants and we sang 'God Defend New Zealand'. There was that intense feeling of togetherness which I love and which outsiders can never really understand.

But it's the next performance that counts, not the last one. You savour victory and enjoy the feeling of satisfaction from a job well done, then you prepare for the next challenge. The achievements of the summer of 1989/90 are in the scorebook and the pressure on us is to perform against a vitalised England team.

STATISTICS

to 1 April, 1990

Compiled by Peter Marriott

FIRST-CLASS CAREER RECORDS

	M	*I*	*NO*	*Runs*	*Ave*	*HS*	*100*	*50*	*Ct*
Auckland	5	6	0	290	48.33	90	–	3	2
Canterbury	16	30	4	1555	59.80	192	5	8	4
Derbyshire	156	265	24	10,638	44.14	190	27	52	82
International XI	1	1	0	2	2.00	2	–	–	1
NZ in New Zealand†	37	63	5	2316	39.93	185	8	7	17
NZ Overseas†	74	127	5	4513	36.99	136	9	22	39
NZ Under 23	1	2	0	45	22.50	33	–	–	1
North Island	2	2	0	27	13.50	22	–	–	1
Northern Districts	43	84	3	3301	40.75	145*	5	21	34
President's XI	1	1	0	73	73.00	73	–	1	–
D.H. Robin's XI	1	1	0	0	00.00	0	–	–	1
Total	**337**	**582**	**41**	**22,760**	**42.07**	**192**	**54**	**114**	**182**

† *includes test matches*

Century in each innings of a match

113 & 105 Northern Districts v Auckland, Auckland, 1981-82

John Wright has also bowled: 61.4-7-339-2; best 1-4. His 2 first-class wickets (both for Derbyshire) are: SFAF Bacchus (West Indians) 1980, and Zaheer Abbas (Gloucestershire) 1984.

TEST MATCH CAREER RECORDS

Against each country

	M	*I*	*NO*	*Runs*	*Ave*	*HS*	*100*	*50*	*Ct*
England	17	32	2	1083	36.10	130	3	5	6
Australia	16	30	2	1040	37.14	141	2	3	8
West indies	10	18	0	535	29.72	138	1	3	4
India	9	15	2	804	61.84	185	3	3	5
Pakistan	11	19	0	576	30.31	107	1	3	5
Sri Lanka	5	7	0	162	23.14	48	–	–	6
Total	**68**	**121**	**6**	**4200**	**36.52**	**185**	**10**	**17**	**34**

As captain/Not captain

	M	*I*	*NO*	*Runs*	*Ave*	*HS*	*100*	*50*	*Ct*
As captain	11	19	2	893	52.52	185	3	3	8
Not captain	57	102	4	3307	33.74	141	7	14	26
Total	**68**	**121**	**6**	**4200**	**36.52**	**185**	**10**	**17**	**34**

Test hundreds

(10)

110	New Zealand v India	Auckland	1980-81
141	New Zealand v Australia	Christchurch	1981-82
130	New Zealand v England	Auckland	1983-84
107	New Zealand v Pakistan	Karachi	1984-85
119	New Zealand v England	The Oval	1986
138	New Zealand v West Indies	Wellington	1986-87
103	New Zealand v England	Auckland	1987-88
185	New Zealand v India	Christchurch	1989-90
113*	New Zealand v India	Napier	1989-90
117*	New Zealand v Australia	Wellington	1989-90

ONE-DAY INTERNATIONAL CAREER RECORDS

	M	*I*	*NO*	*Runs*	*Ave*	*HS*	*100*	*50*	*Ct*
World Cup	14	14	0	422	30.14	69	–	2	3
World Series Cup	43	43	1	1263	30.07	84	–	10	22
World Championship of Cricket	4	4	0	31	7.75	22	–	–	1
Asia Cup	2	2	0	66	33.00	42	–	–	–
Sharjah	4	4	0	119	29.75	55	–	1	–
others	55	54	0	1357	25.12	101	1	5	18
Total	**122**	**121**	**1**	**3258**	**27.15**	**101**	**1**	**18**	**44**

SHELL CUP CAREER RECORDS

	M	*I*	*NO*	*Runs*	*Ave*	*HS*	*100*	*50*	*Ct*
Auckland	7	7	0	223	31.85	96	–	2	–
Canterbury	16	15	0	595	39.66	102	1	4	3
Northern Districts	10	10	0	158	15.80	32	–	–	–
Total	**33**	**32**	**0**	**976**	**30.50**	**102**	**1**	**6**	**3**

ONE-DAY MATCHES FOR DERBYSHIRE

	M	*I*	*NO*	*Runs*	*Ave*	*HS*	*100*	*50*	*Ct*
Benson & Hedges Cup	31	30	2	1005	35.89	102	2	4	8
Natwest Bank Trophy[1]	12	12	2	555	55.50	87*	–	5	2
Refuge Assurance League[2]	93	93	6	2729	31.36	108	2	19	32
Total	**136**	**135**	**10**	**4289**	**34.31**	**108**	**4**	**28**	**42**

[1] *from 1981 – previously known as the Gillette Cup*

[2] *from 1987 – previously known as the John Player League*

Hundreds

(4)

102	Derbyshire v Worcestershire	B&H	Chesterfield	1977
101	Derbyshire v Glamorgan	B&H	Cardiff	1979
103	Derbyshire v Worcestershire	JPL	Worcester	1982
108	Derbyshire v Warwickshire	JPL	Coventry	1983